CHAMPIONING TECHNOLOGY INFUSION

IN TEACHER PREPARATION

A Framework
for Supporting
Future Educators

EDITED BY ARLENE C. BORTHWICK, TERESA S. FOULGER, AND KEVIN J. GRAZIANO

International Society for Technology in Education
PORTLAND, OREGON • ARLINGTON, VIRGINIA

Championing Technology Infusion in Teacher Preparation
A Framework for Supporting Future Educators
Edited by Arlene C. Borthwick, Teresa S. Foulger, and Kevin J. Graziano

Editor: *Emily Reed*
Copy Editor: *Barbara Hewick*
Proofreader: *Angela B. Wade*
Indexer: *Kento Ikeda*
Book Design and Production: *Kim McGovern*
Cover Design: *Edwin Ouellette*

Library of Congress Cataloging-in-Publication Data available.

Names: Borthwick, Arlene, editor. | Foulger, Teresa (Teresa S.), editor. | Graziano, Kevin J., editor.
Title: Championing technology infusion in teacher preparation : a framework for supporting future educators / edited by Arlene Borthwick, Teresa Foulger, and Kevin Graziano.
Identifiers: LCCN 2019049892 (print) | LCCN 2019049893 (ebook) | ISBN 9781564848345 (paperback) | ISBN 9781564848369 (epub) | ISBN 9781564848352 (mobi) | ISBN 9781564848376 (pdf)
Subjects: LCSH: Teachers—Training of—United States. | Educational Technology—Study and teaching (Higher)—United States.
Classification: LCC LB1715 .C47 2020 (print) | LCC LB1715 (ebook) | DDC 370.71/1—dc23
LC record available at https://lccn.loc.gov/2019049892
LC ebook record available at https://lccn.loc.gov/2019049893

First Edition
ISBN: 978-1-56484-834-5
Ebook version available.

Printed in the United States of America

ISTE® is a registered trademark of the International Society for Technology in Education.

About ISTE

The International Society for Technology in Education (ISTE) is the premier nonprofit organization serving educators and education leaders committed to empowering connected learners in a connected world. ISTE serves more than 100,000 education stakeholders throughout the world.

ISTE's innovative offerings include the ISTE Conference & Expo, one of the biggest, most comprehensive ed tech events in the world—as well as the widely adopted ISTE Standards for learning, teaching, and leading in the digital age and a robust suite of professional learning resources, including webinars, online courses, consulting services for schools and districts, books, and peer-reviewed journals and publications. Visit iste.org to learn more.

Related ISTE Titles

Design Ed: Connecting Learning Science Research to Practice, by Angela Elkordy and Ayn Keneman

Learning First, Technology Second: The Educator's Guide to Designing Authentic Lessons, by Liz Kolb

Edtech for the K–12 Classroom: ISTE Readings on How, When and Why to Use Technology, edited by Diana Fingal

About the Editors and Contributors

Arlene C. Borthwick is professor emerita and former associate dean and professor at the National College of Education, National Louis University in Chicago. She has served as chair of the American Association of Colleges of Teacher Education's (AACTE) Committee on Innovation and Technology and as a member of the ISTE Board of Directors. She was president of the ISTE Special Interest Group for Teacher Educators from 2006–2008 and co-led an ISTE-sponsored study tour to New Zealand in 2010. She was nominated by ISTE to serve on the NCATE Board of Examiners (2008–2016) and subsequently served as a site visitor for the Council for the Accreditation of Educator Preparation (CAEP). Her areas of research have included school-university partnerships, design of online teaching, multimedia authoring and coding, and college-level leadership for integration of technology in teacher preparation programs. She served as an officer in American Educational Research Association's (AERA) Action Research SIG and was a founding editor of an online journal on practitioner research, i.e.: *inquiry in education.* She co-edited an ISTE book, *Transforming Classroom Practice: Professional Development Strategies in Educational Technology,* and has served as a reviewer for the *Journal of Digital Learning in Teacher Education* and the *Journal of Educational Computing Research.* She received the ISTE "Making IT Happen" award in 2008.

Teresa S. Foulger is an associate professor of educational technology and program coordinator for educational studies (BAE) in the Mary Lou Fulton Teachers College at Arizona State University (ASU). She has expertise in leading educational transformation and seeks to advance the use of technology for teaching and learning. Her research interests include technology integration, technology infusion in teacher preparation, professional development, and organizational change. She co-authored international research that led to the development of the Teacher Educator Technology Competencies (TETCs). She served as president of the ISTE Teacher Education Network from 2011–2015 and received the Making IT Happen award from ISTE in 2019. She also has served as the cochair of the TPACK Special Interest Group of the Society for Information Technology and Teacher Education (SITE). She is an associate editor for the *Australasian Journal of Educational*

Technology, is an executive board member and associate editor for the *International Journal of Teaching and Learning in Higher Education*, and is on the editorial review board for the *Journal of Digital Learning in Teacher Education*. Teresa's research on the adoption of technology infusion at ASU resulted in a sequence of peer-reviewed journal articles and numerous research awards, including the Outstanding Research Article Award (2014 and 2019) from the *Journal of Digital Learning in Teacher Education*; Best Practice Award for the Innovative Use of Technology (2017, with colleagues) from the American Association of Colleges for Teacher Education's (AACTE) Committee on Innovation and Technology; and the Best Research Paper Award (2014) from the American Educational Research Association (AERA), Technology as a Change Agent in Teaching and Learning Special Interest Group. You can learn more about her at education.asu.edu/teresa-foulger.

Kevin J. Graziano is a professor of teacher education in the School of Education at Nevada State College. He teaches educational technology courses to preservice and inservice teachers and conducts research on teachers' technology integration in the classroom. Kevin is the recipient of the 2012 Nevada System of Higher Education Board of Regents' Teaching Award. In 2012, Kevin received a Fulbright Specialist grant from the US Department of State, Bureau of Educational and Cultural Affairs. He provided training on educational technology to preservice teachers at Sakhnin College in Sakhnin, Israel. In 2012, Kevin also completed two international fellowships at the University of the Sunshine Coast in Queensland, Australia, and the Marino Institute of Education in Dublin, Ireland, where he trained teacher educators and preservice teachers on photovoice and technology. During his sabbatical in 2015, Kevin worked with teachers at a newcomer high school to flip the math classroom. He coauthored international research that led to the development of the Teacher Educator Technology Competencies (TETCs). He is the former chair of the Consultative Council for the Society for Information Technology and Teacher Education (SITE), former chair of the American Association of Colleges for Teacher Education's (AACTE) Committee on Innovation and Technology, and former co-chair of SITE's mobile learning SIG. He is also a contributor and co-editor of *Online Teaching in K–12: Models, Methods, and Best Practices for Teachers and Administrators* (2016) published by Information Today. You can learn more about him at kevingraziano.wixsite.com/portfolio.

Contributors

Ray Buss is an associate professor of educational psychology and educational research in the Mary Lou Fulton Teachers College at Arizona State University. He teaches research and methodology courses and supervises doctoral students in the college's highly recognized EdD program in the Division of Educational Leadership and Innovation. Together with colleagues, he explores how infusing technology instruction into the college's teacher preparation courses and student teaching affect technology integration by teacher candidates as they work toward conducting instruction in their classrooms. He also conducts research that focuses on doctoral students' development of identities as educational leaders and educational researchers and examines instructional issues and outcomes in the doctoral program.

Jon M. Clausen is an associate professor of educational technology and secondary education at Ball State University Teachers College. He has served as chair of the American Association of Colleges of Teacher Education's Committee on Innovation and Technology, teaches educational technology courses, is the director of the New and Emerging Support for Teaching with Technology (NESTT) Learning Labs, and is coordinator for the educational technology programs at Ball State University. His areas of research include technology integration within teacher education; technology use to support teacher learning, preparation, and development within instructional contexts; and preparing teachers within an immersive community-engaged teacher education program. You can learn more about him at drjmclausen.com/Home.html.

Liz Kolb is a clinical associate professor of education technologies at the University of Michigan in Ann Arbor, Michigan. She teaches courses in education technology for the undergraduate elementary, undergraduate secondary, and master's and certification programs. She authored *Toys to Tools: Connecting Student Cell Phones to Education* (published by ISTE in 2008), *Cell Phones in the Classroom: A Practical Guide for the K–12 Educator* (published by ISTE in 2011), *Help Your Child Learn with Their Cell Phone and Web 2.0* (published by ISTE in 2013), and *Learning First, Technology Second* (published by ISTE in 2017).

Michael McVey is a professor of teacher education in the College of Education at Eastern Michigan University. He teaches educational technology courses to preservice and inservice teachers and conducts research on emerging technologies and their impact on teaching practice. He serves as an elected school board trustee and a member of the ISTE Board of Directors. He has also authored almost thirty book reviews related to international trends in education for UNESCO's *International Review of Education*.

Punya Mishra is an associate dean of Scholarship & Innovation and professor in the Division of Educational Leadership & Innovation in the Mary Lou Fulton Teachers College at Arizona State University. He also has an affiliate appointment in the Herberger Institute for Design and the Arts. He is internationally recognized for his work in technology integration in teaching, the role of creativity and aesthetics in learning, and the application of design-based approaches to educational innovation. He has received over $7 million in grants and published over 100 articles and edited 3 books. He is an award-winning teacher, an engaging public speaker, as well as an accomplished visual artist and poet. You can learn more about him at punyamishra.com.

Julie A. Moore is an associate professor at Kennesaw State University where she teaches in the instructional technology master's, specialist, and doctoral programs and is program coordinator for the department's EdD program. Her research interests include the design and implementation of virtual learning communities for teachers, supporting teacher technology integration through virtual coaching, and the use of social media for teacher professional learning. She has served as the Teacher Education Division president for the Association for Educational Communications and Technology (AECT) and is currently a track co-chair for the Online Learning Consortium's (OLC) Accelerate conference.

Robert D. Muller is the dean of the National College of Education, National Louis University in Chicago. Previously he directed Strategy and Business Development at SRI Education, a division of SRI International, and formerly served as director of the Regional Educational Laboratory, Appalachia. He was deputy assistant secretary for vocational and adult education at the US Department of Education during the Clinton and Bush administrations. A consultant on education policy and management at the federal, state, and local levels, he was adjunct professor at Georgetown University and the University of Maryland. He holds an EdD from the University of Pennsylvania and an MPP from Harvard Kennedy School.

Sheryl Nussbaum-Beach is a twenty-five-year educator who has been a classroom teacher, technology coach, charter school principal, district administrator, university instructor, and digital learning consultant. She is the chief executive officer of Powerful Learning Practice, a professional learning and digital consulting company that serves clients worldwide. She is a sought-after national and international presenter, and she co-authored the book, *The Connected Educator: Learning and Leading in a Digital Age,* published by Solution Tree Press. Sheryl served on the ISTE Board of Directors for the last five years and currently serves on the advisory board for EdTech Digest.

Audra K. Parker is a professor and academic program coordinator in elementary education in the School of Education at George Mason University in Virginia. In addition to teaching courses in elementary methods and management, she partners as a university facilitator at Garfield Elementary, a PDS site. Her research includes innovations in clinical teacher preparation in elementary education and elementary organizational structures. She has published research in the *New Educator, Action in Teacher Education*, and *School-University Partnerships*, and she serves as a leader in the field of clinical teacher preparation through active engagement in NAPDS (National Association for Professional Development Schools), ATE (Association in Teacher Education), and AACTE (American Association of Colleges for Teacher Education).

Seth A. Parsons is an associate professor in the School of Education and the Elizabeth G. Sturtevant Center for Literacy at George Mason University in Virginia. His award-winning research focuses on teacher education and development, teacher instructional adaptations, and student motivation and engagement. He has published his research in *Review of Educational Research, Teaching and Teacher Education, Elementary School Journal,* the *Journal of Educational Research,* and other outlets. Seth is co-editor of *School-University Partnerships*, the journal of the National Association for Professional Development Schools (NAPDS). He is currently president-elect of the Association of Literacy Educators and Researchers (ALER).

Denise A. Schmidt-Crawford is an associate professor of educational technology, the director of the Center for Technology in Learning and Teaching, and the associate director of the School of Education at Iowa State University. Her research focuses on teachers' development of technological pedagogical content knowledge (TPACK), and her teaching interests include using technology as a tool for innovation in schools and teacher education. She co-authored international research that led to the development of the Teacher Educator Technology Competencies (TETCs).

She is the past president of the Society for Information Technology and Teacher Education (SITE) and serves as an editor for the ISTE *Journal of Digital Learning in Teacher Education*.

David A. Slykhuis is a professor of science education, assistant dean of the College of Natural and Health Sciences, and director of the Math and Science Teaching Institute at the University of Northern Colorado. He co-authored international research that led to the development of the Teacher Educator Technology Competencies (TETCs). He is the past president of the Society for Technology and Teacher Education. He was recently selected to serve as a member of the American Association of Colleges of Teacher Education Innovation and Technology Committee. He is also the chair of the National Technology Leadership Summit.

Ji Soo Song is an advocate committed to educational equity. As senior policy and advocacy associate at ISTE, he analyzes policy issues related to state edtech standards, educator credentialing systems, and edtech funding streams. Prior to ISTE, he served as a City Year AmeriCorps Member at a Title I elementary school in the District of Columbia, where he taught third grade mathematics and robotics, and received the WilmerHale Civic Innovation Award. Ji Soo was also an undergraduate intern at the US Department of Education's Office of Educational Technology (OET), where he supported development of the National Education Technology Plan and OET "Dear Colleague" Letter.

Joseph South is chief learning officer at ISTE and a national educational technology leader focused on evidence-based learning transformation. He formerly served as the director of the US Department of Education's Office of Educational Technology. In this role, he was an adviser to the secretary of education and developed national policy, including policy to advance educational technology in teacher preparation. He also formed public-private partnerships to assist state and local education leaders in transitioning to digital learning. He is a strong proponent of the active use of technology by learners. He holds a doctorate in instructional psychology and technology from Brigham Young University.

Debra R. Sprague is an associate professor in the School of Education at George Mason University in Virginia. Her research includes technology and teacher education and the affordances of emerging technologies. She has published her research in *Computers in the Schools, Journal of Interactive Online Learning*, and *Contemporary Issues in Technology and Teacher Education*. She is actively involved in the Society for Information Technology in Teacher Education (SITE) and served as the editor for the *Journal of Technology and Teacher Education* from 2001–2012. She also served as the chair of the SIG-TACTL for the American Education Research Association (AERA) from 2016–2017.

Melissa Warr is a doctoral candidate in the Mary Lou Fulton Teachers College at Arizona State University. Her research blends teacher education, design, creativity, and technology. She is currently exploring design perspectives on teachers' professional learning and identity. She is also a violinist and regularly performs with religious and community groups. Her scholarship is available on her personal website at melissa-warr.com.

Jo Williamson is a professor of instructional technology at Kennesaw State University (KSU). Prior to her work at KSU, she served as the director of educational technology for the Georgia Department of Education, the director of Area One Technology Hub for the Illinois State Board of Education, and the technology director for Waukegan, Illinois, public schools. She has authored two ISTE books on the Technology Coach Standards and served as the regional program chair for ISTE 2007 and 2014. She holds an MA from the University of Kansas and a PhD from the University of Illinois.

Contents

SECTION I
Planning for Technology Infusion

SECTION II
Implementing Technology Infusion

CHAPTER 5

Professional Expectations for Teacher Educators:
The Teacher Educator Technology Competencies (TETCs).................. 95

David A. Slykhuis, Denise A. Schmidt-Crawford, Kevin J. Graziano, Teresa S. Foulger

CHAPTER 6

The Necessity of Preparing Teacher Candidates to Teach Online.................. 113

Michael McVey

Contents

SECTION III
Evaluating Technology Infusion

CHAPTER 10

Evaluating Technology Infusion: Teacher Candidate and Program Outcomes 191

Ray R. Buss

SECTION IV

Advancing Technology Infusion

CHAPTER 11

What Can We Achieve Together? A Call to Action for the Future of Technology Infusion in Teacher Preparation Programs 215

Joseph B. South, Ji Soo Song

A Systems View of Technology Infusion

PUNYA MISHRA
MELISSA WARR
ARIZONA STATE UNIVERSITY

Let us begin with a story, a story about a car factory in Fremont, California, and how it changed over time. In the beginning, this factory, run by General Motors (GM), was one of the worst factories in their lineup—inefficient and sloppy. As reported by Adler (1993) and Glass and Langfitt (2010), nobody associated with the factory was happy—not the workers, not the managers, and not even those who would eventually drive the cars. Factory workers were so unhappy that they purposely messed up cars—scratching them, adding extra bolts to make the doors rattle, even putting the engines in backward. The union made it almost impossible for employees to be fired. Absenteeism was high, and drug and alcohol abuse ran rampant. The result was a whole lot of wasted time, energy, and money. Eventually, GM closed the factory (Adler, 1993).

A year later, the factory was reopened, the result of a collaboration between GM and Toyota, and it was a completely different story. The plant ended up becoming one of their most profitable and efficient car factories, and within a couple of years, it was meeting and exceeding every industry standard in terms of quality and efficiency. So, what changed? Well, let's start with what did *not* change. The workforce did not change. The new factory included 85% of the previous employees, including the same union leaders. The brand did not change. For the first four years after the factory reopened, it continued to produce Chevrolets.

What had changed were the systems and culture. In addition to financial investment, Toyota brought their team-based production system to the factory. Toyota had a record of consistently turning out high-quality cars, and they believed their production system was key. To start the project, Toyota brought GM employees to Japan, where they worked in Toyota factories next to Toyota employees. In the Toyota production system, workers were put into teams of four or five employees. They rotated assignments to stave off boredom. When workers were behind, others offered assistance. Whereas in Fremont the assembly line never stopped, at Toyota, if a team had a problem, they could pull a cord and a team-chosen tune would play, informing a manager that help was needed. If necessary, workers could stop the production line to fix problems. The focus was on quality, not quantity. Employees received bonuses for finding ways to make their work more efficient, resulting in new innovations such as special tools and processes. This was a new kind of factory culture—one where managers and laborers worked together and respected one another to create a product they could all be proud of.

The results were astounding. The new factory's quality met the same high standards as the Japanese factories. Workers enjoyed coming to work, absenteeism dropped, and overall production increased. Finally, according to the Consumer Report Reliability Index, the quality of the cars themselves improved (Adler, 1993).

This is the difference that the thoughtful design of systems and culture can make.

The obvious question that readers of this foreword must be asking is, What does the story of the turn-around of a car company have to do with technology infusion, the topic of this book? Essentially, we argue that most teacher preparation programs have seen technology integration as being "somebody else's problem" (Koehler, Mishra, Hershey, & Peruski, 2004). Technology and teaching are domains ruled by different groups of people—teacher educators, who are in charge of pedagogy and learning; and technologists, who are in charge of technology. The solution that emerges from this division is often that of providing a stand-alone technology course to teacher candidates who are taught by technology faculty. In contrast, a framework for technology infusion suggests technology integration should be a concern of the *entire* teacher preparation program, not only that of educational technology faculty. What is needed is a programmatic and systemic approach where the charge is a shared responsibility among all teacher preparation faculty.

There are complex historical precedents that have led to the "somebody else's problem" situation. Scholars have commonly labeled applying technology to teaching and learning as technology integration. Early attempts at integration laudably focused on learners and how they could harness new digital tools for new kinds of learning. For example, Jonassen's mindtools placed technology as a knowledge construction tool, emphasizing that students should be learning with, not from, technology (Jonassen, Carr, & Yueh, 1998). Others have emphasized that technology integration must focus not on the technology itself, but on the teaching and learning the technology enables (Knezek, Christensen, Miyashita,

& Ropp, 2000; Mills & Tincher, 2003; Norum, Grabinger, & Duffield, 1999). Teachers and teacher educators became the focus of attention with the advent of the Technological Pedagogical Content Knowledge (TPACK) framework (Mishra & Koehler, 2006). The TPACK framework described the need for teachers (and teacher candidates) to simultaneously call on their knowledge of technology, pedagogy, and subject matter content. Though the focus on teachers and teacher knowledge was a valuable insight provided by TPACK, the framework does not address how best to develop that knowledge in a teacher preparation program.

We argue that perhaps there has been an inordinate focus on the teacher as the central adopter and agent of change, and we have neglected the role of systems and culture in technology integration efforts. We do not argue that the research has completely neglected the impacts of external barriers, systems, and culture on technology integration. Indeed, much research has considered both internal and external barriers (Ertmer & Ottenbreit-Leftwich, 2013; Rogers 2000), compared the impact of individual versus systemic factors on technology integration (Reid, 2014; Teo, 2015), and emphasized the need for systemic change (Ellsworth, 2000; Fullan, 2007). However, most of this work has focused on studying how the *current* system interacts with and affects teacher actions and beliefs, not on the type of influence a *new* system might have on technology use in education. And *this* is the lesson of the car factory in Fremont, California, with which we began our foreword—that *one can thoughtfully design not just tools and experiences but also systems and culture.*

We argue that it is productive to see tools, processes, experiences, systems, and culture as overlapping spaces of design, what we have called the Five Spaces for Design in Education (Figure F.1).

Each circle in the model depicted in Figure F.1 represents a space for design activity. Although design occurs across all the spaces, in each space the outcome of design is focused on a particular category of product: artifacts, processes, experiences, systems, or culture.

Although technology is not distinctly mentioned in the diagram, one can easily see how technology fits within each of these spaces. For instance, artifacts could be digital artifacts such as apps or websites, while processes could be technology-assisted lesson plans, and so on. It is also important to note that the complexity of the design spaces increases as we go from artifacts to culture. This is not to say that creating a good educational app is easy—rather that it is a relatively tame problem compared to changing systems and culture. These spaces, though they appear nested within each other, do influence meaning-making bidirectionally. Thus, effective design in any design space requires an awareness of all design spaces.

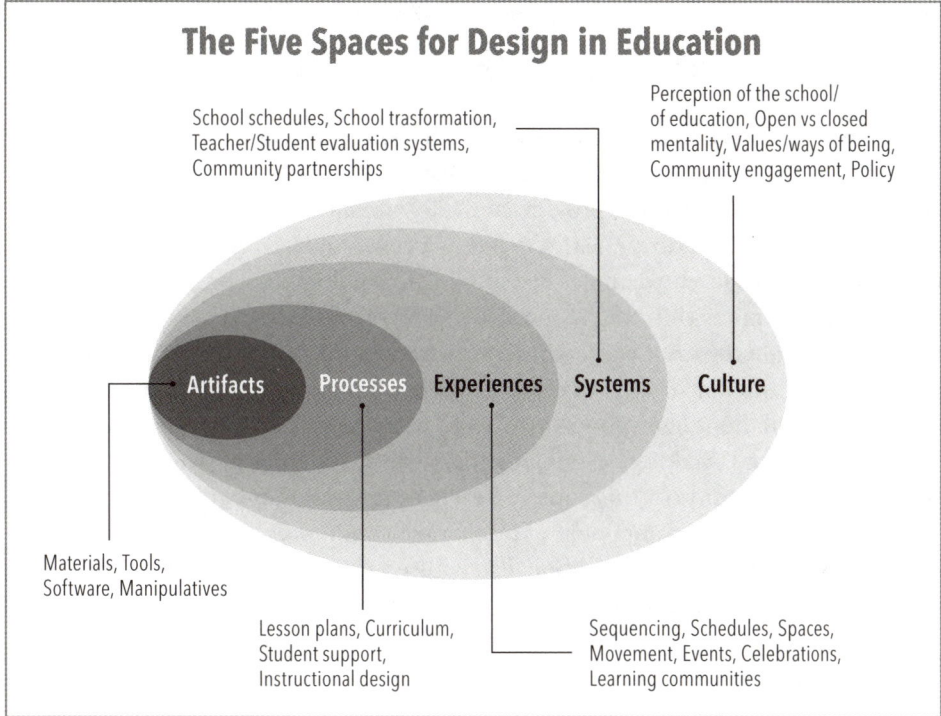

Figure F.1 The Five Spaces for Design in Education (see Warr, Mishra, & Scragg, 2019). Image property of Punya Mishra, Ben Scragg, and Melissa Warr.

We believe that the Five Spaces for Design in Education provides a broad vision of technology in education and emphasizes the importance of designing systems and culture. Most research on technology in education has focused on knowledge needed to design artifacts and processes, and sometimes experiences, but has at times ignored systems and culture which, as we saw in the Fremont factory, can entirely change how artifacts, processes, and experiences gain meaning and are used. Systematic, sustainable change requires attention to all five spaces of design: artifacts, processes, experiences, systems, and culture. This brings us to what we mean by technology infusion. *Whereas technology integration typically focuses on a particular instance when technology is used for teaching or learning, technology infusion is a program-deep and program-wide effort in teacher preparation programs to help teacher candidates learn how to effectively teach with technology.* It empha-sizes redesigning experiences, systems, and cultures of teacher education systems rather than focusing on stand-alone technology integration courses and tool-spe-cific applications. It infuses technology into the culture of the teacher preparation program, enabling rich experiences for teaching and learning with technology.

The chapters in this book explore elements of a technology infusion framework. Teacher education is a complex system, consisting of multilayered and deeply contextual environments that provide students with a range of experiences to help them prepare for the future. Clearly, creating a coherent learning experience for teacher candidates (even when not considering technology) in complex contexts such as these requires thinking at the level of systems and culture. Additionally, teacher education does not work within a vacuum but is driven by structures, visions, and policy constraints that can be both internal to the organization (such as existing regulations, conventions, etc.) and external (such as the needs for certi-fication, and so on). Making sustainable change in these types of situations is often fraught with ambiguity. In this context, teacher preparation programs that seek to make technology a key component of teacher education need to be seen as learning organizations—they are organizational structures adapted to a purpose. Change efforts need to consider relevant situations, constraints, and contexts. This is just a roundabout way of suggesting that the task the authors of these chapters have taken on is not an easy one.

Establishing a technology infusion framework is hemmed in by multiple social, organizational, interpersonal, and structural constraints. Thus, technology infu-sion is complicated, requiring negotiation and thoughtful design with multiple stakeholders. That is what makes technology infusion difficult. And yet, it is only through this deep engagement with systems of teacher education that technology infusion can truly take hold and allow for the development of the next genera-tion of educators. This is not an easy task, but it is an important one. We praise the editors of this book and the authors of each of the chapters for taking on this challenge. The theories of change, the data and practical evidence they provide, and, as importantly, the stories they tell, will be invaluable to others who take on this challenge. We believe this broader perspective, that of technology infusion, requires expanding our focus to include experiences, systems, and culture to help *all* teachers effectively integrate technology into teaching and learning.

References

Adler, P. S. (1993). The learning bureaucracy: New United Motor manufacturing, Inc. In B. M. Staw & L. L. Cummings (Eds.), *Research in Organizational Behavior* (Vol. 15, pp. 111–194). Greenwich, CT: JAI Press.

Ellsworth, J. (2000). *Surviving change: A survey of educational change models.* Syracuse, NY: ERIC Clearinghouse on Information and Technology.

Ertmer, P. A., & Ottenbreit-Leftwich, A. (2013). Removing obstacles to the pedagogical changes required by Jonassen's vision of authentic technology-enabled learning. *Computers and Education, 64*(May), 175–182. doi.org/10.1016/j.compedu.2012.10.008

Fullan, M. (2007). *The new meaning of educational change* (4th ed.). New York, NY: Teachers College Press.

Glass, I., & Langfitt, F. (2010, March 26). 403: NUMMI. In *This American Life.* www.thisamericanlife.org/403/transcript

Jonassen, D. H., Carr, C., & Yueh, H.P. (1998). Computers as mindtools for engaging learners in critical thinking. *TechTrends, 43*(2), 24–32. doi.org/10.1007/BF02818172

Knezek, G., Christensen, R., Miyashita, K., & Ropp, M. M. (2000). *Instruments for assessing educator progress in technology integration.* Denton, TX: Institute for the Integration of Technology into Teaching and Learning.

Koehler, M. J., Mishra, P., Hershey, K., & Peruski, L. (2004). With a little help from your students: A new model for faculty development and online course design. *Journal of Technology and Teacher Education, 12*(1), 25–55. www.learntechlib.org/p/14636

Mills, S. C., & Tincher, R. C. (2003). Be the technology: A developmental model for evaluating technology integration. *Journal of Research on Technology in Education, 35*(3), 382–402.

Mishra, P., & Koehler, M. J. (2006). Technological pedagogical content knowledge: A framework for teacher knowledge. *Teachers College Record, 108*(6), 1017–1054.

Norum, K. E., Grabinger, R. S., & Duffield, J. A. (1999). Healing the universe is an inside job: Teachers' views on integrating technology. *Journal of Technology and Teacher Education, 7*, 187–203.

Reid, P. (2014). Categories for barriers to adoption of instructional technologies. *Education and Information Technologies, 19*(2), 383–407. doi.org/10.1007/s10639-012-9222-z

Rogers, P. L. (2000). Barriers to adopting emerging technologies in education. *Journal of Educational Computing Research, 22*(4), 455–472. doi.org/10.2190/4UJE-B6VW-A30N-MCE5

Teo, T. (2015). Comparing pre-service and in-service teachers' acceptance of technology: Assessment of measurement invariance and latent mean differences. *Computers & Education, 83*, 22–31. doi.org/10.1016/j.compedu.2014.11.015

Warr, M., Mishra, P., & Scragg, B. (2019). Beyond TPACK: Expanding technology and teacher education to systems and culture. *Society for Information Technology & Teacher Education International Conference*, 2233–2237. www.learntechlib.org/primary/p/208009

Champions as Water Carriers: Prioritizing Technology Infusion in Teacher Preparation

ARLENE C. BORTHWICK
NATIONAL LOUIS UNIVERSITY

TERESA S. FOULGER
ARIZONA STATE UNIVERSITY

KEVIN J. GRAZIANO
NEVADA STATE COLLEGE

> Change that is well managed and well led is much more likely to be beneficial and accomplished more quickly. Whether institutions apply formal frameworks and theories or generic best practices, more institutions are including change management as a component of new initiatives and organizational development.
>
> — Grajek, S., & The 2017–2018 EDUCAUSE IT Issues Panel, 2018, p. 14.

We have been hoping for change. We have research, articles, and even books that clarify the concepts and strategies for leadership and change. But what we need are champions—a champion at each institution who brings vision, motivation, and tenacity, and who is supported by a culture that embraces innovation.

Infusing technology in teacher preparation is the vision. Hard work will be required, as exemplified by the champion who is also willing to serve as a water carrier. According to Walker (2018), carrying water is the "invisible art of leading from the back" (p. 133). Champions are individuals who provide support through their interactions, serving as a conduit to elevate priority setting, decision making, and achievement. Champions who are water carriers know when to step forward and when to lead from the sidelines, staying attentive to needs and timing. They also know when to retreat and regroup to be more strategic. Consider the scenarios below—examples of the kind of well-managed change, hard work, and water carrying that is needed by champions of technology infusion.

Sound Familiar?

Picture yourself in one of these situations:

Scenario 1. The subject line in an email from the dean of the School of Education read, "Outcomes of the Spring State Legislative Session." The email announced that the governor had signed a long-awaited bill for the construction of a new, state-of-the-art, 85,000-square-foot education building. The dean, delighted with the news, wrote: "Securing the funding for a new education building is something we have been working on for years. Now is the time to think big, share your vision for the space, and design a building that will help us place the School of Education on the map for its innovative technology." The dean ended his email with a request: "Take time over the summer to think about your dreams for embedding technology into the new building. Be prepared to discuss your ideas at the fall retreat."

Scenario 2. With an eye to the future, the College of Education Technology Committee at a large university lobbied the dean to accept the "challenge" issued by the Department of Education Office of Educational Technology (DOE/OET) to more adequately prepare teacher candidates to effectively use technology in support of teaching and learning. Following a proud moment when their institution was listed among other innovative institutions on the DOE/OET website (tech.ed.gov/edtechtprep) that were willing to step up to this call, the committee quickly added references to the principles outlined in a DOE/OET policy brief to the college's technology plan document. These principles included program-deep and program-wide experiences for teacher candidates and establishing systems of professional learning for faculty. As the committee reviewed the revised technology plan, they realized that a lot of the statements in the document were philosophical and "aspirational." They did not really have an action plan and, further, did not have access to resources to support specific programmatic changes and faculty training. The academic year was coming to a close, and there would be several new committee members next year; they elected an incoming chair in anticipation of next year's committee work.

Scenario 3. Due to the increase in virtual K–12 schools opening across the US, the dean from a small liberal arts college announced at a faculty meeting that she wanted the college to develop a teacher preparation program focused on training a cadre of teachers with a credential in K–12 online teaching. She noted that, as outlined in the college's new strategic plan, key stakeholders such as teacher educators, liberal arts and sciences faculty, administrators and teachers from K–12 virtual schools, and instructional designers would be invited to be at the table from the onset of planning for the new program. An educational technology faculty member spoke up, insisting that planning for the new program must include someone to provide leadership to technology infusion throughout the curriculum, rather than in just one or two courses. Another faculty member expressed concern that even with significant resources devoted to development of the program, how could they be sure newly enrolling students would find the program of value to their future employment?

The faculty and staff from all three scenarios above were faced with deciding "What next?" Ideally, they will all work toward a similar outcome: that is, the infusion of technology throughout their programs. However, as outlined in the scenarios, each representing a different context, the participants must overcome obstacles that are unique to their situation.

> **Scenario 1 Obstacle.** *Funding* for technology is just one element in achieving desired goals.

> **Scenario 2 Obstacle.** Fluid *participation* of faculty and staff, as well as lack of action planning, can lead to the ball being dropped.

> **Scenario 3 Obstacle.** Untested *instructional methods* may lead to failed or unsustainable programming or lack of enrollment.

Obstacles such as these must be considered and addressed in planning when programs are working to build capacity for effective change in teacher preparation. Given the complexity of teacher preparation programs, champions carefully ponder, "How should we proceed?"

A Vision for Technology Infusion

We believe that technology, when used in innovative and powerful ways, can equalize educational opportunities (especially in areas of diverse needs). We have been calling a program-deep and program-wide effort to address technology an "infused" approach. Some colleges and schools of education have eliminated a stand-alone educational technology course for an infused approach. We are aware that other colleges and schools of education are considering this or other alternative methods for improving the way they prepare teacher candidates to teach with technology.

The vision for technology infusion is that teacher candidates are supported throughout all aspects of their preparation and that they are proficient in teaching with technology by the time they enter the field as certified teachers. For this vision to come to fruition, any and all individuals associated with a preparation program need to be responsible for and responsive to infusing technology. Thus, an infused program involves *all the systems and personnel* surrounding teaching and learning in preparation programs, including teacher educators, administrators, professional developers, instructional designers, field supervisors, district and school administrators, mentors, etc.

A large-scale change effort like this does not happen overnight, and long-term change requires close oversight of incremental adjustments. Success in academic transformation depends on educational leaders' commitment and strategic goals for leveraging technology and effective pedagogical practices (Grajek, S. & the 2017–2018 EDUCAUSE IT Issues Panel, 2018). In most cases, even with a strong leader who is focused on discovery, adoption, and implementation of new strategies (Freeman et al., 2017), a cultural acceptance of a systemic effort to adopt a technology-infused approach takes time. As experienced at Arizona State University, a cultural acceptance may not be attained for several years (Foulger, Wetzel, & Buss, 2019), and even then, preparation programs should be forewarned that needs shift, personnel changes, and visions evolve, making ongoing leadership, support, and championing all the more important (Buss, Foulger, Wetzel, & Lindsey, 2018).

At the core of each of the scenarios above lies an organizational champion, an "enlightened change maker who is personally committed to mutual values, rather than self-centered ones, and relentlessly driven by possibilities" (Thompson, 2009, p. 6). Change champions assist in instituting a change; advocating for and promoting the change from within, they are instrumental in the implementation of the change (Warrick, 2009). Champions for technology infusion are concerned with continually advancing a long-term change effort. In doing so, they rely on these skills:

- Champions are key communicators of the change and work to deescalate conflict when necessary.

- Champions problem solve to remove barriers of change, while at the same time they create supports for the change.

- Champions promote new ideas for change, supporting the vision and motivating others to share in this experience.

- Champions believe in the change, are driven by the vision, and are energized by their passion for change.

- Champions are the driving force of organizational change, leading their teams through the change, toward innovation.

If you are reading this book, you are probably a champion for technology in education.

Champions are leaders of systems. The International Society for Technology in Education (ISTE) Standards for Education Leaders, Visionary Planner, describe the role of leaders as evaluating progress on the strategic plan, making course corrections, measuring impact, and scaling effective approaches (The International Society for Technology in Education, 2018). Walker (2018) confirms that leaders who are effective at supporting system-wide efforts where teams are involved are persistent. They are not necessarily good at giving large-group inspirational speeches, but rather create inspiration by circulating "widely, talking to everyone with enthusiasm and energy" (p. 170). In addition, Walker's research supports the importance of "servant" leadership, where an individual is willing to serve in a functional role, assist others, and step up when needed. "A water carrier can improve a team by focusing on shoring up weaknesses and enforcing high standards" and expectations to move the group forward (Walker, p. 145).

Why Is Technology Infusion Important?

The contributors to this book, all of whom are faculty and staff engaged in the preparation of teachers within their own institutions, agree that *effectively* preparing teacher candidates to integrate technology is a priority. And we are not alone.

In 2016, the US Department of Education's Office of Educational Technology issued a policy brief entitled *Advancing Educational Technology in Teacher Preparation* and invited teacher preparation and technology leaders to a White House summit in Washington, D.C. The importance of teacher preparation was highlighted in this call to teacher educators across the nation. As reported in the policy brief and affirmed at the summit:

> Schools of education should work with P–12 schools and school districts to provide meaningful opportunities for pre-service teachers, in-service teachers, school and district leadership, and faculty to co-learn and collaborate to better understand and use technology as a tool to transform teaching and learning experiences for learners of all ages. (Office of Educational Technology, 2016, p. 4)

Further, as researched by a working group of teacher education faculty that was formed at the summit, teacher preparation institutions need to address six areas in their systematic approach to infusing technology: related research; faculty time, incentives, apathy, and competing demands; leadership and pedagogy; technical skill, training, and communities of practice; financial investment and speed of new trends; and connection between PK–12 and higher education (Kolb, Kashef, Roberts, Terry, & Borthwick, 2018).

The US Department of Education's National Educational Technology Plan (NETP) calls for a common vision and collaboration across institutions to create action plans for learning that is enabled through technology (Office of Educational Technology, 2017). The NETP specifically directed teacher educators to take more responsibility for the preparation of teacher candidates to "use technology to realize each state's learning standards from day one" upon their entry to the field as certified teachers (p. 35). Further, the NETP confirmed most state-adopted standards include relevant uses of technology.

> Schools should be able to rely on teacher preparation programs to ensure that new teachers come to them prepared to use technology in meaningful ways. No new teacher exiting a preparation program should require remediation by his or her hiring school or district. Instead, every new teacher should be prepared to model how to select and use the most appropriate apps and tools to support learning and evaluate these tools against basic privacy and security standards. It is inaccurate to assume that

because pre-service teachers are tech savvy in their personal lives they will understand how to use technology effectively to support learning without specific training and practice. This expertise does not come through the completion of one educational technology course separate from other methods courses but through the inclusion of experiences with educational technology in all courses modeled by the faculty in teacher preparation programs. (Office of Educational Technology, 2017, pp. 35–36).

The vision put forth by the National Educational Technology Plan clearly puts the onus for technology integration on all teacher educators.

The evidence is clear that establishing a strong connection between PK–12 and higher education is essential in providing powerful learning experiences for teacher candidates during clinical practice (Brenner & Brill, 2016). In their study of early career teachers, Brenner & Brill examined practices in teacher preparation that supported and "prohibited" technology integration and transfer of skills. Prohibiting factors included "having only one instructional technology-related course; and limited opportunities to practice with technology in content-specific and methods courses" (p. 141). The status of technology in teacher preparation has also been reflected in "SpeakUp" surveys of K–12 students, parents, administrators, and, more recently, teacher candidates. Beginning in 2009, Project Tomorrow (tomorrow.org), in collaboration with Blackboard, surveyed "tomorrow's teachers." Candidate responses about their experiences, knowledge, and aspirations were compared to those of inservice teachers and administrators. Results confirm the relevance of topics covered in various chapters in this book, including the importance of infusion of technology in methods courses, modeling by faculty and classroom teachers, and clinical practice (Project Tomorrow, 2013, 2017).

On a broader level, results from an international survey conducted in 2018 by the Organisation for Economic Co-operation and Development (OECD) in forty-eight countries confirmed inadequate preparation of new teachers.

Only 50% of teachers across the OECD received training in the use of ICT [Information and Communication Technology] for teaching as part of their formal education or training, and only 43% of teachers felt well or very well prepared for this element when they completed their initial education or training. (Organisation for Economic Co-operation and Development, 2019, p. 29)

For US respondents, the percentage of teachers reporting that use of technology for teaching was part of their teacher preparation program was higher, at 63%. However, only 45% of these individuals felt well prepared or very well prepared for using technology for teaching (Organisation for Economic Co-operation and Development, 2019).

Leading the Way to Infusing Technology in Teacher Preparation

Championing Technology Infusion in Teacher Preparation: A Framework for Supporting Future Educators was written by twenty education experts and practitioners in the field. The book targets readers who support technology integration curriculum and innovative delivery methods in teacher preparation institutions, including deans and other administrators in colleges/schools of education, teacher education faculty, educational technology faculty, faculty developers, field experience supervisors and cooperating teachers, and others serving teacher candidates in their field-based experiences.

This book is sequenced to help readers understand the big picture of technology infusion and leadership, as well as targeted aspects of a framework for technology infusion, including curriculum design, clinical practice, teacher induction, program evaluation, and related expectations for teacher educators. Separate chapters can stand alone and may be useful for study and reference at various points during a change process.

The book is divided into four sections:

> **Section I: Planning for Technology Infusion.** Background chapters on technology infusion in teacher preparation, frameworks for organizational change, and technology use in PK–12 teaching and learning.

> **Section II: Implementing Technology Infusion.** Methods and guidance for enhancing technology infusion in teacher preparation, with leadership suggestions for program-wide and program-deep adoption through appropriate curriculum design; expectations for teacher educator knowledge, skills, and dispositions; clinical experiences; and teacher induction.

Section III: Evaluating Technology Infusion. Methods and guidance for assessing candidate outcomes and reviewing program- and college-level processes and progress leading to program-deep and program-wide technology infusion focused on candidate learning.

Section IV: Advancing Technology Infusion. A vision and action steps for nation-wide collaboration for technology infusion in teacher preparation, including the role of state-level government entities and NGOs.

Table P.1 at the end of the preface provides a brief overview of the content of each chapter.

Audience and Use of This Book

Championing Technology Infusion in Teacher Preparation: A Framework for Supporting Future Educators is an ideal read for leadership and teams to thoughtfully examine their current preparation programs and consider their unit's framework for advancing technology infusion, facilitating action planning, and implementing change. The content and organization of the book are particularly appropriate for "book club" use, with chapter-by-chapter discussion and planning by groups of faculty, staff, and external partners. University, state-level, and nongovernment organization (NGO) leaders will benefit from how this book addresses change from a multisystems approach and establishes a national vision for transforming teacher preparation.

Throughout the text, readers will find references to research, theory, and practice. Each chapter concludes with a list of "Getting Started Resources," facilitating access to additional pertinent information. These resources will allow readers to more fully explore and understand the ideas and information presented in each chapter as they seek to adopt a customized approach to advancing their framework for technology infusion. As well, the index at the end of the book provides a quick and useful list of topics of interest.

A Commitment to Technology Infusion from the Editors and Contributors

As editors of this book, we came together with very different histories surrounding educational technology but with a common passion: *to help colleges and schools of education, across the country and internationally, be more effective in their efforts to prepare teacher candidates to teach with technology.* We invited the chapter authors to join us due to their unique area of expertise related to advancing technology infusion. Like ISTE's Visionary Planners, we want to encourage professionals throughout the field to "share lessons learned, best practices, challenges and the impact of learning with technology with other education leaders who want to learn from this work" (International Society for Technology in Education, 2018, p. 1). Together, we are committed to ensuring successful change in the field, and we hope you will join us, working as both water carrier and champion for technology infusion!

References

Brenner, A., & Brill, J. (2016). Investigating practices in teacher education that promote and inhibit technology integration transfer in early career teachers. *TechTrends: Linking Research & Practice to Improve Learning, 60*(2), 136–144. doi.org/10.1007/s11528-016-0025-8

Buss, R., Foulger, T. S., Wetzel, K. A., & Lindsey, L. (2018). Preparing teachers to integrate technology into K–12 instruction II: Examining the effects of technology-infused methods courses and student teaching. *Journal of Digital Learning in Teacher Education, 34*(3), 134–150.

Foulger, T. S., Wetzel, K., & Buss, R. (2019). Moving toward a technology infusion approach: Considerations for teacher preparation programs. *Journal of Digital Learning in Teacher Education, 35*(2), 79–91. doi.org/10.1080/21532974.2019.1568325

Freeman, A., Adams Becker, S., Cummins, M., Davis, A., & Hall Giesinger, C. (2017). *NMC/CoSN Horizon Report: 2017 K–12 Edition.* Austin, TX: The New Media Consortium.

Grajek, S., & The 2017–2018 EDUCAUSE IT Issues Panel. (2018). Top 10 IT issues, 2018: The remaking of higher education. *EDUCAUSE Review*, 10–59. bit.ly/3asQFcq

International Society for Technology in Education. (2018). ISTE Standards for Education Leaders. www.iste.org/standards/for-education-leaders

Kolb, L., Kashef, F., Roberts, C., Terry, C., & Borthwick, A. (2018). Challenges to creating and sustaining effective technology integration in teacher education programs. bit.ly/2LJ6kdL

Office of Educational Technology. (2016). *Advancing educational technology in teacher preparation: Policy brief.* tech.ed.gov/teacherprep

Office of Educational Technology. (2017). *Reimagining the role of technology in education: 2017 National Education Technology Plan update.* tech.ed.gov/netp

Organisation for Economic Co-operation and Development. (2019). *TALIS 2018 results (Volume I): Teachers and school leaders as lifelong learners.* Paris, France: OECD Publishing. doi.org/10.1787/1d0bc92a-en

Project Tomorrow. (2013). *Learning in the 21st Century: Digital experiences and expectations of tomorrow's teachers.* Irvine, CA: Project Tomorrow.

Project Tomorrow. (2017). Speak Up Research Project, Tomorrow's Teachers Speak Up, 2017 Data [Unpublished raw data].

Thompson, M. (2009). *The organizational champion: How to develop passionate change agents at every level.* New York: McGraw Hill.

Walker, S. (2018). *The captain class: A new theory of leadership.* New York, NY: Random House.

Warrick, D. D. (2009). Developing organization change champions: A high payoff investment! *OD Development Practitioner, 41*(1), 14–19.

Table P.1 Content Overview for Championing Technology Infusion in Teacher Preparation: A Framework for Supporting Future Educators

Section or Chapter and Authors	Topic	Overview	Theoretical and/or Conceptual Framework
FOREWORD A Systems View of Technology Infusion *Punya Mishra and Melissa Warr, Arizona State University*	Technology infusion as systems and culture change	The authors of the foreword argue that technology development in teacher preparation has been limited by a lack of attention to systemic factors. Technology infusion, with its emphasis on addressing systems and culture in teacher preparation, offers a better way forward.	• Systems change • Organizational change
PREFACE Champions as Water Carriers: Prioritizing Technology Infusion in Teacher Preparation *Arlene C. Borthwick, National Louis University* *Teresa S. Foulger, Arizona State University* *Kevin J. Graziano, Nevada State College*	Vison and rationale for technology infusion in teacher preparation and use of this book	The preface presents the vision and rationale for technology infusion in teacher preparation. The authors address obstacles that may exist and suggest that champions are needed to ensure that technology infusion is a priority in schools and colleges of education. The preface provides an overview of the contents and best use of the book for achieving successful change.	• Leadership • Teamwork

Continued

Section or Chapter and Authors	Topic	Overview	Theoretical and/or Conceptual Framework
Section I. Planning for Technology Infusion Background chapters on technology infusion in teacher preparation, frameworks for organizational change, and technology use in PK–12 teaching and learning.			
CHAPTER 1 Design Considerations for Technology-Infused Teacher Preparation Programs *Teresa S. Foulger, Arizona State University*	Defining technology infusion Design considerations for program-wide, program-deep efforts to address technology integration	It is important that colleges/schools of education create a customized approach for how they address technology in their curriculum. In a technology-infused preparation program, technology integration is addressed by *all* instructors in a program-deep and program-wide manner. With this vision in mind, the goal for this chapter is to provide program planners with research-based design considerations and theoretical frameworks that will help them establish a personalized vision, initiate efforts, and expand upon their technology infusion initiatives.	• Developing Technological Pedagogical Content Knowledge (TPACK) • Technology integration • Technology infusion
CHAPTER 2 Building Capacity for Technology Infusion through Systemic Change in Colleges and Schools of Education *Robert D. Muller, National Louis University*	Organization development for technology infusion	This chapter proposes a framework for leaders of colleges/schools of education, to help guide their thinking through the choppy waters of technology-driven change. The first section briefly summarizes why and how technology integration and infusion approaches should be important to leaders of programs designed to prepare and advance teachers. The chapter proposes a framework for leaders to attend to the interrelated web of functions and roles that comprise complex organizational systems, and identifies some of the common pitfalls that impede change and recommendations for mitigating them.	• Technical vs. adaptive problems (Heifetz & Linsky) • Change management (Fullan; Kotter) • Networked Improvement Communities (NICs) (Bryk, Gomez, Grunow, & LeMahieu) • PELP Coherence Framework (Childress, Elmore, Grossman, & Johnson)

Continued

Section or Chapter and Authors		Topic	Overview	Theoretical and/ or Conceptual Framework
CHAPTER 3	Rethinking Teacher Preparation: Learning from the PK–12 Edtech Story *Sheryl Nussbaum-Beach, Powerful Learning Practice*	Technology integration and infusion in PK–12 education	This chapter describes PK–12 initiatives and limitations in educational technology. Based on PK–12 needs, the chapter discusses implications for the role of teacher preparation programs in preparing teacher candidates to be visionary, forward-thinking leaders of change who are fully prepared to hit the ground running once they complete their programs. Teacher candidates need to personally adopt the values and dispositions that drive the use of new pedagogies connected to digital learning environments.	• Collaborative, connected educators • PK–12 drivers for change • Four domains of Future Ready Leadership
Section II. Implementing Technology Infusion Methods and guidance for enhancing technology infusion in teacher preparation.				
CHAPTER 4	Frameworks That Scaffold Learning to Teach with Technology *Liz Kolb, University of Michigan*	Using appropriate frameworks to support teacher candidates in their development of TPACK	This chapter describes four frameworks in educational technology—SAMR, PICRAT, TIM, and Triple E—and proposes how each might be used as a scaffold in teacher preparation programs for teacher candidates who are learning how to teach with technology. This chapter calls on teacher educators to use the frameworks as tools to improve their effectiveness with integrating technology into their teaching. Recommendations are provided for which framework to use during various phases of teacher preparation.	• Technology Integration Matrix (TIM) • Substitution, Augmentation, Modification, Redefinition (SAMR) • Passive, Interactive, Creative and Replaces, Amplifies, Transforms (PICRAT) • Triple-E Framework

Continued

Section or Chapter and Authors	Topic	Overview	Theoretical and/or Conceptual Framework
CHAPTER 5 Professional Expectations for Teacher Educators: The Teacher Educator Technology Competencies (TETCs) *David A. Slykhuis, University of Northern Colorado* *Denise A. Schmidt-Crawford, Iowa State University* *Kevin J. Graziano, Nevada State College* *Teresa S. Foulger, Arizona State University*	Technology competencies for teacher educators	This chapter introduces the Teacher Educator Technology Competencies (TETCs) in the context of technology infusion efforts and explains how teacher preparation programs and teacher educators can provide a strategic effort to help *all* teacher educators prepare to teach with technology, teach about technology, and support teacher candidates as they become proficient users of technology in their teaching. The TETCs represent the knowledge, skills, and attitudes *all* teacher educators need. This chapter also explores approaches for how teacher educators can address professional expectations and development related to teaching with technology throughout the teacher preparation program.	• Research-based tech competencies for teacher educators • Frameworks for professional development of teacher educators
CHAPTER 6 The Necessity of Preparing Teacher Candidates to Teach Online *Michael McVey, Eastern Michigan University*	Preparing teacher candidates to teach online	The tools and applications for online instruction appropriate for PK–12 teaching have increased in quality, and soon, access to them will be nearly universal. The consequence of this vastly improved online platform is that many teaching activities traditional to the physical classroom may move beyond those classroom walls and into a *virtual* teaching space. Teacher preparation programs need to prepare teacher candidates to use web-based tools and related instructional design in their teaching practice. This chapter describes how programs should be modeling online instructional strategies, providing teacher candidates opportunities to practice online teaching throughout their programs, and assessing teacher candidates as they expand their capacity to use online tools in blended or fully online PK–12 learning environments.	• Community of Inquiry (CoI) (Garrison, Anderson, & Archer)

Continued

	Section or Chapter and Authors	Topic	Overview	Theoretical and/ or Conceptual Framework
CHAPTER 7	Technology Infusion in Clinical Experiences *Debra R. Sprague, Seth A. Parsons, and Audra K. Parker, George Mason University*	Considerations for mutually beneficial school-university partnerships to support clinical practice	Since the National Council for the Accreditation of Teacher Education published its Blue Ribbon Panel Report in 2010, teacher preparation has experienced a shift to resituate clinical experiences at the core of teacher preparation. Inherent in this turn toward clinically centered teacher preparation are mutually beneficial school-university partnerships. One outcome of these efforts is an opportunity to support theory-to-practice connections. In this chapter, we explore how clinically centered teacher preparation affords opportunities for a program-wide and program-deep approach to address technology infusion. We suggest school-university partnerships afford teacher preparation programs opportunities to actualize technology infusion through both course-based field assignments as well as field experiences (e.g., student teaching) to help teacher candidates develop their ability to integrate technology.	• Clinical experience • Development of practice
CHAPTER 8	Technology Integration in the Induction Years: The Importance of PK–12 Partnerships *Jo Williamson, and Julie Moore, Kennesaw State University*	Teacher induction and transfer of learning from preservice to inservice	It is easy to think that teacher induction is exclusively the purview of PK–12 schools and districts, but this landscape is changing. In this chapter, we assert that a program-deep and program-wide technology preparation experience will transition into a graduates' first few years of teaching. To help teacher educators envision new roles and responsibilities related to graduates' early-career success, this chapter provides a review of what is known about teacher induction and new teachers' technology use. The chapter concludes with three practical strategies and meaningful resources to help teacher preparation programs support inductees' technology integration.	• Sociocultural theories of learning • Zone of proximal development (Vygotsky)

Continued

Section or Chapter and Authors	Topic	Overview	Theoretical and/or Conceptual Framework
Section III. Evaluating Technology Infusion Methods and guidance for assessing candidate outcomes and program- and college-level processes and progress.			
CHAPTER 9 Leadership for Technology Infusion: Guiding Change and Sustaining Progress in Teacher Preparation *Jon M. Clausen, Ball State University*	Leading transformational change for technology infusion in teacher preparation programs	In order for technology infusion to be successful, leaders at the upper administrative levels within teacher preparation programs must facilitate change, prioritize competing initiatives, and shape the change process for faculty and teacher candidates. Education leaders can draw on several theories, frameworks, and tools to support change. This chapter discusses the essential role of leadership for those who seek to promote and support the advancement of technology infusion within their teacher preparation programs and offers suggestions for how education leaders can initiate the process of transformational change for technology infusion.	• Diffusion of innovations theory (Rogers) • Change process (Fullan) • Concerns-Based Adoption Model (Hall & Hord)
CHAPTER 10 Evaluating Technology Infusion: Teacher Candidate and Program Outcomes *Ray R. Buss, Arizona State University*	Assessing teacher candidates' progress in a technology infusion program	This chapter provides information for teacher educators and college/school of education leaders on two ways to assess the effectiveness of technology infusion. First, this chapter focuses on evaluating the ultimate outcome of technology infusion, the development of teacher candidates' technology integration abilities, defined as their capabilities to teach K–12 students using technology. The chapter describes four theoretical perspectives that have influenced assessment efforts related to technology integration—the technological pedagogical content knowledge (TPACK) framework, the self-efficacy perspective, the Theory of Planned Behavior, and the Decomposed Theory of Planned Behavior. Secondarily, complementary assessment work in which teacher candidates evaluate effectiveness of their technology-infused program is discussed.	• TPACK • Self-efficacy • Theory of Planned Behavior (Ajzen) • Decomposed Theory of Planned Behavior (Sadaf, Newby, & Ertmer)

Continued

Section or Chapter and Authors	Topic	Overview	Theoretical and/or Conceptual Framework
Section IV. Advancing Technology Infusion Vision and action steps for nationwide collaboration for technology infusion in teacher preparation.			
CHAPTER 11 What Can We Achieve Together? A Call to Action for the Future of Technology Infusion in Teacher Preparation Programs *Joseph B. South, and Ji Soo Song, International Society for Technology in Education*	Sustaining technology infusion in teacher preparation through collaborative efforts of NGOs, government agencies, and education institutions	In the past decade, an explosion of access to technology in American schools has contributed to a fundamental change in the teaching environment. More classrooms than ever are equipped with the connectivity and devices necessary to leverage digital teaching opportunities. Yet, teachers continue to report that they do not feel well prepared to integrate new technologies across student learning experiences. As highlighted throughout *Championing Technology Infusion in Teacher Preparation*, teacher preparation represents a critical juncture in tackling this issue. This concluding chapter highlights five key areas that stakeholders from the public, private, and nonprofit sectors can collaboratively engage to systemically and sustainably improve teacher preparation pipelines and ensure that all teachers are prepared to use technology effectively from day one: setting a vision, incentivizing mastery, building capacity, prioritizing funds, and leveraging accountability.	• Interagency collaboration

Note: Brief biographical information for each of the contributors and editors is located in the front matter of this book.

SECTION I

Planning for Technology Infusion

This section includes background chapters on technology infusion in teacher preparation, frameworks for organizational change, and technology use in PK–12 teaching and learning.

CHAPTER 1
Design Considerations for Technology-Infused Teacher Preparation Programs
by Teresa S. Foulger

CHAPTER 2
Building Capacity for Technology Infusion through Systemic Change in Colleges and Schools of Education
by Robert D. Muller

CHAPTER 3
Rethinking Teacher Preparation: Learning from the PK–12 Edtech Story
by Sheryl Nussbaum-Beach

CHAPTER 1

Design Considerations for Technology-Infused Teacher Preparation Programs

TERESA S. FOULGER
ARIZONA STATE UNIVERSITY

Overview

It is important for colleges/schools of education to create a customized approach for how they address technology integration in their preparation programs. In a technology-infused teacher preparation program, technology integration is addressed by *all* instructors in a program-deep and program-wide manner. With this vision in mind, the goal for this chapter is to provide program planners with research-based design considerations and theoretical frameworks that will help them establish a unique vision for their program, initiate efforts, and expand upon their technology infusion initiatives.

Introduction

The 2017 US Department of Education's Office of Educational Technology's National Educational Technology Plan (NETP) reported that "many preservice teacher education graduates feel unprepared to use technology to support student learning as they transition to teaching and using technology effectively in the classroom" (Office of Educational Technology, 2017, p. 8). This report motivated some preparation programs to more substantively support teacher candidates as they learn to teach with technology. Typically, programs address teaching with technology through an isolated, stand-alone course taught by educational technology faculty. The NETP called for colleges/schools of educations to restructure their curriculum from a single course to a programmatic approach, representing a complete paradigm shift that calls for teacher educators "to ensure preservice teachers' experiences with educational technology are program-deep and program-wide rather than one-off courses separate from their methods courses" (p. 14). Because educational technology faculty presumably have more knowledge about technology integration and how to teach about it, moving forward with this idea requires "other" faculty take responsibility for supporting teacher candidates learning to teach with technology within the context of preparation courses.

Scenario: A Potential Threat or an Opportunity?

In 2011, the dean of the Mary Lou Fulton Teachers College at Arizona State University called faculty together to discuss her ideas for improving our preparation programs. As a large-scale program, we provide certification coursework for PK–12 teachers following a professional development school (PDS) model with school-based coursework and student teaching. During that meeting, she proposed eliminating the three-credit educational technology course as well as the assessment course to make room for more content methods courses and a full year of student teaching. As a member of the educational technology faculty team, I had worked closely with my colleagues for many years to keep the content of the technology course relevant for our teacher candidates. By then, most schools had high-speed Wi-Fi connections, and rapid advancements in educational technology had produced pockets of schools with strong interest in advancing the use of technology for teaching and learning. Our team was apprehensive about giving a head nod to the dean's proposal because it would mean eliminating our course from preparation programs. But we also saw some relevance to her idea. In the research we conducted about our course content and pedagogy, students had expressed concerns that coursework only partially prepared them to integrate technology in their future classrooms (Wetzel, Foulger, & Williams, 2008).

I began thinking about how I viewed technology "integration." I promoted technology as a seamless and nearly invisible aspect of good teaching, used as a tool to teach subject matter (e.g., mathematics, science, social studies, language arts content) in ways that enhanced learning opportunities. But was I "practicing what I preached" by teaching a course where educational technology was the main curricular focus and teaching about math, science, social studies, or language was of lesser concern?

It took a few weeks before the idea of eliminating the technology integration course fully sank in. Should we just let it go? The faculty realized this *could* be a good idea *if* we figured out a way to weave the technology integration curriculum into other courses, especially where the content was better represented. Yet, we wondered: What would giving up our course mean to the future of technology's presence in our preparation programs? Could we build and sustain a different approach? On a personal level, I was hired to support educational technology in the college. How would my professional identity fare if we moved in this direction?

Once we accepted the dean's proposal to eliminate the educational technology course, we decided to propose a new plan: technology infusion. Technology infusion was our way of addressing technology in a program-deep and program-wide manner, and the new plan ended up heightening the level of importance for technology throughout our college's preparation programs.

We are not aware of other colleges of education infusing technology throughout their programs at the level of infusion seen at ASU. The remainder of this chapter provides ideals, lessons learned, and expanding visions based on our experience and with the intent of supporting other colleges of education who want to adopt their own technology infusion model. Although what follows is framed by the long-standing ASU initiative, the section below is written conceptually in order to allow other colleges of education to imagine the application of technology infusion within their own contexts.

A High-Level Definition for Technology Infusion

The previous scenario occurred five years prior to the release of the NETP (Office of Educational Technology, 2017). While adopting our new approach, which was influenced and strengthened by the NETP call for colleges/schools of education to consider a *program-deep* and *program-wide* approach to support teacher candidates to develop technology integration skills, we began to differentiate between the terms "technology integration" and "technology infusion." The following are working definitions we use at ASU to help frame our conversations around this initiative:

Technology Integration. Any learning experience where technology is seamlessly used by educators (PK–20) and/or learners within the context of a learning process and in a manner that enhances the experience and/or outcome in some way(s). A PK–12 example of technology integration might include sixth graders using probes during their science class to import data to a spreadsheet, then analyzing the data and generating a bar graph to report their findings. An example of technology integration in a preparation program might include teacher candidates enrolled in a language arts methods course working in small groups to research reading strategies, then compiling and sharing best practices with their classmates through a digital presentation.

Technology Infusion. A program-deep and program-wide approach within a teacher preparation program to help teacher candidates learn how to leverage technology in their future teaching (i.e., in PK–12 classrooms). Throughout an infused program, teacher candidates experience:

- a course-specific and developmentally appropriate *technology integration curriculum* (e.g., as part of a science methods course, candidates learn how to effectively use probes in their PK–12 science classroom),

- *technology integration models* that emulate best practices (e.g., teaching strategies of their instructors, PK–12 mentors who excel with technology integration in the classroom, and video-based PK–12 teaching scenarios that showcase the application of technology integration theory and practice), and

- *developmentally appropriate and iterative practice, feedback, and reflection* about teaching with technology (e.g., lesson planning exercises, practice teaching experiences, formal practicums, and student teaching).

A preparation program that infuses technology assures that, upon graduation, teacher candidates have the skill set to teach with technology as well as the self-efficacy needed to do so (e.g., Foulger, Buss, Wetzel, & Lindsey, 2015). This means, ideally, that all courses and field experiences in a preparation program would be taught by faculty who are competent in teaching about the integration of technology within their content area (Foulger, Graziano, Schmidt-Crawford, & Slykhuis, 2017).

Applying a *program-wide* aspect of a technology-infused approach, nearly every stakeholder and system surrounding a teacher preparation program—administration/leadership, faculty, professional development, technology and technology support personnel, course development, course delivery, field experience, district partnerships, etc.—would support teacher candidates as they develop the skills to proficiently teach with technology. However, successfully adopting a technology-infusion approach requires a systemic view of change, the need to build capacity, and dynamic goals and monitoring.

Applying a *program-deep* aspect of a technology-infused approach, technology integration curriculum would be considered a part of all teacher educators' responsibilities. How teacher educators address technology integration within the context of their course content, integrate technology within course learning goals, and use technology pedagogically would provide impetus for innovative approaches. Once courses are revised as part of an infused program, teacher educators would need to manage the ongoing responsibility of ensuring that how they teach (with technology), what they teach (about technology), and the expectations they place on teacher candidates (for using technology) are all up to date with current technological advancements.

Applying Technological Pedagogical Content Knowledge (TPACK) in Preparation Programs

Administrators, faculty, and other stakeholders can more thoroughly create a vision for technology infusion in their colleges/schools of education when they use theory and research as a guide. The Technological Pedagogical Content Knowledge (TPACK) framework (Koehler & Mishra, 2008; Mishra & Koehler, 2006) is a technology integration framework that can be used as a conceptual guide for technology infusion. As illustrated in Figure 1.1, the TPACK framework helps educators to develop their knowledge of technology (TK), pedagogy (PK), and content (CK), as well as the interrelated knowledge bases that occur when TK, PK, and CK overlap (i.e., TPK, TCK, PCK, and TPACK). To be adept at integrating technology, teachers must apply all three knowledge bases of the TPACK framework and the overlapping knowledge bases.

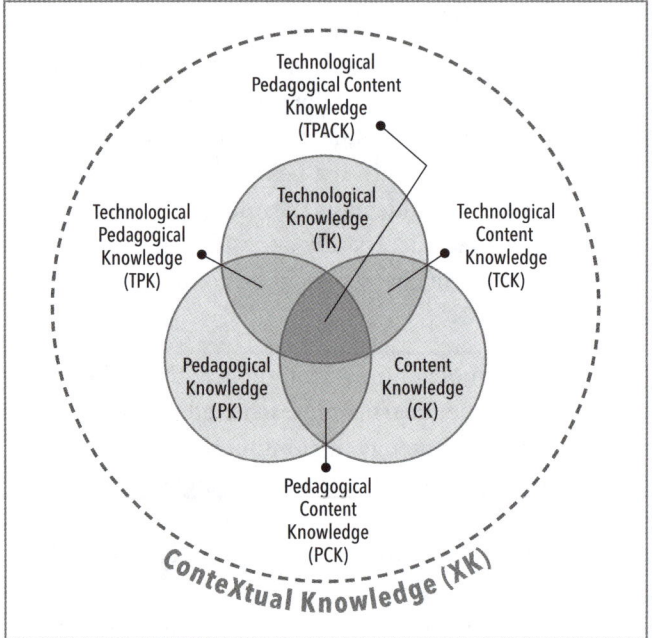

Figure 1.1 The TPACK model demonstrates the weaving together of content knowledge, pedagogical knowledge and technical knowledge, in teaching with technology. Revised version of the TPACK image. © Punya Mishra, 2018. Reproduced with permission.

The Nature of TPACK

Despite extensive research on how teachers can develop TPACK, the concept of TPACK remains nebulous. As Angeli, Valanides, and Christodoulou (2016) state, TPACK is "a unique body of knowledge that goes beyond mere integration or accumulation of the constituent knowledge bases, toward transformation of these contributing knowledge bases into something new" (p. 26). In fact, a study of 260 teacher candidates by Jin (2019) revealed that the growth of teacher candidates' TPACK was not necessarily correlated to growth in their TK, PK, and CK. It seems that developing the knowledge bases of TK, PK, and CK separately may not equate to improved TPACK overall.

Because we do not fully understand how TPACK develops, we also do not know the way(s) in which the knowledge bases should interrelate throughout the teacher preparation process. We are certain, however, that gaining proficiency in TPACK is a developmental process (i.e., it takes time and experience). This poses a challenge for teacher preparation programs attempting to address TPACK through a one-shot, stand-alone course.

TAKEAWAYS

As they plan their technology infusion approach, colleges/schools of education should consider that teacher candidates' development of TPACK involves advancing their knowledge of technology, pedagogy, and content, as well as learning how these three knowledge bases interrelate. This can only be accomplished over time.

Emphasizing TPACK's Contextual Knowledge

An effective technology-using teacher must be proficient with navigating unique school settings. The TPACK framework addresses this need with an additional knowledge base, contextual knowledge (XK), which accounts for the situated nature in which the other knowledge bases of TPACK must be applied by teachers. Mishra (2019), a visionary leader in the field of educational technology, notes that XK is "something that we (as teacher educators) can act on, change, and help teachers develop. … [A] lack of [XK] limits the effectiveness and success of any TPACK development, or a teacher's attempts at technology integration" (p. 2).

To emphasize the development of XK in teacher candidates, coursework must help teacher candidates account for local variables in field placements and future employment. For example, certain student, classroom, and school factors can influence the use of technology with PK–12 students, including but not limited to access to PK–12 online learning tools, the existence of online or hybrid models for learning, equipment maintenance and troubleshooting support, the school-based culture surrounding innovation, and community values surrounding technology use.

TAKEAWAYS

As they plan their technology infusion approach, colleges/schools of education should consider how they might support teacher candidates' development of contextual knowledge.

Developing TPACK through Practical Experience

According to the TPACK theory, the development of the three knowledge domains and a working knowledge of how they relate to one another in practice is tantamount to good teaching. Applying this idea to preparation programs, a longitudinal study by Mouza, Nandakumar, Yilmaz Ozden, and Karchmer-Klein (2017) confirmed that teacher candidates needed opportunities to "practice, or model effective integration of content, pedagogy, and technology during their undergraduate content instruction" (p. 15). This study also demonstrated that in the absence of educational technology coursework, opportunities for TPACK to develop were limited. In another study by Bell, Maeng, and Binns (2013), teacher candidates reported that practical aspects of learning to teach with technology were helpful. This included pedagogical supports such as modeling by instructors, peer collaboration, and feedback and reflection after teaching lessons during field experiences.

TAKEAWAYS

As they plan their technology infusion approach, colleges/schools of education should consider how to provide teacher candidates with experiences that will help them gain the practical aspects of teaching with technology in PK–12 settings.

Developing TPACK through a Long-Term Trajectory

Research by Niess and colleagues on math methods courses (Niess, 2011; Niess et al., 2009) validates the idea that learning to teach with technology is a developmental process. In these studies, researchers conducted observations over a four-year period to analyze how teachers integrated spreadsheets as learning tools into their mathematics classrooms. Findings revealed that teachers progressed through five stages, from an initial awareness of technology's role in teaching mathematics to the ultimate ability to evaluate the results of a learning experience integrated with technology. Specifically, the five stages are as follows:

1. Recognizing (knowledge): where teachers are able to use the technology and recognize how it aligns with mathematics content, yet do not integrate the technology in teaching and learning of mathematics.

2. Accepting (persuasion): where teachers form a favorable or unfavorable attitude toward teaching and learning mathematics by using an appropriate technology.

3. Adapting (decision): where teachers engage in activities that lead to a choice to adopt or reject teaching and learning mathematics by using an appropriate technology.

4. Exploring (implementation): where teachers actively integrate teaching and learning of mathematics with an appropriate technology.

5. Advancing (confirmation): where teachers evaluate the results of the decision to integrate teaching and learning mathematics with an appropriate technology. (Niess et al., 2009, p. 9)

See Figure 1.2 for a graphical representation of how TK, PK, and CK have been shown to advance to TPACK through the five stages of development for math teachers. Curriculum in a technology-infused program should help teacher candidates learn to integrate technology in developmentally appropriate ways.

TAKEAWAYS

As they plan for their technology infusion approach, colleges/schools of education should consider how teacher candidates' development of TPACK, through the developmental stages, can best be supported in a program-wide manner (i.e., across the span of courses).

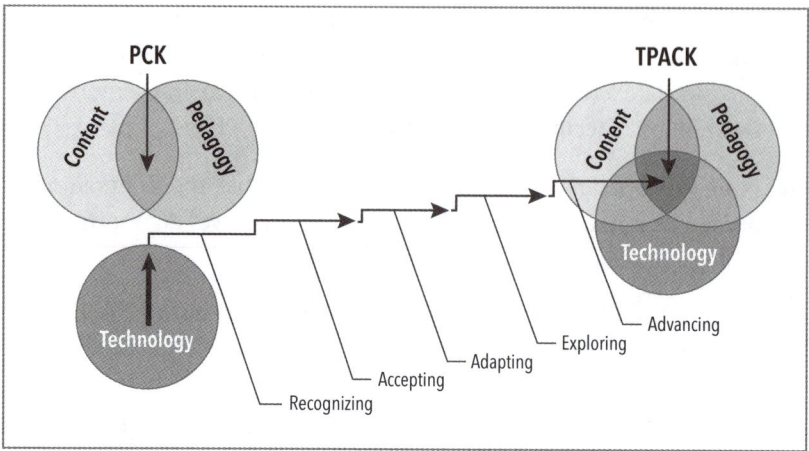

Figure 1.2   Reproduced by permission of the lead author, Margaret L. Niess. Niess, M.L., Ronau, R.N., Shafer, K.G., Driskel, S.O., Harper, S.R., Johnston, C., Browning, C., Ozgun-Koca, S. A. & Kersaint, G. (2009). Mathematics teacher TPACK standards and development model, originally printed in *Contemporary Issues in Technology and Teacher Education, 9*(1),4–24.

Administrative Role in Implementing Large-Scale Change

Educational change expert Michael Fullan claims that proposing a good idea is merely the beginning of an innovation and that the hard work of adopting change requires strong leaders (2001, 2008). In the case of adopting a technology infusion model, change is targeted on all courses, which mandates that faculty join together to do the hard work of program revisioning and course development. Strategic and effective professional development of faculty is necessary, including part-time faculty. Additionally, the systems surrounding programs, coursework, and faculty professional development must align to support a technology infusion initiative.

The support needed of administrators for this type of change to take root is no small undertaking. Administrators must provide leadership in appropriate and helpful ways. This means staying abreast of needs, not just in the initial stages, but in ongoing and ever-changing ways as technology infusion efforts advance (Graziano, Herring, Carpenter, Smaldino, & Finsness, 2017). An unwavering responsiveness to current needs is especially important when competing initiatives arise (Foulger & Clausen, 2019).

TAKEAWAYS

Administrators of colleges/schools of education should continually adjust their support in efforts to keep technology infusion initiatives moving forward, especially when competing initiatives arise.

Development of Teacher Educators' TPACK

Findings from an ASU comparative case study on technology infusion in the Mary Lou Fulton Teachers College depicted a possible pathway for teacher candidates to attain TPACK. These findings may be relevant as a way to scaffold candidates' experiences in a technology-infused program. The study compared teacher candidates' experiences in a stand-alone course to their experiences in a technology-infused methods course. Both groups generally advanced their TPACK with no difference in growth rate (Buss, Wetzel, Foulger, and Lindsey, 2015).

However, students expanded their TK and TPK at faster rates in the stand-alone course, whereas students in the technology-infused approach developed CK and PK faster. This demonstrates that the stand-alone course more thoroughly addressed technology's influence on pedagogy, whereas the technology-infused approach more intentionally addressed content and pedagogy. It is noteworthy that the stand-alone course was taught by educational technology experts and emphasized learning new technologies, while the technology-infused methods courses were taught by subject-matter experts with strengths in content and pedagogy.

Because the responsibility of teaching about technology was new to the majority of methods course instructors (Buss, Wetzel, Foulger, and Lindsey, 2015), we suspect this gap could be lessened over time through a combination of experience and additional professional development. Consequently, we have crafted professional development that is ongoing and guided by the following three needs and design principles:

- Because our teaching is situated across four campuses and within many school districts across our state, we offer foundational professional development online to span this geographical gap.

- Because most professional development needs are specific to courses and those teaching those courses, targeted professional development is course specific.

- Because of faculty transitions and employment of part-time faculty, whenever possible professional development is archived online and made available for faculty new to a course (e.g., via websites, recorded sessions, course-specific instructor networks).

TAKEAWAYS

As they plan for their technology infusion approach, colleges/schools of education should address the limited TPACK of teacher educators through carefully planned opportunities for professional development.

The "Wicked Problem" of Developing TPACK in Teacher Candidates, and the Champion that Is Required

At ASU, we have increasingly become aware that adopting a technology infusion approach mandates support from almost every system in our college. A change of this magnitude is a "wicked problem." Wicked problems, as originally defined (Rittel & Webber, 1973), are innovations characterized by their social complexity and lack of a predetermined stopping point to improvements. One advance toward a solution could lead to another, next concern.

Thompson (2009) goes beyond the generic idea of "leadership" by outlining the function of champions as "enlightened change makers who are personally committed to mutual values, rather than self-centered ones, and relentlessly driven by possibilities" (p. 6). Champions within an organization have a heightened sense of awareness of change, maintain strong communications, and strive to be opportunistic; they are driven by emotional energy and a sense of urgency and a strong sense of personal purpose. As mentioned in the preface to this book, the journey to technology infusion requires leaders to embrace the role of a champion. At ASU, the research and implementation team has served in this capacity through the following shared functions:

Continually Seek a Shared Vision. At ASU, our vision for technology has continually developed. We have found it important to maintain the right amount of risk so as to advance stakeholders with a vision that feels appropriate.

Root Decisions in Local Context. We have tried to be conscious about realities of current PK–12 needs and to couple this with our vision for possible uses of technology as well as innovative uses of technology. It has been important for us to have a sense for what portion or extent of the vision can be addressed in the field and to nudge appropriately.

Seek Incremental Change. As we work with stakeholders, we have a mindset that supports continual, long-term change dedicated to advancing the shared and continually changing vision in incremental ways.

Maintain Constant Communication. As we strive to grow technology infusion, appropriate communication is our strongest tool. We know that the more buy-in we have, and the more active engagement we instill, the stronger this initiative will be.

Lead in All Directions. We seek to continually influence administrators and other leaders in our preparation programs, as well as working laterally with colleagues, support staff, and other stakeholders who are directly involved or indirectly influence the success of technology infusion.

Be Helpful. We have found it imperative to be supportive so those involved can advance their practice, but only as their readiness allows. We have experienced that timing is critical; furthermore, the right amount of nudge is necessary.

Keep Technology in the Forefront. Especially when other initiatives arise that can compete for attention, we have found it imperative to maintain our focus on advancing infusion. Keeping technology infusion in the forefront takes a continual positive mindset. We have found it most helpful to recognize frustration as an opportunity for reflection and regrouping and possibly as a time to advance the vision.

TAKEAWAYS

Colleges/schools of education should recognize from the onset that adopting a technology infusion approach is a complex and long-term change process that will benefit from a dedicated champion or team of champions who fulfill multiple functions.

The Stages of Technology Infusion at ASU

For our teacher candidates to demonstrate greater achievement using our technology infusion approach versus a one-semester course, "technology" had to be seamlessly woven into the fabric of teacher preparation programs. Given that adoption of a technology infusion approach affects the entire teacher preparation system, including the PK–12 partnership schools where our teacher candidates participate in a yearlong student teaching experience, even after years of diligent effort we are still growing in organizational capacity for technology infusion at ASU. Our experience may be helpful to others undertaking this large initiative.

We did not initially plan a pathway for advancing the technology infusion effort in our college. Instead, we took a step toward our vision, then adjusted our efforts based on our research. We learned that contextual concerns such as leadership capacity, support, and acceptance of the idea were critical. To date, we have progressed through what we have labeled as two stages: benchmarking the educational technology course (Stage I) and infusing methods courses (Stage II). Currently in Stage III, full infusion, we are advancing our effort more diligently within all courses and into field experiences. We are also reviewing how to measure the progress of teacher candidates as they learn how to teach with technology. Figure 1.3 depicts the conceptual differences between the three stages.

In Figure 1.3, the dots represent faculty or support personnel. A red dot represents someone with strong TPACK (e.g., educational technology faculty, professional, instructional designer). A pink dot represents someone with a strong understanding of teaching (content) and has the additional responsibility of supporting teacher candidates learning how to teach with technology. A gray circle is someone who has not (yet) been exposed to technology infusion. A dot or circle that is touching a black line represents someone teaching a course; red dots that are distant from a black line represent technology experts who support course development or delivery but are not an instructor of record.

Technology Infusion Adoption Stages

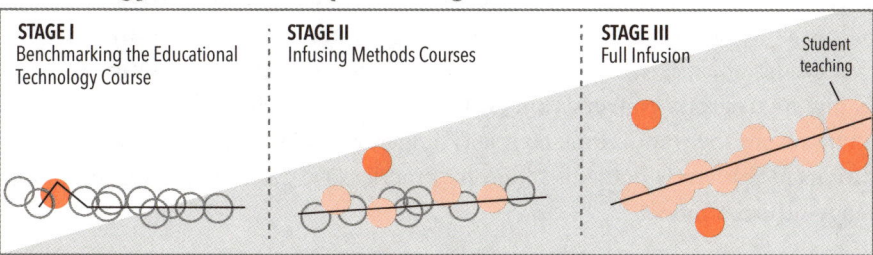

STAGE I
Benchmarking the Educational Technology Course

STAGE II
Infusing Methods Courses

STAGE III
Full Infusion

Student teaching

Figure 1.3 Stages for the adoption of a technology infusion approach. Image property of Teresa S. Foulger.

The black line represents the educational technology curriculum within the span of a preparation program. When a line is on an angle, technology integration builds. In Stage I at ASU (prior to 2011), educational technology faculty taught the educational technology course, which was benchmarked for best practices. During Stage II (2012 to 2018), methods courses were infused. The ultimate vision (Stage III, beginning 2019) is that all courses, including student teaching, will be infused, and technology integration curriculum will be established across the span of an entire preparation program.

Program administrators should seek to develop a process to advance their vision, one step at a time, in ways that make sense for their college/school of education. For ASU, the focus of each stage grew out of the prior stage. The following sections describe each stage in detail.

STAGE I: Benchmarking the Educational Technology Course at ASU

The semester prior to eliminating the stand-alone educational technology course was a one-time opportunity to review the course's content and delivery. The stand-alone course had always been taught by educational technology faculty, including myself. The faculty had worked together for many years, and for the most part, we felt that the activities were interesting and engaging for students and very relevant to PK–12 classrooms.

Because we knew that adopting a technology infusion approach would be a long-term change project, we decided to use research to guide our program's transformation. To begin, we benchmarked the stand-alone course. Benchmarking is a process of comparing a given circumstance against a standard. We conducted a study of 110 teacher candidates spread across five courses taught by three different faculty members, in order to determine benchmarks (i.e., standards we did not want to lose as we launched our technology infusion approach). In a study of our teacher candidates' experiences, survey data assessing ASU teacher candidates' TPACK and focus group conversations with teacher candidates revealed four benchmarks from the stand-alone course (Foulger, Buss, Wetzel, & Lindsey, 2012). Implications of this study helped us identify practices we desired to maintain in our technology infusion model.

Benchmark 1: Technology Skills. Teacher candidates expressed the need for support as they "learn how to learn technology" within the context of specific teaching circumstances. They also desired deep knowledge of important technology tools, as well as awareness of other tool choices for a given content area.

Benchmark 2: Technology Access in the Field. In the stand-alone course, certification-related coursework introduced teacher candidates to visionary uses of technology. Some teacher candidates expressed struggles related to limited access to technology in the field, as well as other roadblocks that inhibited their ability to practice teaching with technology.

Benchmark 3: Orientation of Class Content and Access to Resources. Teacher candidates noted that the process-oriented, hands-on approach of the stand-alone course allowed them to get familiar with technology tools. However, the content by which tools were shared (e.g., a mathematics activity) was often a mismatch for their grade level and subject interests.

Benchmark 4: Teaching and TPACK. Even with limited exposure to the technology tools (TK), teacher candidates were confident in their ability to troubleshoot and expressed little concern over using technology in PK–12 classrooms. However, although they had created units of instruction that involved use of technology, they expressed feeling only moderately prepared to actually use technology to support teaching and learning (TPACK) (Koehler & Mishra, 2008; Mishra & Koehler, 2006).

STAGE II: Infusing Methods Courses at ASU

Once the benchmarking phase was complete, we decided to work with methods course instructors to help them address technology into their courses. For example, an educational technology specialist collaborated with the course coordinators of a social studies methods course to develop assignments that addressed technology integration within the context of the social studies content. A master shell was created for the course so that others teaching the course could use the detailed material. As a part of this phase, the division director established that, moving forward, master shells would be used in our college to ensure that those assigned to teach a given course would have access to appropriate activities, rubrics, policy, etc., that were cocreated for that course by faculty experts and a professional developer.

Additionally, the professional developer created four sequenced, web-based modules on digital citizenship that were strategically placed across the breadth of the program within courses that were fitting. Because the delivery of the digital citizenship modules are web-based, they are monitored and updated on a regular basis by the professional developer to guarantee currency and relevance. This pilot of web-based pedagogy was selected due to the critical nature of the digital citizenship content and our interest in making sure that content was presented with fidelity and appropriate accountability measures for teacher candidates. However, we suspect that in the future, instructor knowledge on digital citizenship might stay limited because the modules are "siloed" and do not necessarily require course instructor expertise.

During a two-year longitudinal study exploring Stage II, we measured the development of teacher candidates' ability to teach with technology via a survey measuring teacher candidates' TPACK knowledge domains (Schmidt et al., 2009). We found knowledge domains increased between the beginning of their teacher preparation courses and their student teaching experience. Based on data collected at ASU, teacher candidates appreciated opportunities to learn about TPACK as a basis for improving their technology integration skills, and they recognized the influence student teaching had on their growth. They planned to integrate technology into their work as certified teachers, and they understood the importance of helping their future PK–12 students learn about digital citizenship (Buss, Foulger, Wetzel, & Lindsey, 2018).

STAGE III: Full Infusion as the Current Vision at ASU

As we moved forward with our vision, we realized that in addition to teaching about technology integration, course instructors should also model teaching with technology. This posed four problems: (1) the course would need to stay innovative and on the cutting edge of technology; (2) faculty with expertise in the course topic, but whose strength is not in teaching with technology (TCK or TPACK), would need ongoing support to keep their courses current; and (3) it would be challenging to create professional development models that effectively address faculty attrition and the use of part-time instructors in our college. Where field experiences and student teaching were concerned, (4) some schools and classrooms were ill-equipped with technology tools and Wi-Fi, making it difficult for teacher candidates when they are asked to practice teaching with technology.

At ASU, we determined that in a fully infused program, all experiences need to provide opportunities for teacher candidates to develop their capability to teach with technology. Although we have not yet reached the full vision of Stage III, we believe this is a more thorough approach than the original, stand-alone educational technology course of our preparation programs prior to 2011.

Three Essential Pillars of a Technology-Infused Program

Colleges/schools of education wishing to begin or advance a technology infusion approach will need to define their curriculum, provide teacher candidates with models, and provide opportunities for them to practice teaching with technology. These efforts should be conducted in a way that will strengthen teacher candidates' self-efficacy in teaching with technology, as well as provide them with a basis for being committed and intentional about using technology as certified teachers.

Technology Integration Curriculum that Spans Certification Programs

Through coursework, teacher candidates engage in a curriculum that connects technology to content-relevant pedagogy and fosters continual growth in their TPACK. The technology integration curriculum should span the breadth of the entire preparation program (i.e., be spiraled and developmentally appropriate), taught within courses that are not solely dedicated to educational technology, and even be addressed in arts and sciences coursework that is outside college offerings. Existing guidelines could support the champions of technology infusion, program administrators, advisory councils, etc., in colleges/schools of education during curriculum development. For example, the ISTE Standards for Educators (iste.org/standards/for-educators) could inform the curriculum used in postsecondary courses, and the ISTE Standards for Students (iste.org/standards/for-students) could help teacher candidates strive to meet the needs of PK–12 students during field experiences. Additionally, some content-focused organizations address teaching with technology through their own standards. For example, the National Council of Teachers of Mathematics (NCTM) Principles and Standards for School Mathematics (2000) promote the use of technology by students as an instructional strategy critical to teaching math content and an "essential component to the [learning] environment" (p. 5). In the NCTM guidelines, "technology" is one of the Six Principles for School Mathematics, with a notation that technology makes it "possible and necessary to reexamine what mathematics students should learn as well as how they can best learn it" (p. 3). Following these and other such guidelines from content organizations where technology is explicitly called out as an essential component of teaching and learning, it is critical that colleges/schools of education align their technology integration curriculum with national guidelines as well as state licensing requirements to ensure that candidates meet the expectations established by accrediting agencies and visionary organizations.

Learning Experiences that Model Innovative Uses of Technology

Through coursework, teacher candidates participate in university-level learning experiences that model innovative uses of technology. This means all teacher educators, even those teaching general education required courses, mentors, and field experience supervisors, etc., would be adept at using technology for teaching, including developing activities and practices that involve technology in the hands of teacher candidates as learners. Moreover, ideally, models for technology integration would span the breadth of the entire preparation program and would be evident even in the general education coursework completed by candidates in the arts and sciences.

Opportunities for Practice and Reflection

Throughout their preparation experiences, teacher candidates have many opportunities to practice integrating technology in a variety of settings. Practice cycles are developmentally appropriate and include cycles of feedback and reflection. Expectations from their performance expand as teacher candidates progress through their program.

Development of Self-Efficacy and Intentionality

Through coursework, teacher candidates establish and develop a vision for their future PK–12 students, including the use of technology that is specific to content and contextual factors. This means teacher candidates are goal oriented throughout their program and by graduation they believe in their ability to successfully integrate technology as a certified teacher, even considering realities of the field when they graduate.

Grow Your Own Vision and Technology Infusion Model

My colleagues and I have found the adoption of technology infusion at ASU to be beneficial. Our progression of technology infusion is within the context of an undergraduate, traditional university preparation setting. While ideas and frameworks shared within this chapter may apply to similar settings, about 20% of teachers new to the field are prepared through nontraditional programs. Additionally, more than 20% of teachers are prepared in states other than where they teach; this necessitates that colleges/schools of education account for "preparation" in a broader sense and beyond their state boarders (Office of Postsecondary Education, 2016). Indeed, further research is needed in the field to better understand the difference between technology integration being taught during an isolated course or set of strategic experiences and through a program that is fully infused with technology. Our work and data that we have collected suggest that under the right conditions, this is a good direction to go.

Leaders who are contemplating how to address the charge in the NETP (Office of Educational Technology, 2016; Office of Educational Technology, 2017) should consider an infused approach. However, before launching into such a large and expansive effort, colleges/schools of education should take time to explore and create structures for success. Iterative cycles of research and program development at ASU have led to our current framework for technology infusion. Upon reflection of our work to date (Foulger, Wetzel, & Buss, 2019), we recommend that other colleges/schools of education consider the following factors as influential in decisions about the design of their technology-infused model:

- Develop a contextualized and dynamic vision.

- Establish the dedication of stakeholders' time, effort, and persistence.

- Leverage pressures from challenging circumstances.

- Ensure leadership capacity and commitment.

- Tap the expertise of educational technology faculty by offering them alternate responsibilities.

- Provide resources to sustain the effort, evaluating progress along the way.

- Allocate resources for professional development, which would be needed by all faculty.

- Plan for ongoing, long-term, and sustained efforts.

Most importantly, administrators and faculty considering a technology infusion approach should realize that as a response to change, faculty as well as teacher candidates may push back (e.g., Rogers, 2003); thus, faculty and staff need to make the necessary plans to account for a possible decline in student satisfaction (Foulger, Wetzel, & Buss, 2019). However, the long-term expected benefits can be expected to outweigh the setbacks felt from adopting this innovation.

The chapters that follow address several elements of a technology infusion effort. Consideration of these topics can help administrators and faculty design and advance their technology infusion framework and effort more comprehensively and systematically. Proponents who are planning, promoting, or participating in technology infusion will want to consider this book's content as they plan their initial design, develop a long-term plan, evaluate progress, and further implement technology infusion initiatives in their school/college of education.

I would like to acknowledge those who have been involved with the technology infusion effort in the Mary Lou Fulton Teachers College at Arizona State University for their hard work and dedication to technology: Keith Wetzel, Ray Buss, LeeAnn Lindsey, Stacey Pasquel, Jodie Donner, and Man Su. Without their championing of the research and adoption process, the insights presented in this chapter would not have been possible.

—TERESA S. FOULGER

Getting Started Resources

Arizona State University. (n.d.) Technology infusion publications and proceedings education.asu.edu/tech-infusion

This website contains information about ASU's change process, informed by a series of iterative research studies. The site includes a reference list of journal articles and conference proceedings that may be helpful to other colleges and schools of education undertaking a similar approach.

Foulger, T. S., Wetzel, K., & Buss, R. (2019). Moving toward a technology infusion approach: Considerations for teacher preparation programs. *Journal of Digital Learning in Teacher Education, 35*(2), 79–91.

The story of the technology infusion approach at ASU is shared in this article. Reflections by ASU faculty, gleaned from five years of iterative cycles of action research, revealed factors that shaped the adoption of technology infusion, including administrative leadership and support, dedicated professional development, and sustained efforts. The article concludes with a list of considerations for administrators and faculty in colleges/schools of education when adopting a technology infusion approach.

Rogers, E. M. (2003). *Diffusion of innovations* (5th ed.). New York, NY: Free Press.

This book provides a comprehensive look at how an innovation is adopted by an organization. It provides an understanding of the complexities through a systems perspective of organizational change. Research and practical considerations in this update of Rogers's seminal work are invaluable for technology infusion champions.

Thompson, M. (2009). *The organizational champion: How to develop passionate change agents at every level*. New York, NY: McGraw-Hill.

This book is a good pre-read for anyone considering approaching their administrators with the idea of moving toward a technology infusion approach. The content moves beyond understanding leadership by addressing the unique skills needed for anyone, at any level within an organization, who has a mission to address organizational and societal needs.

Office of Educational Technology. (2016). *Advancing educational technology in teacher preparation: Policy brief.* bit.ly/2XhWWor

In this policy brief, the US Department of Education's Office of Educational Technology states that new graduates from colleges/schools of education are ineffective at integrating technology in their teaching and asks teacher educators to work together as innovators to develop program-deep and program-wide ways to better address this need.

References

Angeli, C., Valanides, N., & Christodoulou, A. (2016). Theoretical considerations of Technological Pedagogical Content Knowledge. In M. C. Herring, M. J. Koehler, and P. Mishra (Eds.), *Handbook of Technological Pedagogical Content Knowledge (TPACK) for Educators* (2nd ed., pp. 11–30). New York, NY: Routledge.

Bell, R. L., Maeng, J. L., & Binns, I. C. (2013). Learning in context: Technology integration in a teacher preparation program informed by situated learning theory. *Journal of Research in Science Teaching, 50*, 348–379.

Buss, R. R., Wetzel, K., Foulger, T. S., & Lindsey, L. (2015). Preparing teachers to integrate technology into K–12 instruction: Comparing a stand-alone technology course with a technology-infused approach. *Journal of Digital Learning in Teacher Education, 31*(4), 160-172.

Buss, R., Foulger, T. S., Wetzel, K. A., & Lindsey, L. (2018). Preparing teachers to integrate technology into K–12 instruction II: Examining the effects of technology-infused methods courses and student teaching. *Journal of Digital Learning in Teacher Education, 34*(3), 134–150.

Foulger, T. S., Buss, R. R., Wetzel, K., & Lindsey, L. (2012). Preservice teacher education: Benchmarking a stand-alone ed tech course in preparation for change. *Journal of Digital Learning in Teacher Education, 29*(2), 48–58.

Foulger, T. S., Buss, R. R., Wetzel, K., & Lindsey, L. (2015). Instructors' growth in TPACK: Teaching technology-infused methods courses to pre-service teachers. *Journal of Digital Learning in Teacher Education, 31*(4), 134–147. doi.org/10.1080/21532974.2015.1055010

Foulger, T., & Clausen, J. (2019). Visionary guidelines, challenges, and solutions for adopting a technology infusion approach: Suggestions from leaders in the field. In K. Graziano (Ed.), *Proceedings of Society for Information Technology & Teacher Education International Conference* (pp. 2184–2188). Las Vegas, NV: Association for the Advancement of Computing in Education (AACE). www.learntechlib.org/primary/p/207992

Foulger, T. S., Graziano, K. J., Schmidt-Crawford, D., & Slykhuis, D. A. (2017). Teacher Educator Technology Competencies. *Journal of Technology and Teacher Education, 25*(4), 413–448. www.learntechlib.org/p/181966

Foulger, T. S., Wetzel, K., & Buss, R. (2019). Moving toward a technology infusion approach: Considerations for teacher preparation programs. *Journal of Digital Learning in Teacher Education, 35*(2), 79–91.

Fullan, M. (2001). *Leading in a culture of change.* San Francisco, CA: Wiley.

Fullan, M. (2008). *The six secrets of change: What the best leaders do to help their organizations survive and thrive.* San Francisco, CA: Wiley.

Graziano, K. J., Herring, M. C., Carpenter, J. P., Smaldino, S., & Finsness, E. S. (2017). A TPACK diagnostic tool for teacher education leaders. *TechTrends, 61,* 372–379.

Jin, Y. (2019, March). *The nature of TPACK: Is TPACK distinctive, integrative or transformative?* Presentation at the Annual Society for Information Technology and Teacher Education (SITE) Conference, Las Vegas, NV.

Koehler, M. J., & Mishra, P. (2008). Introducing TPCK. In AACTE Committee on Innovation and Technology (Ed.), *The handbook of technological pedagogical content knowledge (TPCK) for educators* (pp. 3–29). New York, NY: American Association of Colleges of Teacher Education and Routledge.

Mishra, P. (2019). Considering contextual knowledge: The TPACK diagram gets an upgrade. *Journal of Digital Learning in Teacher Education, 35*(2), 76–78.

Mishra, P., & Koehler, M. (2006). Technological pedagogical content knowledge: A framework for teacher knowledge. *Teachers College Record, 108*, 1017–1054.

Mouza, C., Nandakumar, R., Yilmaz Ozden, S., & Karchmer-Klein, R. (2017). A longitudinal examination of preservice teachers' technological pedagogical content knowledge in the context of undergraduate teacher education. *Action in Teacher Education, 39*(2), 153–171.

National Council of Teachers of Mathematics. (2000). *Principles and standards for school mathematics.* Reston, VA: Author. www.nctm.org/Standards-and-Positions/Principles-and-Standards

Niess, M. L. (2011). Investigating TPACK: Knowledge growth in teaching with technology. *Journal of Educational Computing Research, 44*(3), 299–317.

Niess, M. L., Ronau, R. N., Shafer, K. G., Driskell, S. O., Harper S. R., Johnston, C., … Kersaint, G. (2009). Mathematics teacher TPACK standards and development model. *Contemporary Issues in Technology and Teacher Education, 9*(1), 4–24.

Office of Educational Technology. (2016). *Advancing educational technology in teacher preparation: Policy brief.* U.S. Department of Education. tech.ed.gov/files/2016/12/Ed-Tech-in-Teacher-Preparation-Brief.pdf

Office of Educational Technology. (2017). *Reimagining the role of technology in education: 2017 National Education Technology Plan update.* tech.ed.gov/files/2017/01/NETP17.pdf

Office of Postsecondary Education. (2016). *Preparing and credentialing the nation's teachers: The secretary's ninth report on teacher quality.* title2.ed.gov/Public/TitleIIReport16.pdf

Rittel, H., & Webber, M. (1973). Dilemmas in a general theory of planning. *Policy Sciences, 4*(2), 155–169.

Rogers, E. M. (2003). *Diffusion of innovations* (5th ed.). New York, NY: Free Press.

Schmidt, D. A., Baran, E., Thompson, A. D., Mishra, P., Koehler, M. J., & Shin, T. S. (2009). Technological pedagogical content knowledge (TPACK): The development and validation of an assessment instrument for preservice teachers. *Journal of Research on Technology in Education, 42*(2), 123–149.

Thompson, M. (2009). *The organizational champion: How to develop passionate change agents at every level.* New York, NY: McGraw-Hill.

Wetzel, K., Foulger, T. S., & Williams, M. K. (2008). The evolution of the required educational technology course. *Journal of Computing in Teacher Education, 25*(2), 67–71.
www.tandfonline.com/doi/abs/10.1080/10402454.2008.10784611

CHAPTER 2

Building Capacity for Technology Infusion through Systemic Change in Colleges and Schools of Education

ROBERT D. MULLER
NATIONAL LOUIS UNIVERSITY

Overview

This chapter proposes a framework for leaders of colleges/schools of education—the institutions responsible for preparing and supporting the ongoing professional development of the vast majority of the nation's teachers—to help guide their thinking through the choppy waters of technology-driven change. The first section briefly summarizes why and how technology integration and infusion approaches should be important to leaders of programs designed to prepare and advance teachers. The chapter proposes a framework for leaders to attend to the interrelated web of functions and roles that comprise complex organizational systems, and identifies some of the common pitfalls that impede change and recommendations for mitigating them.

Why and How Technology Infusion Matters

As modern myth would have it, the invention of the pencil was first seen as a destructive influence on teaching and learning. Fast forward a few hundred years, and the early 21st century has seen an unparalleled pace of technological advances that have also served to disrupt established ideas about teaching and learning. Moore's law, which posits that computing power doubles every two years, may have slowed, but has proven largely true. Consider, for example, the processing speed of today's mobile phone or handheld device compared to just a few years ago, or the power embedded in miniscule microchips in household appliances. And so, with technological advance comes systems and organizational change, opportunities to lead, opportunities to resist, and plenty of ways to stay the same. The question is not whether educational institutions, their people, processes, and structures must embrace technological change but rather how to do so in a manner that advances learning, supports social justice goals, and is coherent and aligned with day-to-day operations and capacity.

This book is about technology integration and infusion, the idea that teaching is technology-enabled and learning is undergirded by appropriate application of digital tools. Technology integration is a precursor to infusion. Mistakenly, the terms are often used interchangeably, but as described in Chapter 1, infusion is an approach to teaching about technology integration that results in teacher candidates being effective with integrating technology. Technology integration in PK–12 classrooms taught by graduates from preparation programs is the intended result and derivative of a program that is infused with technology. Consider, for example, an institution's adoption of a learning management system (LMS). The use of LMS platforms evolved over a complex journey from nonuse in exclusively face-to-face instruction, to sporadic use of course management software by individual faculty, to institution-wide adoption of an LMS, to consistent application of standards for quality of online course design (such as Quality Matters), to planned use throughout program content as well as delivery method. Throughout this book, the authors argue that technology integration and infusion matter—and matter a lot.

Efficiency and Effectiveness

The rationale for technology integration and infusion in teacher preparation is not exclusively an efficiency "do more with less" argument. The goal is not simply to deploy resources efficiently (the "right" way) but also effectively (doing the "right" thing). The efficiency argument for focusing on technology infusion is fundamentally about creating shared vocabulary, common practices, and a community of learners who work together to apply technology as it best suits their needs. The result, while not necessarily just about cost or time savings, is the avoided cost and effort associated with isolated actions. There is an effectiveness argument to be made for ensuring that best practice in technology use is generally applied, and potholes in the information highway avoided. Where digital applications can be used to help differentiate instruction and to model new concepts to advance learning, technology infusion strategies are directly tied to learning goals. Furthermore, as universities undergo metamorphosis from brick and mortar to cyber organizations, they go through a maturation process where technology moves from an individual classroom-based pursuit, to an integrated set of programs and course-level tools, to full infusion throughout the enterprise (McCloskey & Winter, 2012).

Consider the ways in which professional development, instruction, and assessment are all highly dependent on the technologies that enable them. Furthermore, teacher preparation programs are integral parts of ecosystems that extend far beyond university walls. Candidates' clinical experiences, the standards that drive curricula, and methods of instruction and student engagement are shaped by the PK–12 schools and districts where new graduates will teach. Universities, like all organizations, are fundamentally living organisms that are constantly adapting to changes in both external and internal stimuli. The ubiquity, power, and speed of digital technologies break down barriers to focus even greater emphasis on the thoughtful deployment of technology to advance learning.

Perhaps most important, when done well, leaders' efforts to engage entire organizations in thoughtful technology deployment and use can leverage learning theory and brain research in cognitive and noncognitive development. In 1999, the National Research Council described how learning occurs, how expertise develops, and how learning environments can be designed to support learning. The expanded *How People Learn* report (National Research Council, 2000) and the *How People Learn II* update in 2018 (National Academies of Sciences, 2018) have refined and further developed knowledge about the science of learning, the development of the human brain, and how technology can play a key role in learning. For teacher preparation programs, helping candidates understand and design digital learning environments can become part of the foundation of every assignment, not a separate module. This goal poses a fundamental shift for many teacher educators, from considering technology as an "add-on" to becoming part of baseline design assumptions (Jacobson, Levin, & Kapur, 2019; Tondeur et al., 2011). The problem is that this complex undertaking involves virtually every aspect of the teaching enterprise—an adaptive challenge.

Technology Infusion as an Adaptive Challenge

In their provocative work about public leadership, Heifetz and Linsky (2009) posited that contemporary organizations tend to approach issues as technical problems to be solved, rather than adaptive challenges to be understood. Historically, education institutions have approached matters related to technology as technical endeavors—ones which, with the right expertise, time, connectivity, hardware, software, and perhaps a dose of professional development, can be resolved. Technology infusion, on the other hand, is an adaptive challenge. The idea of addressing adaptive challenges is fundamental to learning organizations (Senge, 1990). Adaptive challenges do not lend themselves to easy fixes, nor resolution through unraveling complexity. Rather, adaptive challenges are often ambiguous, paradoxical, nonlinear, and multidimensional. They require an inquiry mindset that brings together diverse perspectives and expertise around common questions. Colleges/schools of education are no exception; leaders therefore need to resist quick fixes and rather face the ambiguity of adaptive problem-solving—posing questions, challenging assumptions, and embracing experimentation.

Technology Infusion as a Systems Design Opportunity

One way to build an adaptive approach is by thinking about technology infusion through the lens of systems theory. Leaders grounded in systems analysis and design-based research methods are more likely to develop robust capacity for finding creative, sustainable, and well-suited technology infusion strategies. Research in systems analysis suggests that significant results and progress can emanate from understanding how complex systems work. Meadows's pioneering work captured the attention of developers of large-scale engineering and technology projects (synthesized in Meadows, 2008); it has since been applied across professions. Bryk, Gomez, Grunow, and LeMahieu take a systems approach to the education reform arena, bringing together research methods, policy change, student-focused outcomes, and continuous improvement (2017). Their work suggests that rather than increasingly narrow research questions designed to meet the methodological specifications of a randomized experimental design study, systems thinking and formation of networked improvement communities to bring together multiple stakeholders around complex educational questions have a much higher likelihood of generating meaningful findings and powerful results. For leaders in teacher preparation institutions in particular, a systems-theory approach is key to thinking about technology integration and infusion, since it touches all facets of organizational life.

Technology Infusion as a Change Management Challenge

At its core, technology infusion is about change (Foulger, Wetzel, & Buss 2018). And with change comes discomfort, resistance, and uncertainty, as well as opportunity, innovation, and enthusiasm. Fullan's keen observations about leading change in education are captured in his many works directed at education leaders (Fullan, 2016). Kotter's framework for leading change remains a time-tested classic (Kotter, 2012), equally germane as education leaders at all levels consider how to advance their technology infusion goals. Leaders of teacher preparation institutions may find Kotter's recommendations helpful, including establishing a guiding coalition, finding quick wins, overcommunicating, and developing explicit strategies to overcome resistance.

Articulating the technology infusion vision is an essential, but insufficient, step to incentivize action. Establishing new norms requires establishing a clear value proposition that appeals to each individual and function in the change process. Then one needs to demonstrate how the establishment of a "new normal," in this case one where technology infusion is a basic precept, is a worthwhile endeavor. Grappling with how the pieces of the organizational puzzle interact and fit together (or not) is an essential piece of analysis. Not only must one consider the internal higher education system dynamics within the college/school of education but also across university functions that influence candidate access and success, program and curriculum, faculty life, and finance. Beyond the walls of the university, the relevant system for leaders in teacher preparation includes the external stakeholders and partners in PK–12 schools and surrounding communities.

This is a lot to keep track of. This book is based on the premise that technology infusion is an important goal for leaders to pursue. How then might leaders of teacher preparation institutions champion technology infusion efforts to build the capacity of their preparation programs?

Creating a Coherence Framework to Guide Action

Achieving technology integration and infusion goals requires organizational alignment and coherence. Harvard's Public Education Leadership Program (PELP) Coherence Model (see Figure 2.1) posits a model for examining the interrelated elements that influence change and how those elements work together or at odds to support organizational goals (Childress, Elmore, Grossman, & Johnson, 2007). The model can be adapted to the setting of a college/school of education and then applied to the challenges of technology infusion and integration. The challenge for leaders is to achieve coherence across all the elements of the model through the alignment of the elements of organizational behavior that drive results.

At the core of the college/school of education is the preparation and development of teachers—the end product and target of technology infusion efforts. The purpose of technology-related investments is to advance the quality of teaching so as to improve educational outcomes for children. As discussed throughout this book, technology infusion involves the ways in which technology is planned and deployed across all parts of the educational enterprise with the ultimate goal of better preparing teacher candidates. Affecting that strategy are the spokes of the wheel, or "slices of the pie," depicted in the PELP model (see Figure 2.1)—the organizational systems and structures, resources, culture, and stakeholders (including internal and external partners) that interact together to produce results. Ability to change is also heavily influenced by an organization's context and environment, represented in the outer ring, of regulations, external funding, and political and policy considerations.

To build the capacity for technology infusion across their teacher preparation institution, leaders must develop strategy and take action in and across each component of the organization. Lack of consistency and alignment may have substantial deleterious effect. For example, a plan to ensure that technology dispositions are infused in assessment processes will have little chance of success if the goal is not reinforced in program curriculum planning and resource allocation. Demonstration of innovative technology tools and use of online learning techniques to help differentiate instruction require concomitant individual faculty skill and reinforcement in program management.

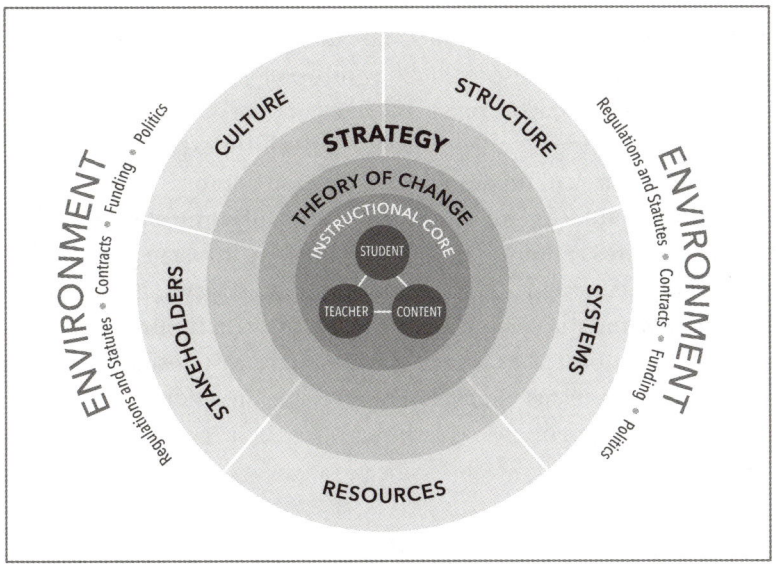

Figure 2.1 The PELP Coherence Framework/Model was developed as part of a collaborative research project—a joint initiative between the Harvard Business School and the Harvard Graduate School of Education—called Public Education Leadership Project (PELP). The original version of this PELP Coherence Framework was adapted from the Congruence Model developed by Michael L. Tushman and Charles A. O'Reilly III.

Systems and Structures

The systems and structures that are inherent in every organization are among the levers available to advance a technology infusion agenda. Consider, for example, the strategic planning process, the development of annual operating plans, and individual performance goal setting and feedback. These are all systems wherein technology infusion intent can be captured. Organizational structures—reporting relationships and operations of organizational units and subunits—are also places for the technology infusion conversation. It is typically in the intersections between different processes, the "white spaces" on the organizational chart, where discontinuities occur and the systems and structures of the organization can either advance, undermine, or simply ignore technology infusion goals. For example, different perspectives between IT personnel and teaching faculty can obscure common goals. Boundary spanners—those individuals who work across units and perspectives—are valuable assets in the change process.

For colleges/schools of education, the program- and curriculum-development process is a prime target for articulating technology infusion goals. Technology infusion is a primary system that cuts across all elements of the institution and is fundamental to candidate learning. Academic leaders can affirm expectations for technology infusion within curriculum design, revision, and approval processes. In addition, technology skills and focus can be gauged by promulgating a technology assessment that is applied across all programs. The technology infusion goal can be made explicit in new program design and in regular program reviews. It can also be emphasized in curricula and master syllabi development. Structurally, technology infusion needs to be captured as part of the functional responsibilities of dean's office personnel, both in terms of developing strategic direction and in terms of measuring, monitoring, and highlighting results.

Resources

Without financial and human resources as inputs to create capacity, there can be no organizational output and impact. How scarce resources are allocated drives what the organization gets done. It is essential to find ways to privilege elements of technology infusion in the resource allocation process. In budget formulation, leaders can seek to identify technology-related priorities, and they can recognize both direct investment and indirect means of advancing a technology-driven agenda. Key to technology infusion is recognizing that, given competition for limited resources and shrinking budgets, direct investment is likely to be scant. And indirect investment provides a valuable tool for leaders, in that it can leverage investments in other areas to ensure a technology-related goal is included. For example, in developing new curriculum or programs, it is possible to require that technology infusion be addressed. In shaping clinical supervision, it is possible to focus on examples of technology use to improve coaching. In course delivery, it is possible to seek ways to better use the existing LMS, videoconferencing capabilities, and assessment instruments to support technology infusion goals.

Technology infusion is not a resource-neutral goal. Investment needs to be both targeted and broadly applied. For example, a targeted technology infusion investment might identify a specific teacher preparation program to pilot and model the infusion of technology across courses and clinical experiences. More broadly, technology infusion could be identified as a college- and school-wide goal and prioritized in discretionary investments—not only in hardware and software but in recruitment, professional development, and retention of faculty and staff.

Culture and People

Embodied in the norms, habits, and underlying values of an organization, culture can also serve to stymie or stimulate new initiatives. How are people motivated? How are decisions made? What are the stories and symbols that describe the organization's ethos? Do recruiting and performance appraisal processes include technology infusion as an important element? These are the elements of culture that shape organizational ethos. A realistic, clear-eyed view of the degree to which the college/school of education is embracing or skeptical, open or insular, passive or proactive, are areas of understanding that will help frame the technology infusion effort. The implications for leaders are to be aware of culture and the forces that shape it, to seek ways to engage in and reinforce aspects of current culture that reinforce technology infusion, and to eschew those aspects of culture that do not. Leaders also must be alert to not inadvertently reinforce behaviors (parts of culture or organizational systems and processes) that in fact undermine and contradict the overall purpose of achieving technology infusion across the organization.

Broadly defined, that people strategy is central to a successful technology infusion effort is well supported in the change management and leadership literature. *Reframing Organizations*, for example, described the multiple "frames" in which organizations and their people operate (Bolman & Deal, 2008). The centrality of human capital and people strategy is also emphasized heavily in the *Good to Great* monograph regarding change in the social sectors (e.g., "Getting the Right People on the Bus" [p. 3]) and of recruitment, retention, and support of high-performing individual faculty and staff (Collins, 2005).

Many colleges/schools of education trumpet a technology-focused rhetoric while simultaneously being bound by well-worn habits that reinforce tradition and history. Leaders must therefore continually be vigilant, searching for models of technology infusion that benefit faculty and students. Further, they must demonstrate in tangible ways how effective application of technology and understanding digital learning environments—and their impact on learning—increase program and candidate success.

Constituents and Stakeholders

One of the more powerful components in the model of organizational or systems coherence for teacher educators lies in the engagement of stakeholders. These are the individuals and groups, internal and external to the organization, who are party to its ability to achieve results. Internal partners primarily are embodied in the faculty and staff who perform the direct work of teacher preparation and go beyond closely allied staff and faculty to include all the functions of the university that can influence educating teacher candidates about how to use technology in teaching and learning. Externally, stakeholders include partner classrooms, schools, districts, and other education institutions and leaders. These individuals and groups simultaneously shape the technology priority of the teacher preparation program and are customers or beneficiaries of the degree to which technology infusion efforts affect teacher candidates.

The college/school of education has a particular advantage in leveraging partners and stakeholders to advance its technology infusion goals, because it is closely tied to those stakeholder needs. The demands facing PK–12 schools translate directly to the relevance of teacher preparation programs, so the increasing need of schools and districts for highly technologically literate educators translates directly to pressure on teacher preparation programs to change the way they address the development of teacher candidates.

Digital Technology Elements of Coherence

Absent from the PELP Coherence Model (see Figure 2.1) as an explicit element is technology, although it is clearly subsumed in structures, systems, resources, culture, and stakeholder considerations. There is a technology component to each element, each of which can be a lever for leaders to use to support technology infusion goals. It is useful for leaders to identify the range of technology applications that shape the teacher preparation program and teacher candidate experience. EDUCAUSE, the nonprofit research and advocacy organization focused on information technology and higher education, describes the digital technology systems, structures, and processes of the university (Abel, Brown, & Suess, 2013). These include hardware and software systems and platforms that enable infrastructure support and organization-wide business processes—for email, data collection and retrieval, human resources systems, and financial management, to name a few. The university's information technology systems setup, including network and facilities, scheduling, and candidate-facing information systems run by the registrar and financial assistance offices, combine to create the overall organizational ecosystem in which programs are delivered and learning can take place.

The provision of instructional content in face-to-face, blended, and online modalities is another consideration. The institution's digital technology backbone also includes the learning management system or systems (LMS) and other learning tools. These support the learning content of courses and related instructional materials and assessment systems. Maximizing the use of an LMS in the delivery of courses should be viewed as a way to model integrating technology to teacher candidates. Use of video observation and annotation; exposure to school-based technology programs and software applications, simulations, and the panoply of applications, software, and hardware in use in contemporary PK–12 classrooms; and assessments (including, for example, creation of an edTPA portfolio for online submission) are all part of the technology integration puzzle.

By considering how technology is deployed across the college/school, decision makers can discern gaps and opportunities that require greater emphasis in technology-related tools. Table 2.1 provides some guiding questions for leaders of technology infusion efforts to begin their analyses.

To effectively address technology integration curriculum using a technology infusion model on an organization-wide scale, the interrelated elements of organizational life need to be understood and influenced. The coherence model depicts the complexity of organizational life and the importance of deconstructing the elements of behavior and performance that must work in concert.

Table 2.1 Guiding Questions for Analysis of Coherence

Coherence Element	Guiding Questions
Strategic Core	Have the key elements of the strategic vision, and its benefit to candidate preparation, been identified and well articulated by leadership?
Structures	What are the organizational structures that are best able to support technology infusion? Which ones might get in the way, and which can be leveraged to your advantage? Consider not only the college/school of education but also clinical experiences.
Systems	What formal and informal systems and processes inform decision making? How can technology infusion goals be incorporated in them? Taking into consideration political and regulatory constraints can figure here.
Resources	What resources are required to advance technology infusion initiatives, and where will lack of investment bring progress to a halt? Consider all resources in addition to direct funding.
Culture	Is the prevailing organizational culture open to experimentation and risk-taking? How can aspects of culture focused on student experience be leveraged to ensure technology is infused across functions?
Stakeholders	Who are the key internal and external stakeholders who can contribute to, or impede, the progress of technology infusion efforts, and how will they benefit from participation? The role of PK–12 partners is an essential element to consider.
Technology	What are the different manifestations of digital technology across all functions of the organization, and how can they be aligned to support the technology infusion effort?

Avoiding Getting Stuck

Technology-infused programs will move toward that goal because they have worked at it. Informed by change theories and the coherence model discussed above, leaders of teacher preparation programs are in pivotal positions to advance curricula, instruction, assessment, and clinical experiences that address the use of technology in teaching and learning across teacher candidates' journey to the classroom. But ambitious efforts like this one often flounder. For example, lack of common language and shared purpose, discomfort with a complex and "messy" process, lack of a robust stakeholder engagement strategy, unclear goals, and an inadequately specified plan can stymie progress. Attending to these elements of institutional life can accelerate change efforts; conversely, lack of support can undermine well-designed initiatives. Each of these elements is discussed below.

Establish Common Language and Shared Purpose

Building a shared understanding of the ways in which technology investments and use are deployed in instruction, assessment, and other processes requires time and focus. Leaders need to work diligently to explain the college/school of education's vision and why the focus on teacher candidates learning to teach with technology is important to results. High-level statements of purpose are insufficient—the general direction must be translated into tangible components relevant to different parts of the organization, as well as to external stakeholders such as the PK–12 schools where field experiences take place. For example, technology infusion efforts will look quite different in administrative or assessment processes than they will in instruction or program development processes. Language describing the technology infusion initiatives should be broad enough to be inclusive, but specific enough to be actionable.

Get Comfortable with Complexity, Ambiguity, and Uncertainty

We live and work in times of turbulent change, accelerated development and diffusion of new technologies, and plenty of distractions. At the same time that external environments may be in the midst of significant instability, internal dynamics can revert to tradition and historical practice as a barrier against the forces of change. The leadership challenge then is to maintain focus on outcomes (educational excellence and student achievement) while embracing new adaptive opportunities. Increasing team members' comfort with new systems and organizational dynamics is an important role of organizational leaders who are working to foster increased technology awareness, use, and integration.

Find Powerful Allies, Build Networks, Highlight Examples and Research

Major change initiatives are fundamentally about persuasion and influence, indirect rather than direct management. As a result, finding voices of allies who influence organizational behavior and direction, as well as seeking examples from peer institutions and other sectors, can help organizations imagine new futures.

Applied research also provides evidence to support change efforts. The networked improvement community approach is a good example to consider (Bryk et al., 2017). Many organizations, and higher education is no stranger here, have a "not built here" reflex that tends to minimize learnings that can be gleaned from cross-organizational and sector comparisons. Examples of how other teacher preparation programs have addressed similar challenges can be powerful tools to drive momentum for change and make it more palpable. Further, every organization is wired with formal and informal networks. Analysis of how decisions are made and who influences behavior, while seeking out the thought leaders and connectors across functions, can help support implementation of technology infusion goals.

Clarify Fuzzy Borders and Unclear Roles

Teacher preparation institutions are complex, dynamic systems that work in concert to prepare and advance educators across their careers. Before initiating a technology infusion effort, it is worth a pause to reflect on how these roles, responsibilities, structures, processes, and perspectives and talents come together to contribute to teacher candidates' experiences and learning. To get to that result, many simultaneous elements of the organizational system need to work together. As technology infusion efforts are undertaken, attention to roles and responsibilities at different junctures of the process is an important step in designing a successful initiative. For some advocates, being involved at the early, strategic stages to structure what technology infusion will look like is the best use of time and expertise. Others are implementers and will be involved in the details of implementation. Leaders and leadership teams should develop plans that recognize not only the diverse functions and parts of the organization and skills of team members but also that their involvement will likely be best applied at different points in the process. Analytic tools such as process and network mapping can be useful here.

Build an Implementation Plan and Sequence Activities

Bold and admirable visions to leverage technology in teacher preparation are not always met by equal attention to implementation. Breaking down the strategy into bite-sized, measurable, and time-sequenced chunks is an important determinant of success. Developing a careful implementation plan that identifies who needs to do what, and when, to accomplish project goals helps drive incremental momentum and engage faculty and staff in different parts of the process. An explicit, sequenced set of implementation steps helps leaders mitigate and manage risks associated with new initiatives, by identifying potential roadblocks before they materialize and identifying contingent actions in the event they are necessary. The action plan should be accompanied by milestones and performance measures to gauge progress and identify need for midcourse adjustment.

Incentivizing Action: A Networked Approach to Implementation

To prompt action, leaders in technology integration must then execute through the roles and responsibilities of the many participants in their organizational ecosystem. The organization's leadership team is responsible for articulating the overall purpose for, and approach to, technology infusion, and for ensuring that technology-related goals are captured in the functions and operational areas under their respective purviews. All levels and roles in the institution have a role to play. For example, at the individual program and course level, technology integration curriculum is reflected in syllabi, candidate assignments, instructor modeling and modalities, and field/clinical experiences. Assessment processes could reflect technology integration in program-embedded technology assessments and in data collected about candidates' and graduates' experiences and achievements.

Program and Curriculum Development

In the curriculum and program development domain, the appropriate use of technology should be an explicit goal for teacher candidates, one based in standards such as those promulgated by ISTE (see www.iste.org/standards). Because technology infusion is a program-deep and program-wide effort involving *all* experiences of teacher candidates, alignment to such standards should be an explicit part of the program and curriculum development and review process. Technology goals should be articulated at the institution, program, and curriculum/course level. There are a myriad of ways in which teacher preparation programs can build technology into learning goals and objectives, assignments, assessment, and portfolio development. For example, candidates could design a technology-based learning intervention, implement it, and assess results. Websites, blogs, and social media can be used as dynamic resources to support learning, as well as opportunities to learn how to use different applications.

Clinical Experiences

The clinical experiences of teacher candidates and educators advancing in their careers provide another focal point for technology infusion initiatives. For example, use of video, and video annotation, is a powerful means of deepening and facilitating coaching and mentoring for teaching with technology. Other aspects of clinical experiences can lend themselves to a technology focus, whether ensuring that candidates are equipped with tools to assess student and classroom technology readiness or that learning technologies are employed throughout the teacher preparation institution's clinical sites. For example, use of video for individual reflection, for group work, and for faculty and mentor feedback is increasingly incorporated into initial teacher preparation programs (Sherin & van Es, 2005). Rubrics for use in observation and student teaching can focus on both teaching with and about technology.

Faculty and Partner Development and Instructional Support

Provision of professional development and instructional support around technology competencies to full-time and part-time faculty is a means of supporting technology infusion in the teaching domain (Foulger, Graziano, Schmidt-Crawford, & Slykhuis, 2017). Faculty employ these tools at different rates and with different degrees of success, and sharing experiences is a powerful learning tool. Professional development for faculty to engage in self-directed teams modeling effective technology use in instruction and inclusion in curricula is a powerful way to develop lasting organizational capacity. Similarly, engaging with school and district partners regarding their technology practices should be a regular practice in informing teacher preparation program development. Schools and districts reflect a wide range of technological sophistication and resources. Faculty and cooperating teachers in PK–12 schools can learn from one another and from other school-site staff. Cooperating teachers and school-based technology coaches or other technology support staff make instructional decisions that use technology in an array of different circumstances, for a range of different student needs.

Accreditation and Assessment

For technology infusion to effectively cascade across the college/school of education, it needs to be a long-term institutional priority and captured in accreditation and assessment processes. The Council for the Accreditation of Educator

Preparation (CAEP) has made technology use an essential cross-cutting requirement for national recognition, ensuring that institutions consider the deployment of technology across programs, clinical experiences, and other activities. ISTE has promulgated standards to which institutions can align their work and which can be used to inform technology-related curriculum development and assessment of candidate outcomes. Individual programs can develop and implement technology assessments to gauge the alignment of their programs and preparation of their candidates according to those standards. Adoption of a systems approach through, for example, the adoption and implementation of a learning management system can serve as a unifying structure for evidence of technology infusion outcomes, including faculty and candidate curation of instructional resources and projects.

In Closing: The Learner View

The ultimate goal of technology infusion in teacher preparation programs is well prepared, versatile, skilled, and compassionate educators—grounded in the science of teaching and learning, committed to helping all children achieve their potential, and lifelong learners themselves—who leverage the power of technology in their practice. Adopting the vantage point of the learner is an effective means of developing a comprehensive technology infusion strategy. The infusion of technology across a college/school of education therefore becomes an embedded and regular theme, not scheduled as an add-on activity or stand-alone initiative. By examining the role of technology in all organizational functions and groups, and levels of responsibility, it is possible to seed a technology-centered and impact-oriented approach to program design and delivery, and preservice teacher supports.

How are teacher preparation programs keeping pace with today's digital world, where every environment is a digital learning environment and digital tools are integral to the most complex and most routine parts of day-to-day life? We imagine teacher preparation institutions that embody the knowledge, skills, and abilities of "digital native" teacher candidates—where the many manifestations of technological advance for teacher candidates are not kludges but infused throughout the organizational being. Leaders of teacher education programs have an obligation to foster environments where technology infusion is at the fore of change efforts, as part of building the colleges/schools of education of the future.

Getting Started Resources

International Society for Technology in Education (ISTE)
  www.iste.org

> Through its website, ISTE provides useful reference material about technology standards for teachers and students, and tools and resources. The ISTE standards, and other resources available through ISTE, are excellent guideposts for leaders of colleges/schools of education interested in technology infusion.

Tondeur, J., van Braak, J., Sang, G., Voogt, J., Fisser, P., & Ottenbreit-Leftwich, A. (2011). Preparing pre-service teachers to integrate technology in education: A synthesis of qualitative evidence. *Computers & Education, 59*(1), 134–144.
  doi.org/10.1016/j.compedu.2011.10.009

> This meta-analysis reviews the literature about trends in technology integration for teacher candidates and the institutional conditions for success. Consider this article as a starting point to frame the issues.

Bryk, A., Gomez, L., Grunow, A., & LeMahieu, P. (2017). *Learning to improve: How America's schools can get better at getting better.* Cambridge, MA: Harvard University Press.

> Bryk, Gomez, Grunow, and LeMahieu posit an approach to data-driven continuous improvement in education that is important for leaders interested in driving change in a systematic, evidence-based, and collaborative manner. Use this work to guide thinking about how to foster, sustain, and change efforts.

Kotter, John. (2012). *Leading change.* Cambridge, MA: Harvard Business Review Press.

> John Kotter's classic, *Leading Change*, is a primer for leaders of change efforts. It focuses in particular on some practical strategies for leaders to employ in creating and executing meaningful change. Although not written with an education audience in mind, the steps identified are actionable and concrete.

Office of Educational Technology. (2016). *Advancing educational technology in teacher preparation: Policy brief.*
  bit.ly/2XhWWor

Office of Educational Technology. (2017). *Reimagining the role of technology in higher education: A supplement to the national education technology plan.*
tech.ed.gov/files/2017/01/Higher-Ed-NETP.pdf

Dabbagh, N., Bass, R., Bishop, M., Costelloe, S., Cummings, K., Freeman, B., … Wilson, S. J. (2019). *Using technology to support postsecondary student learning: A practice guide for college and university administrators, advisors, and faculty* (WWC 20090001). National Center for Education Evaluation and Regional Assistance (NCEE), Institute of Education Sciences, U.S. Department of Education. bit.ly/2UCTSBj

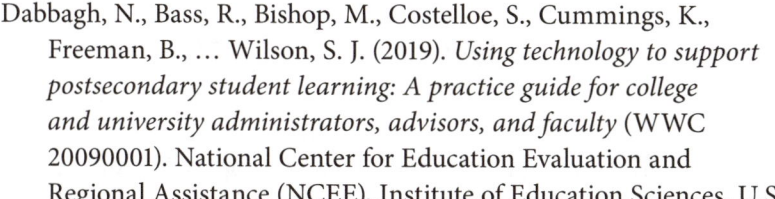

The US Department of Education's technology plan and particular supplement regarding teacher preparation provide a useful introduction to addressing some of the challenges of technology infusion, as well as a broad policy- and practice-focused survey of technology in higher education and teacher preparation.

References

Abel R., Brown, M., & Suess J. (2013). A new architecture for learning. *EDUCAUSE Review, 48*(5), 89–102.

Bolman, L., & Deal, T. (2008). *Reframing organizations: Artistry, choice, and leadership.* San Francisco, CA: Jossey-Bass.

Bryk, A., Gomez, L., Grunow, A., & LeMahieu, P. (2017). *Learning to improve: How America's schools can get better at getting better.* Cambridge, MA: Harvard University Press.

Childress, S., Elmore, R. F., Grossman, A. S., & Johnson, S. M. (2007). *Managing school districts for high performance: Cases in public education leadership.* Cambridge, MA: Harvard Education Press.

Collins, J. (2005). *Good to great and the social sectors: Why business thinking is not the answer.* Boulder, CO: Author.

Foulger, T., Graziano, K., Schmidt-Crawford, D., & Slykhuis, D. (2017). Teacher educator technology competencies. *Journal of Technology and Teacher Education, 25*(4), 413–338. www.learntechlib.org/p/181966

Foulger, T., Wetzel, K., & Buss, R. (2018). Moving toward a technology infusion approach: Considerations for teacher preparation programs. *Journal of Digital Learning in Teacher Education.* doi.org/10.1080/21532974.2019.1568325

Fullan, M. (2016). *The new meaning of educational change* (5th ed.). New York, NY: Teachers College Press.

Heifetz, R., & Linsky, M. (2009). *The practice of adaptive leadership: Tools and tactics for changing your organization and the world.* Boston, MA: Harvard Business Press.

Jacobson, M., Levin, J., & Kapur, M. (2019). Education as a complex system: Conceptual and methodological implications. *Educational Researcher, 48*(2), 112–119.

Kotter, J. (2012). *Leading change.* Cambridge, MA: Harvard Business Review Press.

McCloskey, B., & Winter, M. (2012). *The idea of the digital university: Ancient traditions, disruptive technologies, and the battle for the soul of higher education.* Washington, DC: Policy Studies Association.

Meadows, D. (2008). *Thinking in systems: A primer.* White River Junction, VT: Chelsea Green Publishing.

National Academies of Sciences, Engineering, and Medicine, 2018. *How people learn II: Learners, contexts, and cultures.* Washington, DC: The National Academies Press. doi.org/10.17226/24783

National Research Council. (2000). *How people learn: Brain, mind, experience, and school* (Expanded edition). Washington, DC: The National Academies Press. doi.org/10.17226/9853

Senge, P. A. (1990). *The fifth discipline: The art and practice of the learning organization.* New York, NY: Doubleday.

Sherin, M., & van Es, E. (2005). Using video to support teacher's ability to notice classroom interactions. *Journal of Technology and Teacher Education, 13*(3), 475–491. bit.ly/2XtBGvH

Tondeur, J., van Braak, J., Sang, G., Voogt, J., Fisser, P., & Ottenbreit-Leftwich, A. (2011). Preparing pre-service teachers to integrate technology in education: A synthesis of qualitative evidence. *Computers & Education, 59*(1), 134–144. doi.org/10.1016/j.compedu.2011.10.009

CHAPTER 3

Rethinking Teacher Preparation: Learning from the PK–12 Edtech Story

SHERYL NUSSBAUM-BEACH
POWERFUL LEARNING PRACTICE

Overview

This chapter describes PK–12 initiatives and limitations in educational technology. Based on PK–12 needs, the chapter discusses implications for the role of teacher preparation programs in preparing teacher candidates to be visionary, forward-thinking leaders of change who are fully prepared to hit the ground running once they complete their programs. Teacher candidates need to personally adopt the values and dispositions that drive the use of new pedagogies connected to digital learning environments.

The Current Landscape

With the advent of social media and mobile technology, learning can occur anytime, anywhere—both inside and outside the classroom walls. Emerging technologies can enable learner collaboration, connection, and co-construction of content built around passionate interests in ways never thought possible. With each passing day, new apps and information, personalized and customized with the user in mind, are downloaded to phones and other devices everywhere. These devices and apps are now increasingly valued and embedded into many PK–12 classrooms around the world (Nussbaum-Beach & Ritter Hall, 2012; El-Hussein & Cronje, 2010).

As a professional developer, consultant, and connected learning expert, I have had the unique experience of traveling around the globe to work on digital learning transitions with universities, departments of education, professional associations, and school districts. I have observed several educational technology trends and shifts across the PK–12 landscape. Some of these trends are listed below.

New Learning Models. With exemplary use of technology in the classroom comes new pedagogy. Personalized, competency-based learning environments help to support self-directed learning. Using various technologies, students can design their learning to include self-pacing for mastery. Adaptive learning and artificial intelligence are often at the heart of personalized learning, guiding PK–12 educators on what to teach or reteach and how to organize learning that is individualized (Southern Regional Education Board, 2018).

Assistive Technologies. Teachers design technology use (including devices, applications, and software) to help students work around obstacles or challenges to learning.

Collaborative and Connected Learning. Synchronous and asynchronous platforms, mobile devices, and tools remove space, time, and geographic barriers.

Students as Creators. Makerspace has become a regular focus of libraries in PK–12 schools and communities. Online creation software and multidimensional printers provide opportunities for learners to create innovative projects.

Cybersecurity. In an era of big data, school district servers and "the cloud" may hold personal and sensitive student information that needs protection from unauthorized use and theft and misuse.

1:1 Access in US Districts. The Consortium for School Networking (CoSN) reveals a landscape that is improving, in terms of the number of devices in schools, despite continued worries about equitable access to fast and reliable internet connectivity for all students (Cavanagh, 2018).

Computational Thinking. Students learn to use computational thinking (including thinking about variables, data, and algorithms) as a way to address complex problems and consider possible solutions.

Internet of Things (IoT). The IoT has ushered in the ability to combine big data, artificial intelligence, and machine-driven learning by leveraging microchips that are embedded in devices and objects. This enables data to be shared across machines via the internet. We see evidence of this throughout PK–12 districts in the United States (Newman, 2018).

Parent Expectations. A recent survey confirmed that parents' opinions on the use of mobile devices for educational purposes is generally positive (Ozdamli & Yildiz, 2017). Two-thirds of parents surveyed agreed that effective classroom technology use provides an opportunity for their children to develop college and career skills (Bolkan, 2017). If parents support technology use in the classroom, schools will be more open to providing opportunities for use.

As illustrated in the scenario below, understanding technology as a deep learning curriculum strategy for PK–12 students has fast become an expectation for teachers just entering the profession and seasoned educators as well (Project Tomorrow, 2013).

Scenario: A Day in the Life of a Connected Educator

Before school, Grace scans the new material her fifth grade students have posted to their blogs and changes they have made to the class Google Site. She also comments on revisions to the unit she is codesigning with her colleagues in the threaded discussion happening in the school's project management tool.

School is beginning. Grace's class is comparing local geography and climate to that of New Zealand. A member of Grace's personal learning network lives in Auckland and has arranged a live video chat. During the video session, the teachers and students in both classrooms document the event by snapping photos with their smartphones and making short video reflections to use later in their blogs. She also sends a quick direct message to let her principal know to stop by the classroom for a visit to check out the artifacts created collaboratively with student teams in New Zealand.

Later in the day, Grace introduces a strategy she learned about in one of her online global communities of practice. It plays out exactly as she hoped, pulling in contributions from a hard-to-engage student. Grace makes a mental note to send a thank-you e-card to the teacher in Brazil who suggested the idea.

After school, Grace sees a link from someone in her Twitter learning network to an article on systems-based thinking in education. She reads the article and decides to retweet the link to her followers on Twitter as well as share it with her LinkedIn network. She also saves the citation for the article in her account on Zotero, a free reference tool used to manage bibliographic data and related research materials.

Before turning in for the night, Grace checks her education policy Facebook group. A quick scan compels her to add her own thoughts to a discussion on how to better communicate with legislators regarding equity of technology resources in schools.

The Disconnect

As illustrated in the trends identified at the beginning of the chapter and the scenario above, to be effective in PK–12 education, teacher candidates need to be prepared as digital age teachers and agents of innovation, understanding not only how to effectively use technological tools but also how to help their students become knowledge constructors and global learners. In addition, beginning teachers need to be armed with the skill set necessary to constantly advance their own professional knowledge as well as that of their profession (Jacobsen, Clifford, & Friesen, 2002). However, according to a 2016 study by Project Tomorrow (Evans, 2017), teacher candidates shared that they felt underprepared to use technology when teaching.

According to the International Society for Technology in Education (ISTE), today's PK–12 classrooms need to be intentional about preparing students to "thrive in a constantly evolving technological landscape" (ISTE, 2016, p. 1). ISTE's shift to encompass the evolving nature of technology use is evident in the design of its current student standards, which are very open-ended and point to students being empowered learners, digital citizens, knowledge constructors, computational thinkers, innovative designers, global collaborators, and creative communicators (ISTE, 2016).

In addition to ISTE, other organizations envision the ever-increasing use of technology in PK–12 settings. For example, for years the Horizon Report (Freeman, Adams Becker, Cummins, Davis, & Hall Giesinger, 2017) was the "go to" resource for identifying upcoming trends and challenges in educational technology that K–12 and higher education needed to keep an eye on. In 2014–2017, the Horizon list for K–12 included gaming, Internet of Things, adaptive technology, cloud computing, makerspaces, online learning, robotics, 3D printing, digital badges, and artificial intelligence (Valtonen et al., 2019). I had the privilege of serving on several Horizon Report teams, two with a K–12 focus and one with a higher education focus. These teams were composed of technologists and educators from around the world.

Teacher candidates need to personally adopt the values and dispositions that drive the use of new pedagogies connected to digital learning environments. Teacher preparation programs that embrace the shift from pedagogy as a set of instructional strategies to pedagogy as a set of enablers that maximize inquiry, creativity, and purpose in the learner will be the ones that truly prepare graduates for the classroom of the future (Fullan & Langworthy, 2014). This raises the question: Are college/schools of education up to the challenge?

US Educational Technology Plan as a Driver for Change

As technology and innovation became a priority for school districts across the United States, many tech-enabled initiatives and innovations began to surface. Guiding documents like the National Education Technology Plan (NETP) (Office of Educational Technology, 2017) set a national vision for learning that is enabled by technology. The NETP serves as the flagship educational technology policy document for the United States. It articulates a vision of equity, active use, and collaborative leadership to make everywhere, all-the-time learning possible. As recommended in the NETP, professional development in PK–12 schools began to encourage personalized learning, providing teachers with the ability to connect the "why" of what they learned in their teacher preparation programs to the "how" they needed to bring about meaningful change. Over the last ten years, I personally have witnessed professional learning communities (commonly called PLCs) shift from a top-down design by school districts to teacher-driven entities. In most schools that I worked with or wrote about that adopted a PLC approach, teacher leadership became a respected function of their role.

Other Drivers for Change

Other national reform efforts to encourage digital transformation in PK–12 settings also increased around 2012. The National Council of Teachers of English published a position statement in 2013, redefining literacy to include 21st Century literacies (National Council of Teachers of English, 2013). The Partnership for 21st Century Skills (P21) in association with the National Science Teacher Association (NSTA) created a 21st Century framework that included a content map that combined technology with science and other core content areas (Voogt & Roblin, 2012). The US Department of Education announced that the month of October would be known as Connected Educator Month (US Department of Education, 2013). I was honored to co-lead this US Department of Education sponsored event in which millions around the world "plugged in" to organically offered activities, including webinars, websites, online tours, meet-ups, contests, and virtual projects. Hundreds of schools, districts, and organizations sponsored these activities as a means of leveraging connected opportunities to learn. The National Science Foundation launched the Computer Science for All (CS for All) initiative in 2016 to ensure that computer science education would be available to all students across K–12 classrooms (see nsf.gov/news/special_reports/csed/csforall.jsp). This has enhanced interest in computational and algorithmic thinking.

In addition to the national initiatives springing up in support of technology integration, various teacher-led innovations also began to gain traction in schools: Hour of Code (hourofcode.com/us); Genius Hour (geniushour.com); robotics competitions; video contests; project-, problem-, and passion-based strategies remade to leverage creation tools and enhance personalization of learning (Nussbaum-Beach & Ritter Hall, 2012); flipped classrooms (Bergmann & Adams, 2012); makerspaces (in media centers); and global connections between classrooms in different countries. Augmented and virtual reality have also begun to make their way into PK–12 classrooms, enabling students to gain hands-on application through participation in realistic simulations. (For an example, see naturalhistory. si.edu/exhibits/bone-hall.) More recently, we are seeing artificial intelligence, a type of programed machine intelligence that can outpace and outthink human intelligence, working in conjunction with machine learning, the use of algorithms, and statistics to perform specific tasks without specific instructions. This collaboration between applications is being used to analyze, predict, and customize learning.

All these initiatives and innovations provide a perfect storm to push technology and tech-enabled learning past being an add-on or enhancement in the PK–12 classroom to a place of importance. Technology is deeply embedded into the curriculum and learning process both as a means of student agency and as a driver of assessment, as exemplified by the Science Leadership Academy.

The Science Leadership Academy: An Example of What's Working Well and Why

I recently had the opportunity to chat with Chris Lehmann, CEO and founding principal of the Science Leadership Academy (SLA) in Philadelphia, PA. SLA is an inquiry-driven, project-based high school focused on digital age learning. SLA provides a rigorous, college-preparatory curriculum with a focus on science, technology, mathematics, and entrepreneurship (sla.philasd.org).

I asked Chris directly, "What's working well in terms of technology in your school and why?" He didn't hesitate to identify the culture of SLA as being one where the pedagogy is every bit as important as the technology, and he added, "That is what makes it work. … Traditionally, the schools that have struggled with tech-immersion are ones that have the technology tail wagging the dog." (C. Lehman, personal communication, June 27, 2019). Many times, teachers just starting to use technology in their classrooms will put the focus on the tools and gadgets (technology "tail") rather than the content objectives or solid pedagogy (the "dog"). Lehmann went on to share that the missing ingredient in preparing teachers to work at SLA is not the lack of technology skills per se; it is the investment (or lack of it) in developing effective teacher practice. The new teachers coming into SLA are from some of the best teacher preparation programs in the country. In Lehmann's opinion,

"Schools of education should invest in teaching solid pedagogy, both with and without technology."

I asked Lehmann for a practical example. He explained, "Research in an immersive environment means something very different than when done in a more traditional way." Students are not tied to local resources available at the school. They can garner knowledge about their topic from subject matter experts, access powerful databases, and browse original sources from around the world. With a focus on student individualized learning plans, the school works to involve students through internships and other activities with more than 100 partner businesses, museums, and other organizations. He also mentioned that a tech-immersive environment enables his students "to research their own ideas and conceptualize something new, with the plus of being grounded in research." Lehmann ended our conversation with a strong emphasis on how immersive technologies enabled the Science Leadership Academy to accomplish its goals for learning—specifically, the ability for students to network with the world; collaborate and generate ideas with others; and use technology creatively to build, make, and design artifacts (Lehmann, 2019).

Future Ready Leadership and Future Ready Schools

One of the most satisfying professional opportunities I have ever experienced was in the collaborative leadership of the Future Ready Leaders project (Office of Educational Technology, 2016). To support the vision and goals of the 2016 National Education Technology Plan, the US Department of Education's Office of Educational Technology developed a project geared toward top-level leadership in school districts. The Future Ready Leaders (FRL) project was established under the leadership of Richard Culatta, then director of the US Office of Educational Technology and who now serves as ISTE's chief executive officer, in partnership with Darren Cambridge of the American Institutes for Research (AIR) and myself, Sheryl Nussbaum-Beach of Powerful Learning Practice (PLP).

We began the project with AIR by producing a research synthesis that identified four focus areas aligned with twenty-six key dimensions of future ready leadership. The focus areas of future ready leadership as stated in *Characteristics of Future Ready Leadership: A Research Synthesis* (Office of Educational Technology, 2015) are provided below.

Collaborative Leadership. Commitment to demonstrating strong leadership aptitude, developing the vision, securing the ongoing funding, building a district-wide leadership team, and garnering broad-based support to ensure a successful digital learning transition for students and teachers.

Personalized Student Learning. Personalized pathways for student learning through active and collaborative learning activities, which are aligned with standards, selected through ongoing assessment of students' progress and preferences, and supported by the use and creation of rich content and robust tools.

Robust Infrastructure. Equitable access to bandwidth, wireless networks, hardware, and devices, managed by support personnel for reliable use—both inside and outside school.

Personalized Professional Learning. Ongoing, job-embedded, and relevant professional learning designed and led by teachers with support from other experts to assist other teachers, administrators, and support personnel in making the digital transition. (p. 2.)

Next, through a variety of processes, we looked for and identified district-level leadership teams across the United States that demonstrated in their practice and leadership styles the dimensions of a future ready leader. Based on data we gathered and criteria used, eight districts in Washington, California, Colorado, Iowa, Wisconsin, Illinois, Pennsylvania, and Missouri were selected for site visits and videotaped interviews. The wisdom and practical advice of superintendents and leadership teams in the districts were captured in a report and a comprehensive video set that was created to demonstrate the four areas and twenty-six dimensions (see bit.ly/2vpo7lq).

A companion project took place during President Obama's ConnectEd initiative called Future Ready Schools (FRS). It was spearheaded by the Alliance for Excellent Education (alliance4ed.org). FRS provides schools with resources and support to ensure that local technology and digital learning plans: (1) align with instructional best practices, (2) are implemented by highly trained teachers, and (3) lead to personalized learning experiences for all students, particularly those from traditionally underserved communities.

Future Ready Leadership and Schools: Resources for Colleges/Schools of Education

The FRL research brief mentioned above summarizes evidence-based policies and practices that successful leaders use to leverage technology to enhance teaching and learning. Colleges/schools of education can use the research synthesis to develop deep knowledge of the key dimensions of leadership for technology infusion. In addition, the Future Ready Schools dashboard (futureready.org) includes helpful resources: a framework for planning for future ready learning, guidebooks, case studies, sample micro-credentials, and a blog. These can be used to inform planning, budgeting, faculty hiring and evaluation, policy development, and/or other common tasks related to digital age teacher preparation. These resources can be used to encourage and support discussions for all stakeholders, helping higher education faculty, classroom teachers, student teachers, and school administrators understand what it means to be future ready.

A shift evident in both the research and interviews with school staff is a move toward collaborative leadership. Traditional top-down transactional leaders do not fit well in future ready schools; transformational leadership styles are needed. Colleges/schools of education can use FRL material to understand the research-based dimensions of collaborative leadership. Another aspect of the Future Ready Leaders project that became evident is the need for partnerships. Most of the PK–12 staff interviewed cited partnerships with universities and businesses as vital in helping them with both digital integration and ensuring that their students and teachers became future ready.

Fads and Fantasy: Moving Beyond the Hype

As colleges/schools of education make intentional decisions about what to change in terms of how they prepare PK–12 educators, it is time to assess the evidence about both the limitations and the successes of educational technology in the classroom. There are opposing sides to every issue, and technology is no different. Teacher candidates need to investigate the pros and cons of using various technologies. They should also examine and discuss concerns expressed in the news, such as the need to limit screen time, social media and bullying, and the possible connection of video games to antisocial behavior. For example, some feel that too much screen time can create an addiction (Vinopal, 2019). Other researchers debunk the idea that technology addiction even exists (Ferguson & Ceranoglu, 2014). In terms of bullying, some say that the internet is a dangerous place and we should filter and limit access to selected websites (Bilton, 2014). Conversely, others say we should be teaching digital citizenship (appropriate and responsible behavior online) to empower learners with what they need to know and do to stay safe online (Delzer, 2015). In other words, rather than using fear to guide online behavior, we should look for positive ways to model appropriate use. Another common debate is around the benefits of games as an educational strategy (Parisod et al., 2014). It depends on how the game is used, along with the design of interactive features that play a large role in determining the skills required, including problem solving, critical thinking, and collaboration.

Part of the confusion over the value of digital technologies, however, may be due to how quickly emerging technologies get left behind. In the commotion and fanfare that follows the introduction of a new tool or concept, especially one that is quickly adopted and then may be just as quickly abandoned (like Google Glass, for instance), few are really taking the time to see where pedagogically sound means of use will take us. For example, we have only scratched the surface in understanding what globally collaborating in a Google document can produce in terms of rich learning. When first introduced, everyone "oohed" and "aahed" as we all typed collaboratively on the same sheet of paper in the cloud. Maybe we have moved on too quickly to the "next great thing" rather than looking more closely and documenting aspects of collaborative investigation and knowledge construction in a Google document. Maybe in doing so we have missed important lessons about deep learning (C. Lehmann, personal communication, June 27, 2019). "Technology is neither good nor bad, nor is it neutral" (Kranzberg, 1986, p. 545). But just like any other teaching tool, learning object, or educational strategy, successful technology integration requires deep exploration and appropriate pedagogy before introducing it in the classroom (Okojie, Olinzock, Okojie-Boulder, 2006).

In a policy brief published by the National Education Policy Center at the University of Colorado, Enyedy (2014) writes that "computers in the classroom are commonplace but teaching practices often look similar, as do student outcomes" (p. 3). Enyedy believes that the promise of personalized instruction facilitated by digital technology has fallen short because personalized learning is simply too broad of a term to allow for meaningful evaluation.

The confusion might be a matter of how we are using the technology, perhaps without thinking deeply about pedagogy or outcomes. Or perhaps even the questions we are asking are influencing the lack of return on promises made. What if the questions we asked were directed more at *how* to use the technology to learn in more effective ways or how to leverage the mobile and networked aspects of connected technology as a means of innovation? In other words, just having teacher candidates use technology for technology's sake and then putting a check on their student teaching observation form is not going to produce the types of outcomes we are hoping for in most PK–12 classrooms or schools of education.

Building a Collaborative Culture

What if teacher preparation programs did what they do best: prepared teacher candidates to be effective agents of change using pedagogically sound strategies of inquiry? And what if PK–12 organizations modeled where they are currently strong, using systemic ways to bring meaningful digital reform and technology immersion into the learning space? It seems clear that the two could learn and benefit from and with each other. More and more it seems what is needed is a symbiotic relationship of collaboration between PK–12 schools and colleges/schools of education.

Scott Floyd, chief technology officer at White Oak Schools in Texas, believes that schools of education should provide multiple opportunities for hands-on, minds-on experiences that go beyond just observing as a means of immersing teacher candidates in the realities that await them in the connected classroom and school. "One semester of student teaching simply isn't enough," Floyd shared. "It is a shift in mindset from teaching by reading the chapter and [using] worksheets, to understanding how to personalize learning so that when what they are doing isn't working, they know how to incorporate other tools, technologies, and strategies to ensure success" (S. Floyd, personal communication, June 28, 2019). Teacher candidates need to experience this level of learning in their programs in order to come to schools prepared to teach with technology.

Some colleges/schools of education allow for online experiences and courses as part of their teacher preparation programs. Neil Rochelle, federal programs project lead in Guam, says this is a great idea, but what would be more beneficial in this setting is if beginning teachers came to understand how to create online courses and blended learning experiences. Rochelle's dream is that one day every student will be required to take at least one online course as part of their PK–12 educational experience so that they will be workforce ready, in that they understand how to learn and work in connected spaces. New teacher hires need to understand both how to learn online and how to create quality online learning experiences (N. Rochelle, personal communication, June 30, 2019).

Conclusion

The technology revolution has found its way into every area of society and has the potential to literally transform every elementary through high school classroom around the world (Zucker, 2009). Further, as described at the beginning of this chapter, technology has transformed the way teachers can find each other, interact, and collaborate to create learning environments for their students and grow professionally as educators. Educators who understand not only how to use technology in creative ways but who also have mastered the appropriate technology to personalize learning for all learners are at the forefront of this revolution. Therefore, teacher candidates need and deserve faculty in colleges/schools of education who understand the power of well-integrated and purposeful technology that is grounded in appropriate pedagogical strategies.

A technology-infused approach calls for radically transforming the curriculum and instructional strategies used in teacher preparation. Today's candidates should be given opportunities to:

- learn to develop instruction that enables students to become empowered designers, makers, and producers rather than consumers of information (Gonzalez, 2018).

- learn through participation in and design of online communities of practice-and-build personal learning networks (Nussbaum-Beach & Ritter Hall, 2012).

- become skilled at helping students interact with technology, so the students themselves can control programs, devices, and the apps with which they interact (e.g., Hour of Code, hourofcode.com/us).

The responsibility lies directly with colleges/schools of education to make sure teacher educators graduate as technology-savvy educators who arrive ready on day one to provide deep learning that is technology enhanced. Today's teacher educators should:

- be able to model the design, development, and adaptation of technology-enriched learning environments that enable personalization of learning for students (Nussbaum-Beach & Ritter Hall, 2012).

- focus on the active use of technology to enable learning and teaching through creation, production, and problem solving (Office of Educational Technology, 2017).

- participate in regular professional learning experiences themselves, using technology in ways that will produce transformative learning and teaching (King, 2002).

Teacher education faculty must learn to model and teach about connectedness, creativity, and global collaboration to pass these skills onto their teacher candidates, who will in turn create transformative learning environments that promote equity of access and that produce future ready learners who will affect the world (Nussbaum-Beach & Ritter Hall, 2012).

Getting Started Resources

Office of Educational Technology. (n.d.). Personalized professional learning for Future Ready Leaders. **tech.ed.gov/leaders**

An evidence-based approach leading to digital conversion and change, the Future Ready Leaders project provides a systematic review of research and a personalized playlist for district leaders generated from fifty short videos with high production quality.

Research base: **tech.ed.gov/leaders/research**

Full video library: **bit.ly/2vpo7lq**

Office of Educational Technology. (2014). *The Future Ready District: Professional learning through online communities of practice and social networks to drive continuous improvement.* **bit.ly/2VcNkIX**

This brief summarizes research on the role of online communities of practice and social networks in supporting the professional performance of educators. When high-performance learning is integrated into evidence-based learning that is aligned with district goals and processes, online learning communities and social networks can provide opportunities for personalized professional learning.

Alliance for Excellent Education. Future Ready Schools.
futureready.org

Future Ready Schools supports innovative educators to ensure that each student graduates from high school with the agency, passion, and skills to be a productive, successful, and responsible citizen. This website contains frameworks, reports, resources, videos, webinars, and more, all designed to help PK–12 districts with digital conversion.

Alexander, B., Ashford-Rowe, K., Barajas-Murphy, N., Dobbin, G., Knott, J., McCormack, M., … Weber, N. (2019). *EDUCAUSE Horizon Report: 2019 higher education edition.* Louisville, CO: EDUCAUSE. bit.ly/2WgofP8

This report profiles six key trends, six significant challenges, and six important developments in educational technology as ranked by an expert panel of leaders from across the higher education landscape. New Media Consortium (NMC) originally led the Horizon Report effort. Beginning in 2017, EDUCAUSE continued the NMC work with both sharing the archive of past reports and overseeing the creation of new reports related to higher education.

References

Bergmann, J., & Adams, S. (2012). *Flip your classroom: Reaching every student in every class every day.* Washington, DC: International Society for Technology in Education.

Bilton, N. (2014, September 11). Steve Jobs was a low-tech parent. www.nytimes.com/2014/09/11/fashion/steve-jobs-apple-was-a-low-tech-parent.html

Bolkan, J. (2017, June 29). Report: 2 in 3 parents say classroom tech is key to student futures. bit.ly/2xGntBq

Cavanagh, S. (2018, January 5). Snapshot of K–12 tech landscape: More districts reach 1-to-1, but equity gaps persist. bit.ly/2yUJMn2

Delzer, K. (2015, June 25). How you can become a champion of digital citizenship in your classroom. bit.ly/3bGB8qw

El-Hussein, M.O.M., & Cronje, J. C. (2010). Defining mobile learning in the higher education landscape. *Educational Technology & Society, 13*(3), 12–21.

Enyedy, N. (2014). Personalized instruction: New interest, old rhetoric, limited results, and the need for a new direction for computer-mediated learning. nepc.colorado.edu/publication/personalized-instruction

Evans, J. (2017, May 8). *Teachers' readiness and willingness to adopt digital tools for learning.* bit.ly/2XxKvon

Ferguson, C. J., & Ceranoglu, T. A. (2014). Attention problems and pathological gaming: Resolving the 'chicken and egg' in a prospective analysis. *Psychiatric Quarterly 85,* 103–110. doi.org/10.1007/s11126-013-9276-0

Freeman, A., Adams Becker, S., Cummins, M., Davis, A., & Hall Giesinger, C. (2017). NMC/CoSN Horizon Report: 2017 K–12 Edition. Austin, TX: The New Media Consortium.

Fullan, M., & Langworthy, M. (2014). *A rich seam: How new pedagogies find deep learning* (1st ed.). bit.ly/2Vrxb3y

Gonzalez, J. (2018, May 20). What's the point of makerspace? www.cultofpedagogy.com/makerspace

International Society for Technology in Education. (2016). ISTE standards for students. www.iste.org/standards/for-students

Jacobsen, M., Clifford, P., & Friesen, S. (2002). Preparing teachers for technology integration: Creating a culture of inquiry in the context of use. bit.ly/3c6PD6Q

King, K. (2002). Educational technology professional development as transformative learning opportunities. *Computers & Education, 39*(3), 283–297. doi.org/10.1016/S0360-1315(02)00073-8

Kranzberg, M. (1986). Technology and history: "Kranzberg's laws." *Technology and Culture 27*(3), 544–560.

National Council of Teachers of English. (2013). The NCTE definition of 21st century literacies. ncte.org/statement/nctes-definition-literacy-digital-age

Newman, D. (2018, November). Top 5 digital transformation trends in education for 2019. bit.ly/3eepkNX

Nussbaum-Beach, S., & Ritter Hall, L. (2012). *The connected educator: Learning and leading in a digital age.* Bloomington, IL: Solution Tree Press.

Office of Educational Technology. (2015). *Characteristics of future ready leadership: A research synthesis.* tech.ed.gov/files/2015/12/Characteristics-of-Future-Ready-Leadership.pdf

Office of Educational Technology. (2016). *Getting started: Future ready leaders.* medium.com/@OfficeofEdTech/april-is-future-ready-leaders-month-281ee2e4da49

Office of Educational Technology. (2017). *Reimagining the role of technology in education: 2017 National Education Technology Plan update.* tech.ed.gov/files/2017/01/NETP17.pdf

Okojie, M., Olinzock, A., & Okojie-Boulder, T. (2006). The pedagogy of technology integration. *Virginia Tech JOTS, 32*(2). doi.org/10.21061/jots.v32i2.a.1

Ozdamli, F., & Yildiz, E. P. (2017). Opinions and expectations of parents on integration of mobile technologies to education and school family cooperation. *International Journal of Interactive Mobile Technologies, 11*(4). doi.org/10.3991/ijim.v11i4.6791

Parisod, H., Aromaa, M., Kauhanen, L., Laaksonen, C., Leppänen, V., Pakarinen, A., … Salanterä, S. (2014). The advantages and limitations of digital games in children's health promotion. *Finnish Journal of eHealth and eWelfare, 6*(4), 164–173.

Project Tomorrow. (2013, February 5). Aspiring teachers increasingly prepare for their future jobs online [Press release]. tomorrow.org/speakup/pr/PR_AspiringTeachersReport2013.html

Southern Regional Education Board. (2018). New learning models. www.sreb.org/new-learning-models

U.S. Department of Education, Press Office. (2013, October 18). *U.S. Department of Education celebrates Connected Educator Month 2013.* www.ed.gov/news/press-releases/us-department-education-celebrates-connected-educator-month-2013

Valtonen, T., Hoang, N., Kankaanpää, J., Sointu, E., Kukkonen, J., Smits, A., …
    Laru, J. (2019). Mapping support strategies for pre-service teachers' ICT
    integration: SQD in Finland. Joensuu, Finland: University of Eastern Finland.
    doi.org/10.13140/RG.2.2.32190.64326

Vinopal, L. (2019, May 3). How screen time creates kid 'dopamine
    addicts' with bad habits. www.fatherly.com/health-science/
    screen-time-hurts-kids-dopamine-addiction

Voogt, J., & Roblin, N. (2012). A comparative analysis of international
    frameworks for 21st century competences: Implications for national
    curriculum policies. *Journal of Curriculum Studies, 44*(3), 299–321.
    www.learntechlib.org/p/131784

Zucker, A. A. (2009, Winter). Transforming schools with technology. *Independent
    School Magazine.* www.nais.org/magazine/independent-school/winter-2009/
    transforming-schools-with-technology

SECTION II

Implementing Technology Infusion

The chapters in this section share methods and guidance for enhancing technology infusion in teacher preparation.

CHAPTER 4

Frameworks That Scaffold Learning to Teach with Technology

LIZ KOLB
UNIVERSITY OF MICHIGAN

Overview

This chapter describes four frameworks in educational technology—SAMR, PICRAT, TIM, and Triple E—and proposes how each might be used as a scaffold in teacher preparation programs for teacher candidates who are learning how to teach with technology. This chapter calls on teacher educators to use the frameworks as tools to support teacher candidates in improving their effectiveness in integrating technology into their teaching. Recommendations are provided for which framework to use during various phases of teacher preparation.

Scenario: Modeling Technology in a Math Methods Course

Recently, a field supervisor was observing a teacher candidate teaching a lesson to a classroom of second grade students. The teacher candidate wanted to demonstrate how technology could be integrated to address mathematics standards. The math objective for the lesson was telling time on a dial clock. In her attempt to demonstrate the use of technology to scaffold content learning, the teacher candidate integrated Spheros (www.sphero.com), small robotic balls that can be programmed to move by using an application on an iPad. The students were placed in a small group, were provided two Sphero balls, and asked to sit near one of the floor mats. Each floor mat had a "dial clock" face painted on it. Students were asked to take turns using the iPad to program the Sphero balls to "tell time." The teacher candidate explained to the second-graders that one ball was to represent where the hour hand would be on a dial clock and the other ball was to represent where the minute hand would be on a dial clock. The teacher candidate asked the second-graders to take turns programming the Spheros to roll to the proper spots that would represent 2:00 p.m. on the floor mat.

While the students were working in their groups, the field supervisor observed the students' attempts, interactions, and struggles with the Sphero balls. She noted that, on occasion, some students asked for technical help from their group members. She wondered if the trial-and-error attempt by the second-graders to program the Sphero was overshadowing the learning objective to tell time on a dial clock. As well, she had thoughts about the amount of time and cognitive energy spent programming the Sphero versus attending to the math content.

After the observation, the field supervisor asked the teacher candidate if she felt the lesson with the Sphero balls was an effective way to integrate technology. The teacher candidate answered, "I am not sure." When the field supervisor probed further, the candidate was at a loss as to how to explain the relationship between the learning objective and the use of the technology tool. It was difficult for the teacher candidate to ascertain whether or not technology affected student learning. This made the field supervisor realize the candidate lacked a method or framework to view technology integration, determine the effectiveness of technology, and discuss the impact of technology on teaching experiences.

This scenario posed some significant concerns for the field supervisor, and she began to think about how she might better scaffold her teacher candidates as they learn to teach with technology. Specifically, she wondered:

- How can I support teacher candidates to make informed decisions about when to use technology?

- What scaffolds might I use to provide insight for teacher candidates about the added value technology can bring to content-based learning?

- How can I better frame and discuss technology with teacher candidates after a field observation?

Subsequently, the field instructor decided to analyze the Sphero lesson with the teacher candidate by using the lens of education technology frameworks. Education technology frameworks can be used as instructional guides to scaffold teacher educators and field instructors who work with candidates as related to the above needs. These frameworks can help identify deficits and affordances of technology used during teaching and learning and provide insight that will help generate reflective conversations. In order to understand how various educational technology frameworks can support these reflective conversations, this chapter provides the description of four frameworks, as well as the dialogue that the field instructor could have with the teacher candidate as a result of analysis of the Sphero lesson using these frameworks.

Why Learning How and When to Teach with Technology Is Complicated

As noted in the scenario above, learning to effectively use technology in teaching is not a simple endeavor. It involves simultaneously thinking about technological choices, curriculum goals, and pedagogical opportunities. Technological Pedagogical and Content Knowledge (TPACK) is a conceptual framework commonly used to depict the nature of teaching with technology (Mishra & Koehler, 2006). The framework originated when scholars were discussing prior research by Shulman that defined how effective teachers must employ both content knowledge and pedagogical knowledge, commonly referred to as pedagogical content knowledge (Shulman, 1986). Expanding upon Schulman's work, Mishra and Koehler (2006) positioned technology as an equally important and integral knowledge base to form technological pedagogical content knowledge (TPACK). TPACK emphasizes how these three knowledge bases—technological knowledge (TK), pedagogical knowledge (PK), and content knowledge (CK)—interrelate with one another. The framework also includes a heightened emphasis on teachers' contextual knowledge (XK) when technology is used in their teaching (Mishra, 2019). Applying these knowledge bases within the practice of real-life teaching situations is a challenge for teacher educators as they think about how to best scaffold teacher candidates to account for the unique context of a school and community. In order for a teacher preparation program to effectively infuse technology throughout all coursework, all the knowledge bases (CK, PK, TK, and XK), as well as how they influence one another, should be seamlessly woven into preparation program curriculum. See Figure 4.1 for an illustration of TPACK.

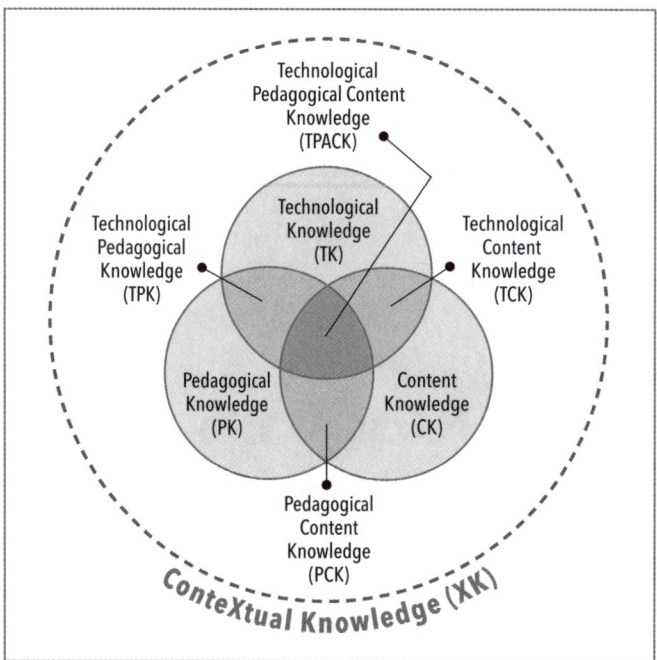

Figure 4.1 The TPACK model demonstrates the weaving together of content knowledge, pedagogical knowledge and technical knowledge, in teaching with technology. Revised version of the TPACK image. © Punya Mishra, 2018. Reproduced with permission.

Four Frameworks to Help Teacher Educators Scaffold Teacher Candidates Learning to Teach with Technology

What follows are four frameworks that can be used by teacher educators and those individuals who work with teacher candidates to support the development of candidates' TPACK. The four frameworks are not an exhaustive list but were selected because they are aligned to and draw on the power of TPACK. Each framework has the ability to provide teacher candidates a way to evaluate and inform instructional tool choices that are supported with research. Because the frameworks have unique affordances and limitations, employing a selection of frameworks will help teacher educators personalize the support they provide teacher candidates.

An overview of each framework is provided in the sections that follow, along with an explanation of how each framework aligns with the knowledge bases in TPACK and selected research that demonstrates the validity of the framework. As a demonstration of how each framework might be used within preparation programs, each framework will be applied to the Sphero scenario. Each section will conclude with general recommendations for appropriate use of the framework based on the developmental needs of teacher candidates across the span of a teacher preparation program.

SAMR

The first framework teacher educators might use as a scaffold with their teacher candidates is the Substitution, Augmentation, Modification, and Redefinition model (SAMR) developed by Puentedura (2013). SAMR is based on four classifications of technology use in the classroom: substitution, augmentation, modification, and redefinition. See Figure 4.2 for an illustration of SAMR. At the substitution classification, students use technology to substitute for a traditional learning activity. As an example, when students write and edit a story using pencil and paper and then type their final stories in Microsoft Word (without using any editing features in Word), they are *substituting* word processing for handwritten work. At the augmentation classification, students use technology to substitute a traditional learning activity, and the substitution provides added value over the traditional method. As an example, students use Word to draft a story and are expected to use the editing features of Word such as spellchecker and grammar check. At the modification classification, students use technology to modify a traditional learning activity in a way that would change what or how it is produced. As an example, students use Word to type a story with embedded links to web-based media, additional resources, and references, making the story interactive for the reader. At the redefinition classification, the traditional learning task is completely changed by the technology tool. As an example, small groups of students work collaboratively in Google Docs to create a script for a podcast that will be shared via a web-based archive with a targeted audience. According to SAMR, learning activities that fall within the classifications of substitution and augmentation apply technology in ways that enhance learning, while learning activities that fall within the classifications of modification and redefinition transform learning (Puentedura, 2013).

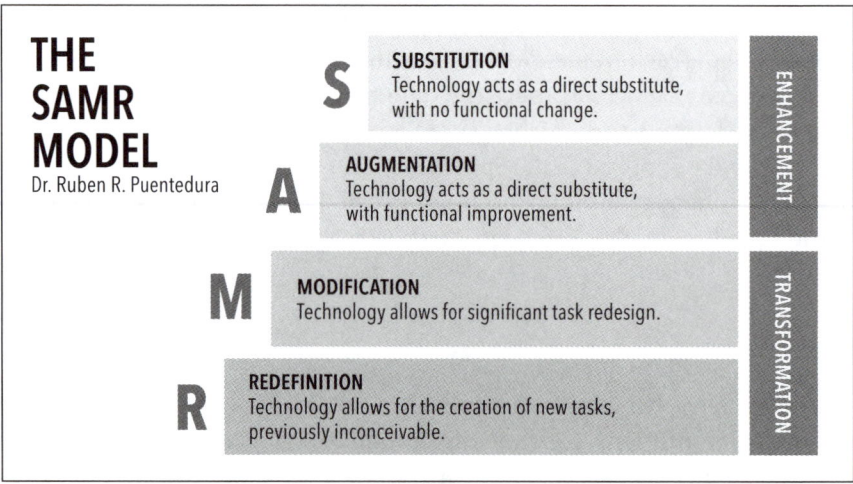

Figure 4.2   Model of the SAMR framework by Lefflerd, distributed under a CC BY-SA 4.0 license.

Puentedura intended SAMR to be used by educators to classify the type of technology used in learning, ultimately hoping that the framework could be used as a tool to enhance the quality of learning with technology in a lesson (2013). Asking teacher candidates to classify the type of technology used in a teaching and learning experience and consider if the activity could be redesigned to "level up" to another classification level (i.e., devising ways to make technology more necessary and powerful) can support candidates to hone their understanding of technological knowledge (TK). While SAMR explicitly stresses the type of technological tool uses (TK), there is minimal emphasis on how using technology might amplify the content learning goal (CK) or allow for more sophisticated pedagogical techniques when using technology (PK). Therefore, the three knowledge bases in TPACK are not necessarily given equal attention, which means candidates may be able to define the type of technology used in a lesson but not necessarily understand the impact of that technology on the content learning goals or explain how pedagogical choices were affected by the technology. With that said, SAMR, focusing on only four identification levels, creates a simple classification structure that new teacher candidates may find beneficial when they are first introduced to the design of instruction that integrates technology.

Thus far, studies that have applied SAMR to evaluate technology use in the classroom (e.g., Azama, 2015; Speirs, 2016) were found to be valid for measuring the use of technology in education at the modification and redefinition levels but not valid at the substitution and augmentation levels (Batiibwe, Bakkabulindi, & Mango, 2017). As the validity of this model is still being researched, teacher preparation programs using the SAMR framework as a tool to support teacher candidates should stay abreast of new research about the use of SAMR.

Analyzing the Sphero Lesson Using SAMR

When the field supervisor and teacher candidate evaluated the Sphero lesson using the SAMR framework, they found learners *substituted* a real dial clock with a floor mat and two Sphero balls representing the hands of a clock. The field supervisor then discussed with the teacher candidate that while the Sphero balls and floor mat were substituting for a traditional way of learning to tell time, the learning goal (telling time on a dial clock) may have been more difficult for the second grade students to master and for the teacher candidate to assess. She shared her observations of the limitations of the technology as the second-graders were learning to tell time: students may have struggled to relate to the Sphero balls as clock hands, students were not given feedback on their process of locating the correct time (either by the teacher candidate or their peers), and students' ability to practice telling time with any sort of repetition or variation in time choice was extremely limited. Thus, the students' skill with telling time was not evident.

Next, the field supervisor suggested the teacher candidate explore using a different tool with the second-graders, one that would better ensure they can tell time in their everyday lives. The supervisor recommended using an educational application called Quick Clocks. Quick Clocks has a realistic representation of a dial clock, includes scaffolds such as visual cues, and provides children multiple attempts with feedback as they manipulate the hour and minute hands in the application. Quick Clocks would augment the learning experience because students could manipulate the clock hands in ways that a traditional dial clock allows and provide students with explicit feedback, making it easier for students to transfer their learning to dial clocks in their everyday lives.

Summary for Teacher Educators Using SAMR

SAMR can be useful for beginning teacher candidates to classify the type of technology used in a learning activity. SAMR may be best used in the early stages of a teacher preparation program. Additionally, SAMR might be useful later in the program in conjunction with other frameworks that could allow candidates to delve into the pedagogical choices surrounding the use of the tool and how the tool affects content learning.

PICRAT

The second framework teacher educators might use as a scaffold with their teacher candidates is called PICRAT, which stands for Passive, Interactive, Creative and Replaces, Amplifies, and Transforms. PICRAT was developed by Kimmons (2016). See Figure 4.3 for an illustration of the PICRAT model. PICRAT was based on an earlier model, RAT (Hughes, Thomas, & Scharber, 2006), with the addition of cognitive thinking elements (PIC) from Bloom's taxonomy (Bloom, 1956). PICRAT helps teacher candidates consider technology use in learning along two knowledge perspectives, PIC and RAT. First, the type of technology used is compared to traditional instructional methods to determine if the way it is used replaces, amplifies, or transforms learning experiences (RAT). The RAT component of PICRAT is similar to SAMR in that it addresses the transformative uses of technology, but it uses different terminology and only has three classification levels instead of four. RAT asks:

- Does the technology *replace* a traditional method (e.g., word processing to replace writing on paper)?

- Does the technology *amplify* a traditional method (e.g., word processing with hyperlinks and graphics embedded to create a digital "book")?

- Does the technology *transform* a traditional method (e.g., scripting a podcast to transform a word-processed book into an audio broadcast)?

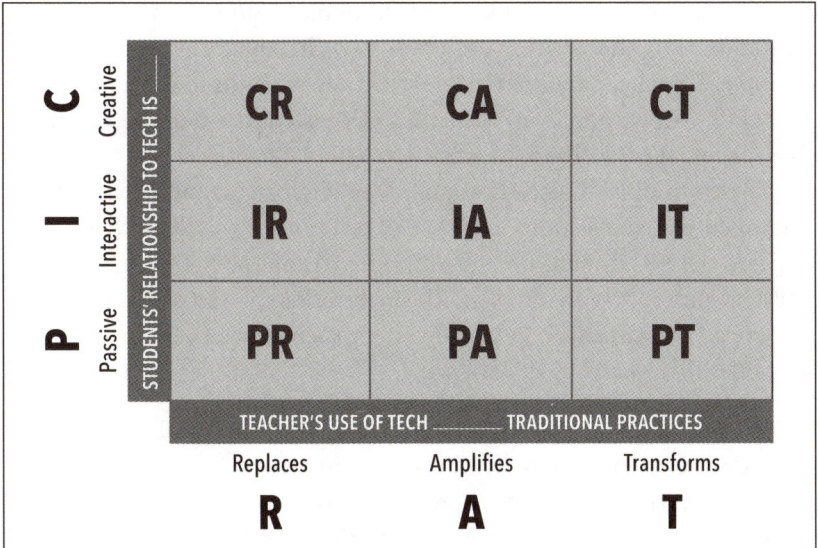

Figure 4.3   Model of the PICRAT framework by Dr. Royce Kimmons, distributed under a CC BY 3.0 license.

The second perspective considers whether students are passive, interactive, or creative (PIC) as they interact with technology. PIC asks:

- Are students *passively* using technology (such as students listening to a podcast)?

- Are students *interacting* with technology on a lower cognitive level (such as students listening to a podcast, then posting a reflection about the topic in the comments section of the podcast)?

- Are students *creating* with technology (such as writing a script for a podcast, then recording and publishing the podcast on the internet)?

PICRAT is represented using a three-by-three3 matrix to demonstrate how a lesson with technology is evaluated from both dimensions at once, PIC and RAT. For example, a teacher candidate who provides a lecture to students using a PowerPoint presentation with slides containing lecture notes (no hypermedia, images, or video) would be considered passive (P) for the PIC dimension and replaces (R) for the RAT dimension, because the way technology is used is not in the hands of the students and the PowerPoint simply replaces a traditional tool/method of presentation of information (a teacher writing out notes on a chalkboard or whiteboard). In another example, a teacher candidate asks fifth grade students to use an interactive lecture tool (www.nearpod.com) through a self-paced lesson delivered on their individual Chromebooks. The fifth grade students interact with the Nearpod lecture by answering multiple-choice questions, drawing images, and reflecting as they respond to open-ended questions. This use of technology would be categorized as interactive (I) on the PIC dimension and amplifies (A) on the RAT dimension, because the students interact individually with the technology, and although the Nearpod slides are all the same (not personalized for each student), the self-paced technology amplifies their learning experience.

Although PICRAT has yet to be fully researched for validity and reliability, the original RAT model has been validated and used in research studies to assess how technology is used in learning (e.g., Blanchard, LePrevost, Tolin, & Gutierrez, 2016; Kimmons, 2015). Future validity studies on the addition of PIC into the model are still needed.

Analyzing the Sphero Lesson Using PICRAT

When the field supervisor reviewed the Sphero lesson with the teacher candidate through the PIC dimension, the lesson was assessed at the interactive (I) level. The students were interacting with the iPad application to adjust the program that moves the two Sphero balls. On the RAT dimension, the lesson was at the replacement (R) level, since the Sphero balls replaced the dial clock hands. The field supervisor provided a word of caution to the teacher candidate: the PICRAT matrix does not evaluate if the learning activity actually helped the students meet the learning goal of telling time. Thus, similar to the SAMR model, the field supervisor shared that while the Sphero activity scored at the interactive level on PIC, it did not necessarily mean the technology was supporting stronger student learning outcomes. Rather, the interactive score on PIC meant that effective pedagogical choices around the technology were in place (such as interactive/hands-on use of the technology), but PIC is not able to measure if the learning objective was met through this activity. Therefore, the supervisor helped the teacher candidate understand that, while the pedagogical choice of interactivity with technology may be appropriate when it comes to best learning practice with technology tools, the learning goal was not necessarily effectively met. Thus, similar to SAMR, the field supervisor suggested a change of tool from the Sphero balls to the Quick Clocks app, so the tool would better associate with dial clocks and amplify the learning by providing practice with feedback for students with using dial clocks, while keeping the sound pedagogical choices around the tool (e.g., interactive/hands on).

Summary for Teacher Educators Using PICRAT

PICRAT builds on SAMR to emphasize not only the classification of technology use but also the level of activity use of the tool. I would recommend teacher educators use PICRAT after teacher candidates have learned to classify technology use and had enough exposure to technology integration that they can compare technology-rich experiences to non-technology experiences. Similar to SAMR, PICRAT does not directly consider learning goals; thus, PICRAT should either be applied in conjunction with other frameworks that more directly address how technology is used to support learning goals or used with an expert teacher educator or field instructor who can help teacher candidates understand the nuances between using sound pedagogy, tool choice, and learning outcomes.

TIM

The third framework teacher educators might use as a scaffold with their teacher candidates is the Technology Integration Matrix (TIM) developed in 2005 and updated in 2011 by researchers at the University of South Florida College of Education (Welsh, Harmes, & Winkelman, 2011). Similar to SAMR and the RAT in PICRAT, TIM emphasizes instructional levels, which are categorized as entry, adoption, adaptation, infusion, and transformation. See Table 4.1 for definitions of instructional levels of technology used in the TIM framework.

TIM also emphasizes meaningful learning environments, which are categorized as active, collaborative, constructive, authentic, and goal directed. See Table 4.2 for definitions of these environments.

Table 4.1 Definitions for Instructional Levels of Technology Use According to TIM Framework

Instructional Levels of Technology Use in the TIM Framework	
Instructional Levels of Technology Use	**Definition**
Entry	The teacher begins to use technology tools to deliver content to students.
Adoption	The teacher directs students in the conventional and procedural use of technology tools.
Adaption	The teacher facilitates the students' exploration and independent use of technology tools.
Infusion	The teacher provides the learning context, and the students choose the technology tools.
Transformational	The teacher encourages the innovative use of technology tools to facilitate higher-order learning activities that may not be possible without the use of technology.

Source: Welsh, Harmes, & Winkelman, 2011

Table 4.2 Definitions for Characteristics of Meaningful Learning Environments According to TIM Framework

Meaningful Learning Environments	
Characteristics of Meaningful Learning Environments	**Definitions**
Active Learning	Students are actively engaged in using technology as a tool rather than passively receiving information from technology.
Collaborative Learning	Students use technology tools to collaborate with others rather than working individually at all times.
Constructive Learning	Students use technology tools to connect new information to their prior knowledge rather than to passively receive information.
Authentic Learning	Students use technology tools to link learning activities to the world beyond the instructional setting rather than working on decontextualized assignments.
Goal Directed Learning	Students use technology tools to set goals, plan activities, monitor progress, and evaluate results rather than simply completing assignments without reflection.

Source: Welsh, Harmes, & Winkelman, 2011

To identify the interrelatedness of instructional levels and meaningful learning environments, the TIM framework is represented by a five-by-five matrix with the two aforementioned characteristics: instructional levels and meaningfulness. TIM encourages teacher candidates to strive for the transformational level of technology use and to meet all five characteristics of a meaningful learning environment. One would think a lesson that is active-transformational, constructive-transformational, goal directed-transformational, authentic-transformational, and collaborative-transformational would be the ultimate achievement for effective technology integration in a lesson. However, the researchers behind TIM caution that it is not appropriate that all lessons be at a transformational level, and note that the matrix level should be dependent on the focus of the learning goal (Welsh, Harmes, & Winkelman, 2011). A 2010 study found the TIM questionnaire (questions associated with the twenty-five cells in the TIM framework) to be a valid and reliable instrument to classify technology use in lessons (Meigs, 2010). TIM has been used in numerous research studies as a support for training teacher candidates and with certified teachers for evaluating a PK–12 teacher and administrator professional development programs (Florida Center for Instructional Technology, 2011).

Analyzing the Sphero Lesson Using TIM

When the field supervisor examined the Sphero lesson with the teacher candidate by using the TIM matrix, the supervisor rated categories as entry or adoption with no category scoring at the infusion or transformation levels:

Active-Adoption. The second-graders did not have a choice in the tool or how the tool was used. The movement of the Sphero balls was to produce the correct time on a clock dial that was represented on the floor mat.

Collaborative-Adoption. The second-graders took turns using the Sphero balls. Because students were in groups and were sharing one set of Sphero balls, they naturally worked with one another when they needed technical help with manipulating the balls, but collaboration related to the content goal of telling time happened only inadvertently and was not encouraged.

Constructive-Adoption. The teacher candidate defined the lesson goal, activity, and technology the students would use; the second-graders had no choice in defining the learning goal or the tool selection. The activity had a right answer (i.e., indication of the correct time on the floor mat).

Authentic-Entry. Using Sphero balls to represent clock hands on a floor mat is not how students tell time in the real world. Thus, this was not an authentic connection to real-life experiences between dial clock hands and Sphero balls.

Goal Directed-Adoption. There was a specific goal in place, with guidelines set by the teacher candidate, but the students did not participate in creating the goal.

To summarize, the field supervisor and teacher candidate found the Sphero lesson scored in the lower end of the TIM framework (i.e., entry and adoption dimensions), meaning the lesson is not as transformative for meeting the learning goal of telling time as the teacher candidate may have hoped. Thus, the field supervisor used the results on the TIM framework to guide the teacher candidate to consider pedagogical strategies and tool choices that might allow the lesson to move toward the transformational side of the matrix (i.e., transformation and infusion dimensions). The field supervisor suggested the teacher candidate change the tool from a Sphero to an interactive educational application (e.g., Quick Clocks) so the students could focus on telling time with dial clocks using an app that could provide explicit feedback. In addition, as the students seemed to be naturally supportive of one another, the field supervisor suggested the teacher candidate consider having students be encouraged to help one another as they work with the educational application. These instructional changes would move the activity from adoption to infusion on the collaborative dimension of the TIM scale, and from entry to adaption on the authentic dimension.

Summary for Teacher Educators Using TIM

TIM has a strong emphasis on the instructional use of the technology tool (entry, adoption, adaptation, infusion, and transformation). TIM also considers the tool in conjunction with the learning context (active, collaborative, constructive, authentic, and goal directed). Using TIM may be overwhelming and difficult for new teacher candidates who have limited experience with lesson development, instruction, and evaluation because of the multiple knowledge bases represented in the five-by-five matrix. Upon initial use, rather than conquering all levels at once, it might make sense for teacher educators to provide scaffolding for teacher candidates using TIM by focusing on one level of the matrix at a time (e.g., the entry level: active-entry, collaborative-entry, adaptation-entry, infusion-entry, and transformation-entry).

Triple E Framework

The fourth framework teacher educators might use as a scaffold with their teacher candidates is the Triple E Framework (Engagement, Enhancement, Extension) developed by Kolb (2017). The framework was designed to guide educators in selecting pedagogical strategies when integrating technology in learning. See Figure 4.4 for an illustration of the Triple E Framework. Triple E examines the learning goals and pedagogical strategies around technology to assess the extent to which learning activities are focused on content goals. Thus, this model stresses the interrelatedness and application of a teacher's pedagogical knowledge (PK), content knowledge (CK), and technological knowledge (TK) in a lesson.

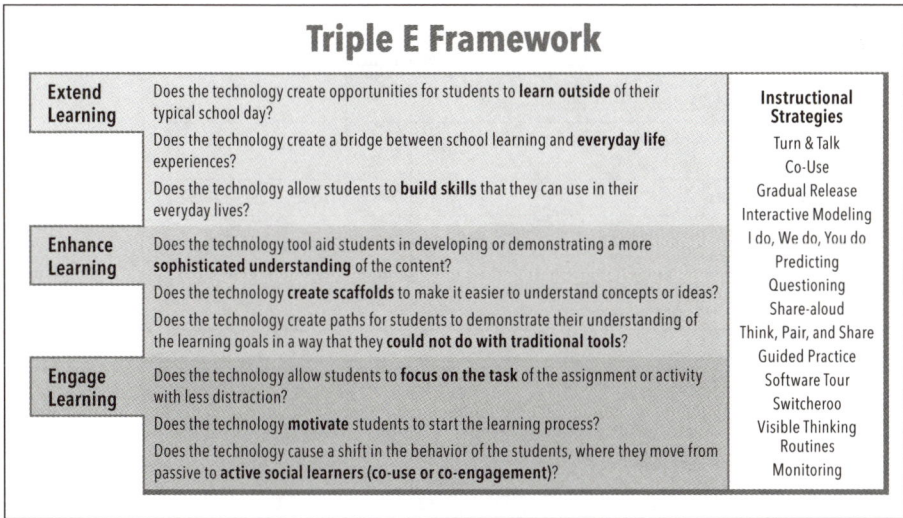

Figure 4.4 Model of the Triple E Framework. Model created by Liz Kolb, found at Tripleeframework.com.

The Triple E defines three aspects of learning with technology: engagement, enhancement, and extension. *Engagement* considers the extent to which students' minds are on the learning goals and undistracted by peripheral elements, and social and active learning occur in the lesson. *Enhancement* considers how students use higher-level cognition when using technology, how the technological tools scaffold the learning, and how technology adds value beyond a traditional experience. *Extension* considers how the technology supports an authentic learning experience, bridges students' everyday lives with classroom learning, and develops soft skills that are integrated into the lesson (e.g., collaboration and critical thinking). A key feature of Triple E is the focus on instructional strategies selected by the teacher that are used in conjunction with the technology.

Triple E Evaluation Rubric: *When to Use Technology* by Liz Kolb

Engagement in the learning	0=No	1=Somewhat	2=Yes
The technology allows students to focus on the assignment/activity/goals with less distraction (Time on Task).			
The technology motivates students to start the learning process.			
The technology causes a shift in the behavior of the students, where they move from passive to active social learners (through co-use or co-engagement).			
Enhancement of the learning goals	**0=No**	**1=Somewhat**	**2=Yes**
The technology tool allows students to develop or demonstrate a more sophisticated understanding of the learning goals or content (using higher-order thinking skills).			
The technology creates supports (scaffolds) to make it easier to understand concepts or ideas (e.g., differentiate, personalize, or scaffold learning).			
The technology creates paths for students to demonstrate their understanding of the learning goals in a way that they could not do with traditional tools.			
Extending the learning goals	**0=No**	**1=Somewhat**	**2=Yes**
The technology creates opportunities for students to learn outside of their typical school day (24/7 connection).			
The technology creates a bridge between students' school learning and their everyday life experiences (connects learning goals with real life experiences).			
The technology allows students to build authentic life soft skills, which they can use in their everyday lives.			

READING THE RESULTS
- 13–18 Points: Exceptional connection between learning goals and tool
- 7–12 Points: Some connection between learning goals and tool
- 6 Points or below: Low connection between learning goals and tool

TOTALS
_____ /18

Figure 4.5 The Triple E Framework Evaluation Rubric. Rubric created by Liz Kolb. Found at Tripleeframework.com.

Triple E evaluates technology integration using a nine-question rubric with a 0–2 grading scale associated with each question. See Figure 4.5 for the rubric. A lesson can score between 0 to 18 points. A lower range score (≤ 6), indicates that the tool and instructional strategies used in conjunction with the tool are not well connected to the learning goal. A midrange score (≥ 7 and ≤ 12) indicates that the tool and/or instructional strategies support some aspects of the learning goal. A high-range score (≥ 13) means the tool and instructional strategies are well connected to the learning goal. Schatzke (2019) found the Triple E Framework to be both a valid and reliable tool for evaluating lesson plans that integrate technology for their effectiveness to meet learning goals.

Analyzing the Sphero Lesson Using Triple E

When the field supervisor used the Triple E Framework to evaluate the Sphero lesson with the teacher candidate, the supervisor's assessment was based on the nine Triple E rubric questions.

Engagement Questions:

1. *Does the technology allow students to focus on the task of the assignment or activity with less distraction?* The Sphero distracted from the goal of telling time because learners focused more on manipulating the Sphero than on telling time. The answer to this question is "not present," with a score of 0 out of 2.

2. *Does the technology motivate students to start the learning process?* Although the Sphero balls did motivate learners because it was a unique and memorable classroom experience, the Sphero was an overcomplicated way to represent hands on a dial clock. Thus, the Sphero balls distracted and/or confused the learners from focusing on telling time on a dial clock. The answer to this question is "somewhat present," with a score of 1 out of 2.

3. *Does the technology cause a shift in the behavior of the students, where they move from passive to active social learners?* While the students worked in groups, occasionally helping each other with the technical aspects of the Sphero, and took turns using the Sphero, no collaborative learning was happening surrounding the learning objective. Yet, the learners were actively using the Sphero. The answer to this question is "somewhat present," with a score of 1 out of 2.

Enhancement Questions:

4. *Does the technology tool aid students in developing or demonstrating a more sophisticated understanding of the content?* The activity did encourage learners to use higher-level cognitive skills, mostly around programming, but programming was not the learning objective. Telling time on a dial clock was the learning objective. Thus, the answer to this question is, somewhat present, with a score of 1 out of 2.

5. *Does the technology create scaffolds to make it easier to understand concepts or ideas?* The Sphero did not do anything to make it easier to understand telling time on a dial clock; in fact, it added complication to the task of telling time. Thus, the answer to this question is "not present," with a score of 0 out of 2.

6. *Does the technology create paths for students to demonstrate their understanding of the learning goals in a way that is not possible with traditional tools?* Learners could have mastered telling time in a more authentic way with no technology scaffolds (such as drawing the minute and hour dial hands on a worksheet with pictures of clocks). The answer to this question is "not present," with a score of 0 out of 2.

Extension Questions:

7. *Does the technology create opportunities for students to learn outside of their typical school day?* The Sphero balls were not a technology that learners would use in the real world to help them tell time. The answer to this question is "not present," with a score of 0 out of 2.

8. *Does the technology create a bridge between school learning and everyday life experiences?* While telling time is a real-world concept, the Sphero balls did not help the second-graders relate telling time in the lesson activity to telling time in the real world. The answer to this question is "somewhat present," with a score of 1 out of 2.

9. *Does the technology allow students to build skills that they can use in their everyday lives?* Learners were required to use some soft skills such as problem solving when programming the Sphero, and they experienced some minimal collaboration. Even though students had opportunities to apply these skills, the use of the skills was not associated with the content objective of telling time on a dial clock. The answer to this question is "somewhat present," with a score of 1 out of 2.

TOTAL SCORE = 5 out of 18

When they discussed the Sphero lesson, the field supervisor and teacher candidate scored the lesson in the low range of the Triple E (≤ 6). The low score indicated that the technological and pedagogical decisions were ill-fitted to meet the learning objective. Using the nine question prompts in the Triple E Framework, the field supervisor discussed with the teacher candidate how the lesson would benefit from adjusting the tool and instructional choices. Knowing the Sphero lesson scored lowest on enhancement (1/6) and extension (2/6), they determined this lesson did not effectively integrate technology in ways that would enhance or extend the learning goal. Therefore, the field supervisor suggested switching from the Sphero balls to an educational application with scaffolding features for telling time (such as Quick Clocks), thus allowing a more pronounced focus on the content. Furthermore, the supervisor suggested integrating authentic discussions around telling time in conjunction with Quick Clocks (extension). The authentic discussions, along with the scaffolded feedback in the Quick Clocks application (enhancement), would ensure a higher score on the Triple E Framework.

Summary for Teacher Educators Using Triple E

Because of the many knowledge bases that come into play using the Triple E Framework, it would be best to use this framework with teacher candidates once they have foundational understanding of technological knowledge, pedagogical knowledge, and content knowledge. Since this tool provides an extensive review of technology integration, it requires teacher candidates to think about how various factors combine when making a judgment on how technology is used; thus, the Triple E Framework would be particularly useful toward the end of a teacher preparation program and during practicums.

Summary of the Sphero Lesson

This chapter analyzed the Sphero lesson through the lens of four technology integration frameworks. Each framework examines various aspects of a lesson with technology tools (e.g., type of technology used, level of active use with the technology, type of learning environment created around the technology, and the alignment of the instructional choices used in conjunction with the tool to meet the learning goals).

As Table 4.3 depicts, the Sphero lesson was assessed using all four frameworks. In the SAMR model, the Sphero balls were substituting for the clock hands, without changing the learning task, leading the field supervisor to conclude that the tool was not benefiting the learning goal any better than a traditional worksheet with dial clocks.

In the PICRAT model, where RAT is similar to SAMR, the Sphero replaced the clock hands (similar to substitution in SAMR). However, the PIC dimension of PICRAT allowed the field supervisor to also measure the lesson in terms of the level of active use of the Sphero balls, concluding that the teacher candidate allowed her students to be hands-on (interactive) with the Sphero. After a discussion of the PICRAT assessment, the field supervisor encouraged a change of tool from the Sphero balls to an educational application (Quick Clocks) that would amplify the learning goal with the feedback and repetition supports built into Quick Clocks and still allow for interactivity.

In the TIM framework, the field supervisor was able to more deeply discuss the Sphero lesson in terms of the type of technology used (entry, adoption, adaptation, infusion, and transformation) at each of the meaningful learning environments (active, collaborative, constructive, authentic, and goal directed). Ultimately, the supervisor found that all five learning environments in the Sphero lesson were at the entry or adoption levels. The field supervisor and teacher candidate discussed how the lesson could move in all five environments toward transformational use through a change of tool (e.g., Quick Clocks) and instructional strategies (e.g., more collaboration when using Quick Clocks).

Using the Triple E Framework, the Sphero lesson scored low (≤ 6) on all three Es, scoring the lowest on enhancement and extension. While the field instructor found some social and active learning occurring in the lesson (engagement), the Sphero lesson was not effective at making the learning of telling time easier than traditional methods (enhancement), and there was a deficit in developing an authentic connection to the students' everyday lives around telling time on a dial clock (extension). Thus, the field supervisor concluded that the Sphero balls did not add value to the learning goal, and she recommended a different technological tool (Quick Clocks) to better support the learning goal.

Although analysis of the Sphero lesson led to a similar conclusion applying each framework, what each framework evaluated in the lesson varied. This illustrates the importance of teacher educators being thoughtful about selecting frameworks that match their instructional goals, as well as the importance of considering the possibility of using multiple frameworks when a more comprehensive evaluation is desired or needed. Another factor to consider is the developmental readiness of teacher candidates.

Table 4.3 Summary of How the Sphero Lesson Was Evaluated in Each Framework

Framework	What Is the Framework Evaluating?	Result	Effective Use of Technology Result	Modifications to Lesson Based on Framework
SAMR	1. Type of technology use.	Substitution Level	Low result: This is an ineffective technology choice.	In order for the lesson to be more effective according to the SAMR model, the lesson should remove the Sphero balls and integrate an educational application on telling time that provides scaffolds and supports to help the students augment how they learn to tell time.
PICRAT	1. Type of technology use. 2. Amount of active use of technology tool.	Interactive and Replacement Levels	Low to Mid result: This is an ineffective technology choice.	For this lesson to be more effective according to the PICRAT model, the lesson should remove the Sphero balls and integrate an educational application on telling time; this would keep the interactivity (manipulating the dial clock in the application) but also allow for opportunities to amplify the learning by providing scaffolds such as feedback to the students in the application.
TIM	1. Type of technology use. 2. Amount of active use of technology tool. 3. Type of learning environment created around the technology.	Levels Achieved on Matrix • Active-Adoption • Collaborative-Adoption • Constructive-Adoption • Authentic-Entry • Goal Directed-Adoption	Low to mid result: This is not an effective technology choice for meeting the learning outcomes.	To make this lesson more effective according to the TIM model, change the Spheros to an educational application using realistic dial clocks that the students could manipulate. This would allow for more authenticity. In addition, allowing the students to collaborate together about dial clocks while using the application would create opportunities for more collaborative learning.

Framework	What Is the Framework Evaluating?	Result	Effective Use of Technology Result	Modifications to Lesson Based on Framework
Triple E	1. Type of technology use. 2. Amount of active use of technology tool. 3. Alignment of instructional choices used in conjunction with the technology tool to meet the learning goal.	5/18 score on Triple E rubric	Low result: This is not an effective technology choice for meeting the learning outcomes.	To make this lesson effective according to the Triple E model, the Spheros should be removed and an educational application that provides realistic dial clocks that students can manipulate should be used. The application would allow for extension of learning by providing a more authentic learning experience of using dial clocks. It would also enhance the learning experience with opportunities for repetition and scaffolded feedback within the application.

Conclusion

Teacher preparation programs should consider using educational technology frameworks as scaffolds to support candidates as they learn to design activities that leverage technology. Table 4.4 provides a comparison of the four frameworks and how they align with the knowledge bases represented in the TPACK framework. This table can guide teacher educators to select a framework that best fits their needs, based on where the teacher candidates are in their learning trajectory.

By using one or more of the four practitioner frameworks shared in this chapter, teacher preparation programs can successfully scaffold learning events geared for teacher candidates to effectively use technology in their teaching. Using an educational technology framework will also support candidate growth in technological, pedagogical, and content knowledge and the interweaving of these forms of knowledge to enhance teaching and learning. Those who design (or redesign) teacher preparation programs can be confident knowing that each of the four frameworks presented in this chapter align with the national ISTE Standards for Educators (International Society for Technology in Education, 2018) on how teacher candidates should be prepared to teach with technology—in particular standards 2 (Leader), 5 (Designer), and 6 (Facilitator).

Table 4.4 A Comparison of Practitioner Frameworks in Educational Technology: TPACK Knowledge Base, Tool, Level of Difficulty, and Recommendations for Best Time to Use Each Framework with Candidates

Comparison of Four Frameworks for Technology Integration					
Educational Technology Framework	What knowledge bases from TPACK are covered in the framework?	What tool is used to measure the technology use in learning?	How complex is the framework for new teacher candidates to learn to use?	Which considerations should be in play when teacher educators use the framework with teacher candidates?	When in the teacher preparation program should the framework be used with teacher candidates?
SAMR	TK	4-Level Scale	Easy	If considering how technology is changing a traditional assignment or learning task, then use SAMR.	Early (introduction to teaching with technology)
PICRAT	TK PK	3x3 Matrix	Medium	If considering how technology is changing a traditional assignment or task and how technology is moving students from passive to active learners, then use PICRAT.	Middle (before student teaching)
TIM	TK PK	5x5 Matrix	Difficult	If considering the type of instructional use and the context of the learning environment around the tool, then use TIM.	Later (during student teaching)
Triple E	PK CK	9-Question Rubric	Medium	If considering how the pedagogical choices used in conjunction with the technology are affecting the learning goals, then use Triple E.	Later (during student teaching)

Getting Started Resources

Florida Center for Instructional Technology. (2011). *The technology integration matrix.* fcit.usf.edu/matrix/matrix.php

The University of South Florida's College of Education created a robust website for teacher educators to learn about TIM. The website includes the TIM matrix, a wide variety of TIM tools for teacher educators to use with their candidates, video case studies of lessons, research, TIM graphical models, and FAQs about TIM.

Kolb, L. (2016). Triple E Framework. tripleeframework.com

Teacher educators can use this website to support their candidates when using the Triple E rubric. The website includes downloadable and interactive rubrics, case studies, sample lessons, models, research, and a blog that provides updates on the framework and examples of how educators are integrating the framework.

Puentedura, R. (2004). Ruben R. Puentedura's Blog.
hippasus.com/blog

This blog includes a wealth of resources related to SAMR such as presentations, podcasts, and videos about SAMR by Dr. Puentedura. Teacher educators can use the models and presentations to help their teacher candidates better understand the original nature of the SAMR model and how each level is defined.

Pulham, E. (2018, May 8). *New framework helps to unlock transformative, creative learning.* Blended Learning Universe.
bit.ly/2w0jezH

This article includes an explanation of the PICRAT model, as well as examples of how to use the model when analyzing technology use in learning. Teacher educators may find this short but informative article useful in thinking about how PICRAT can support teacher candidates to understand the technology choices (type and use) they are making in their lesson planning.

TPACK.org. (2019). **www.tpack.org**

The TPACK website is useful for teacher educators to better understand the conceptual frame behind each form of knowledge in TPACK. The website includes practitioner tools such as short video tutorials, newsletters keeping educators up to date on the evolution of TPACK, and descriptions of how K–12 and teacher preparation programs are using TPACK.

References

Azama, Y. (2015). Effective integration of technology in a high school beginning Japanese class. *Capstones and Theses at Digital Commons: Paper 517.* digitalcommons.csumb.edu/caps_thes/517

Batiibwe, M. S. K., Bakkabulindi, F. E. K., & Mango, J. M. (2017). Is the SAMR model valid and reliable for measuring the use of ICT in pedagogy? Answers from a study of teachers of mathematical disciplines in universities in Uganda. *International Journal of Computing and ICT Research, 11*(1), 11–30. ijcir.mak.ac.ug/volume11-issue1/article2.pdf

Blanchard, M. R., LePrevost, C. E., Tolin, A. D., & Gutierrez, K. S. (2016). Investigating technology-enhanced teacher professional development in rural, high-poverty middle schools. *Educational Researcher, 45*(3), 207–220. edr.sagepub.com/content/45/3/207.short

Bloom, B. S. (1956). *Taxonomy of educational objectives, Handbook I: The cognitive domain.* New York, NY: David McKay.

Florida Center for Instructional Technology. (2011). The technology integration matrix. fcit.usf.edu/matrix/matrix.php

Hughes, J., Thomas, R., & Scharber, C. (2006). Assessing technology integration: The RAT – Replacement, Amplification, and Transformation – framework. In C. Crawford et al. (Eds.), *Proceedings of Society for Information Technology & Teacher Education International Conference* (pp. 1616–1620). Chesapeake, VA: AACE.

International Society for Technology in Education. (2018). ISTE Standards for Educators. Arlington, VA: Author.

Kimmons, R. (2015). Examining TPACK's theoretical future. *Journal of Technology and Teacher Education, 23*(1), 53–77.

Kimmons, R. (2016). *K–12 technology integration.* Montreal, Canada: Press Books.

Kimmons, R., Graham, C. R., & West, R. E. (2020). The PICRAT model for technology integration in teacher preparation. *Contemporary Issues in Technology and Teacher Education, 20*(1). citejournal.org/volume-20/issue-1-20/general/the-picrat-model-for-technology-integration-in-teacher-preparation

Kolb, L. (2017). *Learning first, technology second.* Arlington, VA: International Society for Technology in Education.

Meigs, R. P. (2010). *Development and pilot of the Technology Integration Matrix Questionnaire* (Doctoral dissertation). www.bakeru.edu/images/pdf/SOE/EdD_Theses/Meigs_Russell.pdf

Mishra, P. (2019). Considering contextual knowledge: The TPACK diagram gets an upgrade. *Journal of Digital Learning in Teacher Education, 35*(2), 76–78.

Mishra, P., & Koehler, M. (2006). Technological pedagogical content knowledge: A framework for integrating technology in teacher knowledge. *Teachers College Record, 108*(6), 1017–1054.

Puentedura, R. R. (2013, May 29). SAMR: Moving from enhancement to transformation [Blog post]. www.hippasus.com/rrpweblog/archives/000095.html

Schatzke, S. E. (2019). *A validation study of the Triple E rubric for lesson design: A measurement tool for technology use in the classroom* (Doctoral dissertation). digital.library.unt.edu/ark:/67531/metadc1505198

Shulman, L. S. (1986). Those who understand: Knowledge growth in teaching. *Educational Researcher, 15*(2), 4–14.

Speirs, M. N. (2016). *Assessing teachers' mobile device skills and the integration of technology into their lives* (Master's thesis). dspace.sunyconnect.suny.edu/handle/1951/69691

Welsh, J. L., Harmes, J. C., & Winkelman, R. (2011). Tech tips: Florida's Technology Integration Matrix. *Principal Leadership, 12*(2), 69–71.

Professional Expectations for Teacher Educators: The Teacher Educator Technology Competencies (TETCs)

DAVID A. SLYKHUIS
UNIVERSITY OF NORTHERN COLORADO

DENISE A. SCHMIDT-CRAWFORD
IOWA STATE UNIVERSITY

KEVIN J. GRAZIANO
NEVADA STATE COLLEGE

TERESA S. FOULGER
ARIZONA STATE UNIVERSITY

Overview

This chapter introduces the Teacher Educator Technology Competencies (TETCs) (Foulger, Graziano, Schmidt-Crawford, & Slykhuis, 2017) in the context of technology infusion efforts and explains how teacher preparation programs and teacher educators can provide a strategic effort to help *all* teacher educators prepare to teach with technology, teach about technology, and support teacher candidates as they become proficient users of technology in their teaching. The TETCs represent the knowledge, skills, and attitudes *all* teacher educators need. This chapter also explores approaches for how teacher educators can address professional expectations and development related to teaching with technology throughout the teacher preparation program.

Introduction

We believe one of the great ironies in higher education may be the basic assumption that having a deep understanding of the content in one's field will enable a person to teach that content to a novice in the field. Most colleges/schools of education are an exception to this rule. Generally, teacher educators have completed a teacher preparation program themselves and therefore have been exposed to research-based best practices in pedagogy. However, although teacher educators in college/schools of education may be more prepared to teach or discuss PK–12 education, they may not be prepared to teach with technology.

Teacher candidates are most likely to teach how they were taught, regardless of the pedagogical strategies they learn in their teacher preparation programs (Britzman, 1991; Lortie, 1975). Therefore, if we expect teacher candidates to be prepared to teach with technology, they must experience the best practices of learning with technology while in teacher preparation programs. Faculty modeling the use of technology in teacher preparation courses will increase the ability of teacher candidates to integrate technology into their practice (Koh & Divaharan, 2011). However, modeling the use of technology cannot be limited to a single technology class (Dorfman, 2016; Kajder, 2005). To build capacity for the integration of technology by teacher candidates, teacher preparation programs need to design program-wide and program-deep experiences (Office of Educational Technology, 2017) where the decision to incorporate technology is not left up to an individual instructor in any one course (Murthy, Iyer, & Warriem, 2015). The following scenario illustrates the critical need for teacher preparation programs to infuse technology across the curriculum.

Scenario: Your Dean Identifies a Problem and a Solution

The dean of the college of education holds an annual meeting for leaders from local school districts where teacher candidates are placed for field experiences and where many teacher candidates are hired into the profession. At this meeting, the dean hears from several leaders that students from her college are not well prepared to teach using technology and the districts use their own resources to bring the teacher candidates and new teachers up to the expected level of proficiency for infusing technology into their teaching. The district leaders lament that the college of education is not doing its part to prepare teacher candidates to teach with technology. In fact, the district leaders conclude that the college's teacher education faculty must be assuming that because teacher candidates are "digital natives" (Prensky, 2001) they will naturally be able to teach with technology.

Following the meeting, the dean is determined to change how teacher candidates are prepared to teach with technology and starts gathering information and research on preparing teacher candidates to use technology. The dean knows that in order for teacher candidates to be prepared to teach with technology, they need to be taught by faculty who teach with technology. The dean attended a conference and heard a keynote speaker discuss a recently developed set of competencies for higher education faculty, Teacher Educator Technology Competencies (TETCs). (See www.learntechlib.org/p/181966.) After reflecting again on the meeting with school district leaders, the dean decides to meet with the department chairs to see how they can work together to leverage change so *all* teacher educators working with teacher candidates can become more knowledgeable about and proficient in the TETCs.

Examining the Scenario

Like the school district leaders in the scenario above, the 2017 National Education Technology Plan also places the responsibility of the technology preparation of teacher candidates on colleges/schools of education and in turn on teacher educators (Office of Educational Technology, 2017). A challenging aspect of the above scenario is having all faculty who provide instruction to teacher candidates, even those in the college of arts and sciences, work together to ensure teacher candidates experience teaching and learning with technology throughout their entire teacher preparation program. Furthermore, how do teacher educators develop the needed competencies (i.e., their TETCs), demonstrate proficiency to their department chair or dean, and stay proficient? Charged with this call to action from the US Department of Education's Office of Educational Technology, the authors of this chapter formed a research group to help guide colleges/schools of education in the professional development of teacher educators.

The Critical Need to Address Professional Expectations for Teacher Educators

Researchers argue that teacher candidates enter PK–12 classrooms ill-prepared to teach with technology (Angeli & Valanides, 2009; Ertmer & Ottenbreit-Leftwich, 2010; Kay, 2006; Tondeur, Roblin, van Braak, Fisser, & Voogt, 2013). Other researchers reveal there are just not enough teacher educators who are serving as role models for using technology effectively while preparing teacher candidates to teach (Gronseth et al., 2010; Tondeur et al., 2012; Uerz, Volman, & Kral, 2018). Evidence also suggests that many teacher preparation programs are failing to prepare teacher candidates to use and apply technology in meaningful ways in classrooms (Office of Educational Technology, 2017). Teacher preparation programs must ensure that their teacher graduates, from day one, know that "effective use of technology is not an optional add-on or a skill that we simply can expect teachers to pick up once they get into the classroom" (p. 35).

In a meta-analysis of studies related to teacher candidates' preparation and technology integration, Tondeur et al. (2012) identified twelve critical variables that directly affect teacher candidates' use of technology in practice. Those variables included such faculty characteristics as role modeling, aligning theory and practice, and providing opportunities for candidates to reflect on attitudes about technology. If teacher preparation programs in the United States (and around the world) are charged with the need to prepare teacher candidates to use technology in powerful ways, then teacher educators must establish curriculum for teaching with technology, serve as role models for using technology in teaching, and provide support to teacher candidates for developing the ability to teach with technology. Thus, there is a critical need to address the professional expectations and learning around helping *all* teacher educators develop the competencies—the knowledge, skills, and attitudes—for infusing technology in teaching and learning.

What Are the TETCs?

There is no "one-size-fits-all" approach for colleges/schools of education to address technology infusion that is program-wide and program-deep. Innovation in this area will function best if colleges/schools of education address educational technology curriculum in a way that (a) relies on subject matter (e.g., science content), (b) provides teacher candidates many opportunities to practice teaching with technology spanning the breadth of their program, and (c) maintains the depth of technology integration typical of a course taught by educational technology faculty (Foulger et al., 2017). The goal of the TETC research project was to develop technology competencies that would be visionary, as timeless as possible, and accepted by *all* teacher educators involved in a teacher preparation program (Foulger, Graziano, Slykhuis, Schmidt-Crawford, & Trust, 2016).

What ensued was a yearlong, collaborative research process involving several teacher educators and educational technology experts from across the country and internationally. The process began with a review of literature and was followed by six iterations of revisions, informed by a seventeen-member Delphi panel. The final step involved open public comment. The end result of this highly collaborative, multimethod approach was the Teacher Educator Technology Competencies (TETCs) (Foulger et al., 2017), a set of twelve competencies and related criteria. For a complete list of the competencies and criteria, see www.learntechlib.org/p/181966. In sum, the TETCs

> encourage teacher educators to design instruction that utilizes content-specific technologies to enhance teaching and learning; incorporate pedagogical approaches that prepare teacher candidates to effectively use technology; and support the development of the knowledge, skills, and attitudes of teacher candidates as related to teaching how technology is used by learners in their content area. The TETCs support teacher educators' use of technology to enhance teaching and learning; differentiate instruction to meet diverse learning needs; assess learners; connect globally with a variety of regions and cultures; teach online and/or in blended/hybrid learning environments; and address the legal, ethical, and socially-responsible use of technology in education. The TETCs also encourage teacher educators to engage in ongoing professional development and networking activities to improve the integration of technology in their teaching, engage in leadership and advocacy for using technology, and apply basic troubleshooting skills to resolve technology issues. (Foulger et al., 2017, p. 431)

Endorsing the development of the TETCs, national organizations, whose missions involve furthering the use of technology in education, openly supported the development of the TETCs and served in an advisory capacity throughout the research process. These organizations included the US Department of Education's Office of Educational Technology, Council for the Accreditation of Educator Programs

(CAEP), National Technology Leadership Coalition, Society for Information Technology and Teacher Education (SITE), Teacher Education Network of the International Society for Technology in Education (ISTE-TEN), and American Association of Colleges for Teacher Education (AACTE). In general, these organizations supported the process for developing the TETCs because of their potential to empower teacher educators and education leaders to actively "ensure all students have skilled teachers who actively use technology to meet student learning needs" (International Society for Technology in Education, 2018, 1a).

Professional Learning for Teacher Educators

Teacher educators are experts in their discipline and the pedagogical approaches applied to that discipline. Although teacher educators are typically confident in the content and pedagogy they teach, they often lack the necessary knowledge for strategically infusing technology into their teaching (Uerz et al., 2018). Technological Pedagogical Content Knowledge (TPACK) can be a useful conceptual framework to help position or challenge teacher educators to thoughtfully consider how content, pedagogy, and technology interact with or constrain each construct within the context of an instructional episode (Mishra, 2019; Mishra & Koehler, 2006). Applying recognized professional development approaches like learning by design (Koehler & Mishra, 2005), peer coaching (Joyce & Showers, 1995), and communities of practice (Wenger, 1998) can prove to be successful in facilitating teacher educators' professional growth and their specific knowledge about and application of the TETCs.

Some teacher education institutions are identifying specific strategies for providing teacher educators with useful professional learning opportunities (Tondeur et al., 2012; Uerz et al., 2018). Such professional learning opportunities should be focused on specific pedagogical contexts, inter- or multidisciplinary collaboration, teacher educators' needs and interests, and reflective learning (Uerz et al., 2018). Ping, Schellings, and Beijaard (2018) conducted a systematic review of literature investigating what, how, and why teacher educators learn. They identified four specific learning activities for teacher educators related to professional growth: (1) learning through academic engagement, (2) learning through collaborative activity, (3) learning through attending professional development programs, and (4) learning from reflective activity. These categories also define how teacher educators might be motivated to seek professional learning opportunities around the TETCs. For example, learning through collaborative activity may involve a group of teacher educators within a college/school of education forming a yearlong professional learning community to study and apply the TETCs. It is also important to note the three reasons why teacher educators seek professional learning opportunities: (1) external requirement, (2) personal ambition, and (3) professional role transition (Ping et al., 2018). In general, teacher educators are lifelong learners who seek learning opportunities to improve their own practice, including the infusion of technology.

How to Build Capacity: Applying the TETCs in Teacher Preparation

The following section examines just two of the twelve TETCs, in detail, in order to provide readers with an understanding of the depth required by teacher educators as they seek to become competent in addressing technology within their course content.

TETC 8 in Practice

8. Teacher educators will use technology to connect globally with a variety of regions and cultures.

TETC 8 focuses on teacher educators' use of technology to connect globally with a variety of regions and cultures. The criteria associated with TETC 8 include teacher educators (a) modeling global engagement using technologies to connect teacher candidates with other cultures and locations, (b) designing instruction in which teacher candidates use technology to collaborate with learners from a variety of backgrounds and cultures, and (c) addressing strategies needed for cultures and regions having different levels of technological connectivity.

The Center for Global Education (n.d.) reminds educators that technology should not be considered a supplement for existing curricula, nor should it be limited to technology training courses and professional development alone. Instead, technology should be used to help teachers meet their global learning goals and address standards across multiple curricular areas. Educator goals and standards that specifically relate to using technology to connect globally with others may stem from the ISTE and InTASC standards. For example, ISTE Standard 4, Collaborator, posits that educators will "use collaborative tools to expand students' authentic, real-world learning experiences by engaging virtually with experts, teams and students, locally and globally" (International Society for Technology in Education, 2017). InTASC Standard 3 speaks to developing an effective learning environment. A performance within Standard 3 includes teachers promoting "responsible learner use of interactive technologies to extend the possibilities for learning locally and globally" (Council of Chief State School Officers, 2013, p. 21). Teacher educators need to model global engagement during instruction, allowing teacher candidates to explore, engage, and collaborate with others around the world using technology.

Teacher educators can use global themes such as climate change; equality and inequality; conflict, peace, and security; language and identity; health and development; and science and technology to connect with other teacher candidates or students and teachers from other countries. This can be done using videoconferencing tools such as Facetime, Skype, Skype Classroom, Google Hangouts, Zoom, or the conference feature within an LMS where all students are enrolled in the same course. Teacher educators can take academic content and use gaming, blogs, e-pen pals, and social media such as Twitter, LinkedIn, and Pinterest to design instruction where teacher candidates collaborate with learners from different cultures. For example, teacher candidates in an education foundations course, along with the teacher educator, can individually post tweets on a current education topic (e.g., how the concept of "equity" is interpreted in various locales across the globe) and include a hashtag to their course prefix and number. Teacher candidates can search for tweets on the same topic from individuals around the world and respond to those tweets. Teacher educators can require teacher candidates to post to their LMS class discussion board selected content from their original tweet, what others said about the topic, and new information they learned as a result of using Twitter. Tapping the larger Twitter community, teacher educators can require teacher candidates to participate in discipline-specific Twitter chats with practicing teachers where teacher candidates share resources, gather resources, and build upon their professional networks (Mullins & Hicks, 2019).

Teacher educators should also consider using Google Earth and virtual reality field trips to connect teacher candidates with different cultures and locations. Not all teacher candidates or K–12 students have access to world-class facilities such as museums or can visit locations such as the International Space Station, the Coliseum in Italy, or locations of personal interest such as the town(s) where one's great grandparents were born. With Google Earth, teacher educators can develop cross-curricular assignments that allow teacher candidates to investigate via satellite views of different regions, streets, and specific locations.

Field trips via virtual reality headsets allow teacher candidates to experience world-class facilities and events such as flying an airplane, swimming with sharks, or viewing a human heart without leaving the classroom. Google Expeditions, an immersive education app that allows educators and students to view the world through virtual reality tours, is one example of how teacher candidates and teacher educators can explore the world. These selected examples of how teacher educators can use technology in the classroom to connect globally with different cultures and regions demonstrate to teacher candidates what a global curriculum with the assistance of technology can look like in their future classroom.

In an opinion blog posted to *Education Week*, Soppelsa and Manise (2015) challenged educators and administrators to think about what global competence means to them and whether the process for credentialing new teachers is reflective of the realities of today's classrooms. Colleges/schools of education are encouraged to engage in the same reflective exercise and critically think about how technology is used by teacher educators to connect globally with a variety of regions and cultures. Teacher education administrators should help teacher educators develop skills in globalizing instruction, project-based learning, and conceptual learning with technology. It is critical for teacher preparation programs to provide new learning opportunities that prepare teacher candidates to enter an interconnected world (Moss, Manise, & Soppelsa, 2012). Technology allows teacher educators to develop coursework that integrates global competence into both content and pedagogical development.

TETC 9 in Practice

9. Teacher educators will address the legal, ethical, and socially-responsible use of technology in education.

TETC 9 focuses on how teacher educators address the legal, ethical, and socially-responsible use of technology in education. The criteria associated with TETC 9 include teacher educators (a) modeling the legal, ethical, and socially-responsible use of technology for teaching and learning; (b) guiding teacher candidates' use of technology in legal, ethical, and socially-responsible ways; and (c) providing opportunities for teacher candidates to design curriculum following legal, ethical, and socially-responsible uses of technology.

Digital communications have surpassed traditional means of social interaction and provide an avenue for individuals to stay connected when they might not otherwise be able to do so. Many teacher candidates use social networking tools such as Facebook, Instagram, and Snapchat to stay updated with their friends, classmates, and coworkers. They can also use these tools to connect with organizations and events. Social networking tools afford the ability to connect and communicate with anyone in the world. Even those who are not fully vetted by the individual can be "friended."

While there are many positive and educationally useful elements to social media, negative aspects have also risen, such as cyberbullying. This term has become a catchall phrase for a vast array of online communications designed to "flame," harass, exclude, and impersonate others. With a device connected to social media, social structures, especially those between teacher educators and teacher candidates (and PK–12 teachers and students), are flattened. Literally anyone with a device and internet connectivity can post to a social media account from anywhere, at any time. Teacher educators must help teacher candidates realize the power and the dangers of their social presence, including their online footprint, and help them plan for the legal, ethical, and socially-responsible use of technology. Teacher candidates need to realize that everything that appears on the internet, whether they posted it or someone else did, can be viewed, copied, sent, republished, or otherwise distributed to others. This awareness should be shared with their K–12 students with a warning that images, videos, and text could be viewed and judged by colleagues, parents, and students, and possibly taken out of context.

When selecting technology to use in the classroom, teacher educators often gravitate toward so-called free websites or apps. However, many websites or apps offered as "free" may not be effective pedagogically, and they may pose concerns related to the data collected in the registration process or through the use of the service. Of concern, personal data can then be used to market products targeted to users, or the data can be sold to other companies. Based on this major concern, teacher educators need to teach personal data literacy to teacher candidates, including data analytics generated through the use of some online software, how data are being collected, and why data are being collected (Pangrazio & Selwyn, 2019). The teacher candidates must then teach their PK–12 students how to protect their personal data as well.

Additionally, with the proliferation of web services and apps requiring accounts, teacher candidates need to learn strategies for protecting themselves from getting hacked. Because it may be difficult to remember the plethora of passwords needed for all of today's services, it may be common to reuse a password across multiple platforms. This is a particularly poor practice that may multiply the effect of a single data breach across multiple sites and accounts. Teacher educators should be encouraged to use two-factor authentication whenever it is available.

Another pressing issue for any educator is ensuring that their use of internet-based information is reliable and credible and having the knowledge and ability to identify disinformation or fake news. This is of particular importance when news and information are often shaped to fit an ideological viewpoint. This increases the importance of not relying on a single source for information. Teacher educators should stress the keys to website evaluation (like relevance, accuracy, bias/perspective, reliability (Coiro, 2017)) and the importance of looking for and reading links and pages that say "about us," "philosophy," "background," "biography," or "who am I." Teacher candidates should be encouraged to look for the author or the name of the organization responsible for the webpage and should be taught how to examine the author's credentials in relation to the subject.

Other ethical and socially-responsible technology-related topics for teacher educators to discuss with teacher candidates across the curriculum may include the use of social media in the classroom, the use of cell phones in the classroom, the dos and don'ts of blogging, posting to YouTube, using Creative Commons and Wikipedia as resources, as well as protecting and respecting personal digital information, the use of online netiquette, and plagiarism.

Championing the TETCs

As mentioned in the preface and Chapter 1, any project that involves long-term change and requires professional development can benefit from the participation and support of a champion: someone who is connected, seeks opportunities, and is personally invested (Thompson, 2009). In the case of building capacity for teacher educators to address technology integration (e.g., TETCs) within their courses, the champion could be an IT specialist, instructional designer, instructional technologist, teacher educator, or professional developer. A team made up of individuals with a variety of responsibilities surrounding teaching and learning and officially tasked by their administration would be ideal in leading the effort to advance and support technology infusion (Ping et al., 2018; Uerz et al., 2018).

To target professional learning activities, we recommend leaders within colleges/schools of education administer a survey to gauge teacher educators' individual perceptions of competency for each of the TETCs and related criteria. Additionally, data from the survey could be used to identify (1) any immediate concerns related to teacher educators' understanding of the TETCs and (2) areas where support might create a sustained professional learning trajectory and potentially grow a community of practice. Champions may opt to consider getting started with action steps for selected competencies. TETC 8 and TETC 9, explored in detail above, serve as examples for how to get started with implementing the TETCs for *all* teacher educators.

There is limited professional development research that addresses capacity building for teacher educators as they develop their courses to include the TETCs (Uerz et al., 2018). Because teacher educators are afforded so much autonomy in their own growth and learning, the design of effective professional development will require flexibility to customize TETC-related professional development. Championing the TETCs through professional development needs to be ongoing and sustained by leadership committed to change.

Using the TETCs to Support Change

So, how does the dean in the scenario at the beginning of the chapter meet the goal of having *all* teacher educators in a college/school of education become proficient in the TETCs?

> **Short-Term Support: Assessing and Increasing Faculty Expertise.** In the short term, there is a need to first assess the degree of TETC expertise already being exhibited by teacher educators. Once this is determined, then professional learning can be designed to meet the greatest need(s). Professional learning for teacher educators often takes many different forms, from reading groups to study groups, to conference attendance and participation, to attending face-to-face instruction offered by instructional support centers on campus. Another

alternative, directly related to the TETCs, is the online TETC Professional Development Course supported by SITE and developed by the TETC originators, along with two other teacher educators with expertise in global delivery of faculty professional learning (Slykhuis et al., 2019). This self-paced, four-course sequence is based on a professional development program originally designed for teacher educators that was expanded successfully throughout higher education. The TETC professional development course supports teacher educators in their understanding and application of the TETCs to their own practice; upon completion of the courses, individuals are awarded a micro-credential for each TETC. (For more information on the course, visit site.aace.org/tetc.)

Mid-Term Support: Resources for Course Development and 1:1 Support. In the mid-term, the dean may need to consider allocating resources for teacher educators who are teaching sections of the same course to co-plan solutions for the meaningful integration of technology into their courses. Additionally, colleagues who are technology educators could be given a reduced teaching load specifically so they can support other teacher educators throughout the college with integrating technology in such a way that helps them gain proficiency in the TETCs.

Long-Term Support: College/School of Education Policies and Hiring. In the long term, systematic changes will need to be made to college/school of education policies to ensure that implementation becomes part of the culture of the college/school. To ensure teacher educators are addressing meaningful technology integration as defined by the TETCs, items related to technology integration and the TETCs can be added to annual evaluations and promotion and tenure requirements (Ping et al., 2018). When hiring new teacher educators, screening criteria for applicants can be added to the review and evaluation of the ability of an applicant to integrate technology in a way consistent with the TETCs.

Implementing short-, mid-, and long-term changes in expectations and capacity may be met with resistance by some teacher educators and will require the commitment of resources by the dean. In time, however, the dean and department chairs should begin to receive positive feedback from local school districts about the noticeable change in technology proficiency of the teacher candidates being placed for practicum experiences and the new teachers being hired into the field. The dean should then feel confident the college/school of education is doing its part to prepare teacher candidates who demonstrate that "effective use of technology is not an optional add-on or a skill that we simply can expect teachers to pick up once they get into the classroom" (Office of Educational Technology, 2017, p. 35).

Getting Started Resources

Borthwick, A., Clausen, J. M., Foulger, T. S., & Slykhuis, D. A. (2019, August 8). Preparing new teachers: How collaboration across professional associations can advance technology infusion. [Blog post: American Association for the Advancement of Science: ARISE]. bit.ly/2JpU1BX

This blog post describes how the TETCs and other resources are being used by professional associations to infuse technology, particularly into science, technology, engineering, and mathematics (STEM).

Foulger, T. S., Graziano, K. J., Schmidt-Crawford, D., & Slykhuis, D. A. (2017). Teacher educator technology competencies. *Journal of Technology and Teacher Education, 25*(4), 413–448. learntechlib.org/p/181966

This is the first article that published the twelve Teacher Educator Technology Competencies (TETCs) and related criteria. The article provides a description of how the TETCs were developed and suggests important directions for further research and work in the area.

TETCs. site.aace.org/tetc

This website is a quick reference to access information about the Teacher Educator Technology Competencies (TETCs) and related criteria. Additional TETCs resources are provided.

Schmidt-Crawford, D. A., Foulger, T. S., Graziano, K. J., & Slykhuis, D. A. (2019). Research methods for the people, by the people, of the people: Using a highly collaborative, multimethod approach to promote change. *Contemporary Issues in Technology and Teacher Education, 19*(2). bit.ly/2JcJny3

This article provides a detailed description of the collaborative, multimethod research approach used to develop the TETCs. Researchers interested in learning more about using methods like crowdsourcing, Delphi, and public opinion as part of their research will find this article useful.

Slykhuis, D. A., Schmidt-Crawford, D. A., Graziano, K. J., &
    Foulger, T. S. (2019). TETC Webinar: Applying the Teacher
    Educator Technology Competencies. Sponsored by the Society
    for Information Technology and Teacher Education (SITE).
    youtu.be/adiV46r5YKc

In this webinar, the research team describes how the Teacher Educator
Technology Competencies (TETCs) were developed and suggests how a teacher
educator might apply each competency in their classroom or context.

References

Angeli, C., & Valanides, N. (2009). Epistemological and methodological issues for
    the conceptualization, development, and assessment of ICT–TPCK: Advances
    in technological pedagogical content knowledge (TPCK). *Computers &
    Education, 52*(1), 154–168.

Britzman, D. (1991). *Practice makes practice: A critical study of learning to teach.*
    Albany, NY: State University of New York Press.

Center for Global Education. (n.d.). *Use technology to develop global competence.*
    asiasociety.org/education/use-technology-develop-global-competence

Coiro, J. (2017). Teaching adolescents how to evaluate the quality of online
    information. edut.to/39tqdPo

Council of Chief State School Officers. (2013). *InTASC model core teaching
    standards and learning progressions for teachers 1.0: A resource for ongoing
    teacher development.* Washington, DC: Author.

Dorfman, J. (2016). Exploring models of technology integration into music teacher
    preparation programs. *Visions of Research in Music Education, 28.*
    bit.ly/3ayuK48

Ertmer, P. A., & Ottenbreit-Leftwich, A. T. (2010). Teacher technology change: How
    knowledge, confidence, beliefs, and culture intersect. *Journal of Research on
    Technology in Education, 42*(3), 255–284.

Foulger, T. S., Graziano, K. J., Schmidt-Crawford, D., & Slykhuis, D. A. (2017). Teacher educator technology competencies. *Journal of Technology and Teacher Education, 25*(4), 413–448. Waynesville, NC: Society for Information Technology & Teacher Education. www.learntechlib.org/p/181966/

Foulger, T. S., Graziano, K. J., Slykhuis, D., Schmidt-Crawford, D., & Trust, T. (2016). Invited commentary: The time is now! Creating technology competencies for teacher educators. *Journal of Technology and Teacher Education, 24*(3), 249–256.

Gronseth, S., Brush, T., Ottenbreit-Leftwich, A., Strycker, J., Abaci, S., Easterling, W., ... & van Leusen, P. (2010). Equipping the next generation of teacher: Technology preparation and practice. *Journal of Digital Learning in Teacher Education, 27*(1), 30–36.

International Society for Technology in Education. (2017). ISTE Standards for Educators. www.iste.org/standards/for-educators

International Society for Technology in Education. (2018). ISTE Standards for Education Leaders. www.iste.org/standards/for-education-leaders

Joyce, B. R., & Showers, B. (1995). *Student achievement through staff development: Fundamentals of school renewal* (2nd ed.). White Plains, NY: Longman.

Kajder, S. B. (2005). "Not quite teaching for real:" Preservice secondary English teachers' use of technology in the field following the completion of an instructional technology methods course. *Journal of Computing in Teacher Education, 22*(1), 15–21. editlib.org/j/ISSN-1040-2454/

Kay, R. H. (2006). Evaluating strategies used to incorporate technology into preservice education: A review of the literature. *Journal of Research on Technology in Education, 38*(4), 383–408.

Koehler, M. J., & Mishra, P. (2005). Teachers learning technology by design. *Journal of Computing in Teacher Education, 21*(3), 94–102.

Koh, J., & Divaharan, S. (2011). Developing pre-service teachers' technology integration expertise through the TPACK–developing instructional model. *Journal of Educational Computing Research, 44*, 35–58.

Lortie, D. (1975). *Schoolteacher: A sociological study.* Chicago, IL: University of Chicago Press.

Mishra, P. (2019). Considering contextual knowledge: The TPACK diagram gets an upgrade. *Journal of Digital Learning in Teacher Education, 35*(2), 76–78.

Mishra, P., & Koehler M. (2006). Technological pedagogical content knowledge: A framework for teacher knowledge. *The Teachers College Record, 108*(6), 1017–1054.

Moss, D. M., Manise, J., & Soppelsa, B. (2012). *Preparing globally competent teachers.* Washington, DC: NAFSA: Association of International Educators. Background paper for CAEP commissioners. Washington, DC: NAFSA.

Mullins, R., & Hicks, D. (2019). So I feel like we are just theoretical, whereas they actually do it: Navigating Twitter chats for teacher education. *Contemporary Issues in Technology and Teacher Education, 19*(2), 218–239. www.learntechlib.org/p/187335/

Murthy, S., Iyer, S., & Warriem, J. (2015). ET4ET: A large-scale faculty professional development program in effective integration of educational technology. *Educational Technology & Society, 18*(3), 16–28. www.ifets.info

Office of Educational Technology, (2017). *Reimagining the role of technology in education: 2017 National Education Technology Plan update.* tech.ed.gov/files/2017/01/NETP17.pdf

Pangrazio, L., & Selwyn, N. (2019). 'Personal data literacies': A critical literacies approach to enhancing understandings of personal digital data. *New Media & Society, 21*(2), 419–437. journals.sagepub.com/doi/pdf/10.1177/1461444818799523

Ping, C., Schellings, G., & Beijaard, D. (2018). Teacher educators' professional learning: A literature review. *Teaching and Teacher Education, 75*, 93–104.

Prensky, M. (2001). Digital natives, digital immigrants Part 1. *On the Horizon, 9*(5), 1–6.

Slykhuis, D. A., Foulger, T. S., Graziano, K. J., Hofer, M., Lee, J., & Schmidt-Crawford, D. A. (2019). *TETC Professional Development Course.* Waynesville, NC: The Society for Information Technology and Teacher Education. site.aace.org/tetc/

Soppelsa, B., & Manise, J. (2015, August 19). The top 10 characteristics of globally competent teachers [Blog post]. bit.ly/2UMBpRR

Thompson, M. (2009). *The organizational champion: How to develop passionate change agents at every level.* New York, NY: McGraw Hill.

Tondeur, J., Roblin, N. P., van Braak, J., Fisser, P., & Voogt, J. (2013). Technological pedagogical content knowledge in teacher education: In search of a new curriculum. *Educational Studies, 39*(2), 239–243.

Tondeur, J., Van Braak, J., Sang, G., Voogt, J., Fisser, P., & Ottenbreit-Leftwich, A. (2012). Preparing pre-service teachers to integrate technology in education: A synthesis of qualitative evidence. *Computers & Education, 59*(1), 134–144.

Uerz, D., Volman, M., & Kral, M. (2018). Teacher educators' competences in fostering student teachers' proficiency in teaching and learning with technology: An overview of relevant research literature. *Teaching and Teacher Education, 70*, 12–23.

Wenger, E. (1998). *Communities of practice: Learning, meaning, and identity.* Cambridge, England: Cambridge University Press.

CHAPTER 6

The Necessity of Preparing Teacher Candidates to Teach Online

MICHAEL MCVEY
EASTERN MICHIGAN UNIVERSITY

Overview

The tools and applications for online instruction appropriate for PK–12 teaching have increased in quality, and soon access to them will be nearly universal (Consortium for School Networking, 2018). The consequence of this vastly improved online platform is that many teaching activities traditional to the physical classroom may move beyond those classroom walls and into a *virtual* teaching space. Teacher preparation programs will need to prepare teacher candidates to use web-based tools and related instructional design in their teaching practice. This chapter describes how programs should be modeling online instructional strategies, providing teacher candidates opportunities to practice online teaching throughout their programs, and assessing teacher candidates as they expand their capacity to use online tools in blended or fully online PK–12 learning environments.

Scenario: My Graduates and the Changing Nature of Teaching

For the last two decades, I have helped prepare teacher candidates to use technology in their classrooms. Each year, I have seen emerging technologies alter conversations and expectations about teaching. To keep abreast of these changes, I attend local educational technology conferences, where I often meet graduates who now teach in their own classrooms. When I can, I record a minute or so of impromptu video where they talk directly to my current teacher candidates to let them know what knowledge and skills they think will be valuable for new teachers.

Over the years the conversations I have with my graduates are beginning to change. My graduates used to share news about a new application or tool they were hoping to try in their classrooms. Now, they share how they resolved challenging problems by incorporating flipped or blended models of teaching. Their challenges vary from school to school, but the underlying issues are that the reality of daily living sometimes conspire to disrupt student success. They share stories about students who trickled into morning class because of spotty city bus service, students who had to stay home to look after younger siblings, and students who were chronically absent, not because they disliked school but because a fear of bullying kept them home.

One solution for my new teachers is to engage their students remotely. One teacher streamed his class for a temporarily homebound student. Another set up a video chat so a group member who was ill at home would not miss planning for a project. And another used a flipped model of instruction for his pre-algebra classes. He created and posted online a series of four-minute instructional videos based on a key concept for the week. He broke up each lesson with online questions to ensure student engagement. When students finally came to class, regardless of how late public transit had made them, they had already reviewed the key concepts in the lesson being covered and could jump right into class activities. Some even reported reviewing the videos and taking the brief quizzes on their smartphones during the bus ride to school.

My graduates reported that the blended teaching approach was becoming the new normal for them. They shared with me that transforming some lessons into videos or moving collaborative activities into discussion forums and shared documents not only kept students engaged but also provided new opportunities for teacher candidates to enrich their learning. One teacher told me that she had created unique websites for each of her after-school clubs and sports activities in which students planned and shared insights with each other. Another opened up online homework chats for a half hour each evening to answer questions students (or parents) raised. On occasion, some of my graduates even mentored colleagues who had far more years of teaching experience.

My Reflection on Comments from Graduates

Of deep concern to me was the graduate who pointed out a serious problem in her teacher preparation training. During her studies, she had few opportunities to develop a practical or conceptual understanding of the dynamics of blending online and face-to-face teaching. In examining other programs, it has become increasingly apparent to me that the existing content of many teacher preparation programs will soon need to address directly the shifting focus toward online-supported teaching practices already in the field. Colleagues have sometimes disparaged educational technology as an add-on or a passing fad. The current teaching profession, however, does not reflect such casual dismissal.

With informal professional development through various social media platforms (Carpenter & Krutka, 2015), combined with training, encouragement, and advocacy from organizations such as the International Society for Technology in Education (ISTE) (Thomas & Knezek, 2008) and the Aurora Institute (formerly iNACOL), teachers in the field have increasingly found technology that supports online platforms to be a powerful force for improved student success. And with a growing use of online presence in PK–12 schools, as well as an increase in the number of completely online schools, I would argue that it should be the essential work of schools and colleges of education to build capacity to prepare teacher candidates to learn how to design effective blended and online teaching suitable for PK–12 settings.

One could additionally argue that practices favorable to online teaching can also enrich teaching in the traditional classroom. As a lifelong educator, the liveliest and most engaged classrooms I have encountered use approaches drawn straight from online teaching. Students in these classes meet subject matter experts in virtual environments using videoconferencing. They write plays and podcasts, create videos and animations, and even compose their own music using technology. Students who use technology are both challenged and engaged, and can even continue to work after school using online platforms that allow them to conduct science experiments, work on robotics projects, or participate in group research from their own homes. Producing, creating, thinking, and especially sharing is happening in digital spaces, and perceptive teachers are connecting their physical classrooms with this student enthusiasm for online interaction.

What the Research Says: A Few Key Points

Online learning opportunities are becoming increasingly prevalent in PK–12 across the United States (US). Miron, Shank, and Davidson (2018) discovered a fast-growing virtual school sector in the US with more than 429 full-time virtual schools enrolling almost 300,000 students. In their estimation, in 2015 more than 2.7 million students took roughly 4.5 million supplemental online courses. Moreover, that number is growing not only in the US but also abroad; for example, in South Korea, Japan, and many other countries with robust internet infrastructures, online tutoring is growing and changing the face of supplemental education (Kim, 2016). School districts are also embracing online learning strategies to resolve a variety of practical concerns such as increasing student engagement and preventing disruption by providing online activities in lieu of taking a snow day (Milman, 2014).

Individual states have also recognized the inevitability of online learning and have taken action to prepare their students to be competent as online learners. The Digital Learning Collaborative (2018) noted that five states *require* students to complete an online course to graduate (Alabama, Arkansas, Florida, Michigan, and Virginia). In addition, other states, including Georgia, New Mexico, Massachusetts, and West Virginia, have passed rules or legislation encouraging online learning. Some schools and districts have followed this trend, not waiting for states to mandate online or blended courses, as they already perceive the need for students to gain a degree of comfort with the online learning environment and also see online learning as a way of enabling students to engage in projects in their communities.

The US Department of Education (2011) recognizes blended learning as a strategy that allows schools to be more flexible in awarding credits, provide competency-based education, and enhance project-based learning opportunities. In addition, they note that online learning strategies can enhance personalized learning opportunities through differentiated teaching practices and enhancements to many instructional strategies.

To begin addressing the increased adoption of online learning, teacher educators need to recognize that the tools and features of online education have changed. The days of static, text-heavy, and barely interactive online instruction are behind us. Vastly increased processing speeds, storage capacity, cloud-based storage, graphics resolution, and improved interactive capabilities have also turned handheld devices into powerful new opportunities for teaching and learning inside and outside the physical classroom. Beginning with early research on the use of handheld devices in schools (Norris, Hossain, & Soloway, 2011), handheld devices and smartphones have demonstrated the potential to transform online learning (Pegrum, Oakley, & Faulkner, 2013). Expanding computing power to teachers and students, supported by models such as blended instruction, has created opportunities for teacher educators to be more deliberate about including pedagogical approaches for online teaching in their preparation programs.

A two-pronged approach to building capacity for these skills is for teacher educators, no matter what content they teach, to model online and blended learning methods and provide opportunities for teacher candidates to practice teaching either online or in blended/hybrid learning environments. The Teacher Educator Technology Competencies (TETCs) (Foulger, Graziano, Schmidt-Crawford, & Slykhuis, 2017) for faculty teaching in a technology-infused program include online teaching skills as one of the key competencies: *"Teacher educators will use effective strategies for teaching online and/or blended/hybrid learning environments"* (p. 433).

A recent survey of teacher preparation leaders revealed that some undergraduate and graduate teacher preparation programs are already infusing online teaching skills by discretely teaching how to develop online versions of discussions, course content, and assessments (Graziano and Bryans-Bongey, 2018). These early adopters have embraced a continuum of skills from tool management to the incorporation of instructional design practices for online learners. Although online field experiences are still rare in teacher preparation, there has been incremental growth from 1.3% to

4.1% in the number of PK–12 teacher preparation programs in the US that address online teaching as a component of their curriculum (Archambault et al., 2016).

Several recent approaches to changing pedagogical practices in higher education through technology-infused teaching have had encouraging results. A study conducted in Finland (Sointu et al., 2019) on the implementation of the flipped classroom method in a higher education setting emerged as an innovative solution to emphasize student-centered learning. The authors further concluded that the flipped classroom model successfully integrated pedagogy and technology, and the power of technology integration was clearly visible to candidates. One caveat to adopting the flipped model, even for enthusiastic teachers, is that, all students would need access to a device and the internet at home.

Learning to teach is a complicated task, and addressing skills required to teach online not only requires that teacher candidates are grounded in their content area but that they know the pedagogical function of online tools and can apply them (Mishra & Koehler, 2006). This intersection of pedagogy with technology is of paramount importance, and the task of preparing teacher candidates for physical classrooms must extend to preparing them to teach well in online environments. To accomplish this, teacher candidates need to learn how to use online and blended activities grounded in appropriate learning theory. One approach is to provide opportunities to develop and practice these skills in online settings; for example, the results of a study of novice science teachers (Bell, Maeng, & Binns, 2013) who had opportunities to contextualize technology instruction through authentic practice experiences found that they later integrated technology into instruction more frequently than their peers who had not had such opportunities.

Even for teacher educators, the integration of advanced technology into a course can be a daunting prospect. One helpful strategy is the creation of long-duration professional development academies. Brinkerhoff (2006) observed that general faculty attitudes and self-efficacy improved because of regular interactions with colleagues as they worked in small teams to engage with projects over the course of a year that directly influenced their teaching.

Another strategy for consideration by schools and colleges of education is to adopt well-grounded and well-researched standards for blended instruction such as those released in 2015 by iNACOL (now known as the Aurora Institute). iNACOL's Blended Learning Teacher Competency Framework (see Getting Started Resources) focuses on four domains: (1) mindsets, (2) qualities, (3) technical skills, and (4) adaptive skills.

A Theoretical Framework for Online Teaching and Learning

As colleges and schools of education focus on how to provide a curriculum for teacher preparation that includes training in online instruction, one theoretical model could prove beneficial. Decades after its first appearance, a frequently referenced model relevant to online learning is Community of Inquiry (CoI) (see Figure 6.1). In this framework, teachers create deep and meaningful learning experiences through the interplay of three interdependent elements or presences: the social, the cognitive, and the teaching. These presences exist within the interactions of teachers and their learners (Garrison, Anderson, & Archer, 1999).

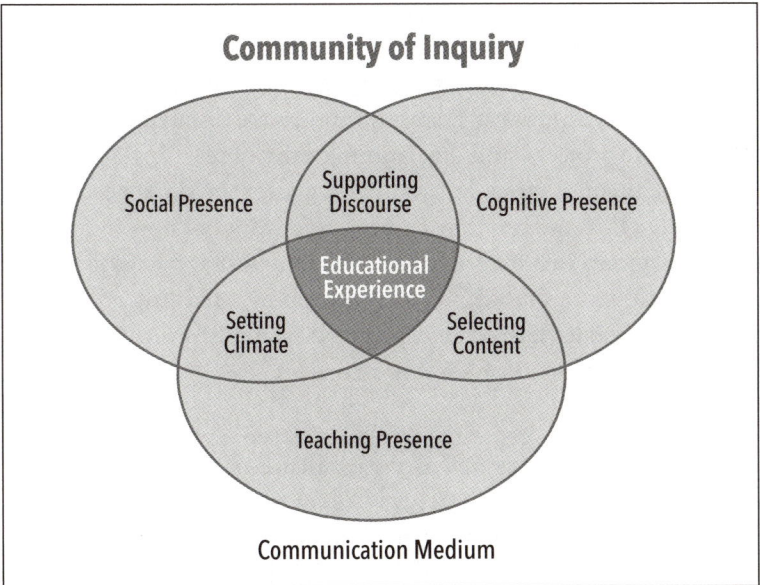

Figure 6.1 Community of Inquiry (CoI) Framework. Reprinted from *The Internet and Higher Education, 2*(2–3), D. Randy Garrison, Terry Anderson, Walter Archer, Critical Inquiry in a Text-Based Environment: Computer Conferencing in Higher Education, Page 19, Copyright 1999, with permission from Elsevier.

Cognitive Presence focuses on how online learners interact and engage with course content and with each other. An event initiates learning that activates curiosity and prompts explorations to seek the answers to questions and the solutions to problems (Shea & Bidjerano, 2009). For this presence, teacher educators and teacher candidates develop skills necessary to ensure the materials used in the course or lesson are appropriate to grade level, reading level, and overall course learning objectives, and are presented in a manner that will lead toward understanding or application of the content. An excellent starting place for developing the skills to use available tools is by curating digital resources. As teacher candidates master the basics of finding relevant online resources to support learning objectives in an online lesson, they also learn to discern which digital artifacts are age or grade-level appropriate or need modifications for English language learners or students with special needs.

Social Presence focuses on the importance of the social-emotional aspects of online learning. This attribute often drives the climate of the course and describes how individuals identify as a part of the learning community within an online course (Garrison et al., 2000). For this presence, teacher candidates would need to develop the skills necessary to engage their students in learning processes by using such techniques as framing appropriate discussion prompts, developing collaborative projects, and determining ways of reaching out to students to encourage them. As teacher candidates master the skills needed for the curation of digital resources, they can begin to work out how to frame those same digital materials in a manner that would interest and engage learners. Teacher educators can model ways of developing a trusting relationship with learners and seek to develop interpersonal relationships within an online class or online components of a traditional class.

Teaching Presence focuses on the teacher candidate as designer and developer of online learning environments, as well as the facilitator of cognitive and social processes in collaboration with learners (Akyol & Garrison, 2013). The improved functionality of learning management systems has enabled a multifaceted approach to designing for online learning. For this presence, teacher candidates would need to develop skills necessary to engage students through techniques in instructional design to effectively present content, activate prior knowledge, provide appropriate practice intervals, and determine ways of assessing knowledge and skills both formatively and summatively. Online teaching requires an intentional coordination of the interactions of learners with each other and with the instructor. Success with the teaching presence requires planning and an understanding of the needs of students.

Teacher candidates would need to practice using all three presences in the CoI framework as they develop an online learning environment either as a stand-alone lesson or in the context of a larger unit. Teacher educators can also use the CoI framework as a basis for reviewing teacher candidate progress as they develop these skills. One excellent strategy for developing the skills needed in all three presences is to provide teacher candidates with their *own* course shells in their methods class or student teaching seminar. It is often possible to set up instructor accounts for teacher candidates, depending upon the learning management system used by an institution, which will allow teacher candidates to create their own learning environments (sometimes known as shells or sandboxes). Some colleges/schools of education have used open-source tools such as Moodle to provide these shells, while others make use of Google Classroom. The learning management system chosen is less important than providing teacher candidates with a space and creative license to design and practice teaching using an online structure.

From a faculty perspective, a little encouragement goes a long way. The CoI framework can support the expectation that teacher candidates will develop an online lesson to enhance their student teaching experience. Intermediary steps that lead toward the skills required of online teaching could dovetail well with skills taught through existing teacher preparation coursework. As an example, take the task of developing an assessment using an online discussion forum. As teacher candidates use their content knowledge to design an online lesson, they may use a discussion forum as a formative assessment tool. This activity would be a good place to practice designing prompts grounded in the content (cognitive presence) and, through careful monitoring of the discussion, to ensure students stay on track and are respectful of each other's opinions (social presence). The overall placement of such an assessment could take advantage of the interactivity of online environments and be designed in such a way that they complement the overall lesson design (teacher presence).

Teacher candidates can further practice formative assessments by developing open-ended questions to supplement a video they might be using as a digital resource. Sites such as TedEd (ed.ted.com) allow teacher candidates the opportunity to create a video and develop a variety of assessments ranging from more constrained multiple-choice questions to less constrained, open-ended questions (Scalise & Gifford, 2006). Google's suite of tools allows for the creation of simple forms and quizzes with relative ease. Certification programs that put teacher candidates on a pathway to develop these resources and provide practice teaching opportunities will help them exercise the creative skills needed to effectively teach online upon graduation.

In my own teacher preparation program, we send approximately 200 teacher candidates each year into the field for student teaching. We have many of the basic technology tools available for them to gain hands-on experiences. Fully 40% of students choose to take their mandatory technology class online, thus gaining direct experience of both learner and teacher in an online environment. That said, there are always students who note that the schools in which they are practicing their teaching are significantly ill-prepared to let technology take a major role in either lesson development or instruction. Despite the sometimes jarring reality, they have seen enough examples of the potential for technology in the classroom so they are challenged, not disillusioned.

Embedding Instructional Design for Teaching Online

Preparing teacher candidates for an online teaching experience means preparing them to overcome challenges caused by the lack of face-to-face exchanges with learners, what Moore (1973) referred to as transactional distance. During online instruction, teacher candidates experience an increase in transactional distance and resulting difficulty in communication with learners; candidates begin to note the difficulty of knowing how well learners have understood their instructions. Teacher candidates cannot scan their online students for typical cues such as gestures and facial signals or cast a quick glance at work in progress. Online-based teaching models can help candidates plan ways to overcome a disruption in communication that may be more natural in face-to-face transactions. This is only one instructional design element pertinent to teacher candidates' preparation.

Strategies for effective teaching in fully online environments can be just as effective for teaching in partial or blended online settings. Modifying a lesson for an online learning environment can reinforce skills that teacher candidates develop in preparation programs geared solely for traditional teaching. Planning to teach students who are remotely situated can improve skills in instructional design as teacher candidates (1) develop a clear pathway for progress through a course or lesson, (2) differentiate instruction for varying learner needs, (3) increase learner engagement through social interaction, and (4) increase access to relevant learning materials. Although teacher preparation programs extensively cover lesson planning, designing for the participation of remote students requires teacher candidates to acknowledge a host of factors that are out of their immediate control. The inability to answer questions or provide interventions the moment they arise means that teacher candidates must clearly introduce online lessons and intentionally design all instructions *in anticipation of* the varied learning needs of students whom they cannot observe (Reiser & Dempsey, 2018).

To anticipate these needs, teacher candidates should understand the sequence of learning activities that led up to their online lesson. They must provide a clear pathway through the online unit, sometimes through built-in redundancy of directions or by including progress markers throughout. As part of the design process, teacher candidates will need to account for the varying learning needs of their students, consider accessibility options, and make appropriate modifications to content and presentation. These modifications are especially important when providing links to websites, online tools, or videos.

The International Society for Technology in Education (ISTE) released the ISTE Standards for Educators (2017), which provide an excellent guide for teacher educators to help teacher candidates master the educational technologies they will encounter as they develop their teaching skills. Some standards fit well with the goals of infusing teacher preparation programs with curriculum that addresses online teaching skills. For example, consider Standard 5:

> **Designer.** Educators design authentic, learner-driven activities and environments that recognize and accommodate learner variability. Educators: Explore and apply instructional design principles to create innovative digital learning environments that engage and support learning.

Teacher educators can take the following approach, grounded in the work of Reiser and Dempsey (2018), to infusing instructional design strategies when preparing teacher candidates to meet ISTE Standard 5.

Analysis. In the instructional design process, teacher candidates must analyze learners, their learning contexts, and the objectives of the instruction. Learning analysis would include an examination of learner skill level, cultural background, attitudes, and motivation. Teacher candidates must also become proficient with helping learners to access content and instruction in online learning systems. Analysis would also include the identification of learning objectives.

Selection. In this time-intensive phase, teacher candidates would become proficient in identifying content sources and selecting lessons to support unit goals. They would also need to learn how to develop new digital content and determine applications and techniques for supporting group interaction as well as methods of assessing learning, both formative and summative.

Implementation. In this phase, teacher candidates would practice the lesson or unit with students either in a real classroom setting or with fellow teacher candidates. The feedback from learners is an essential iterative element of the instructional design process. Through this feedback, they would be able to make informed modifications to the course interface, content, and instruction to meet the needs of learners.

Tools Needed to Teach Online

Access to online tools and applications would allow teacher candidates to learn about ways to engage with learners and to explore how to counter obstacles common in traditional interactions. Most of these tools and applications are common to learning management systems that teacher candidates will encounter in their classrooms. Each of the general categories of tools in Table 6.1 provides what are known in the literature as affordances, with each addressing unique challenges and offering opportunities for the integration of technology into the curriculum. Note that the column labeled "Communication Medium" is based on the Community of Inquiry (CoI) theoretical framework that represents a process of creating meaningful learning experiences through the development of three interdependent elements: social, cognitive, and teaching presence (Garrison et al., 2000).

Table 6.1. Online Tools and Pedagogy

Communication Medium from CoI Framework	Online Tool Example	Skill Overview	Pedagogical Challenge
Social Presence	Live Chat	This synchronous tool can be a stand-alone app but is often built into shared notetaking applications and can enhance collaborative interactions.	Synchronous chats with larger groups require teacher candidates to maintain a sense of order and clarity and develop their skills as moderators.
Supportive Discourse	Discussion Board or Forum	This asynchronous tool enables online learners to conduct in-depth conversations among themselves over a longer period and share images or supporting links and documents.	Online discussions require teacher candidates to develop prompts that will generate relevant discussions leading to deeper inquiry or concept building.
Cognitive Presence	Quiz Tools	Quiz-making tools allow teacher educators to create a variety of question types—from multiple choice to open-ended —that they can use as summative or formative assessments.	Online quizzes require teacher candidates to use the many options of this tool to prompt for deeper understanding by providing enriching and encouraging feedback.
Setting Climate	Form-Making Tools	Online forms can be embedded into websites, documents, and even video and can provide formative data to determine engagement with lesson material.	Form tools require teacher candidates to consider ways of developing formative assessments that encourage and engage students.
Teaching Presence	Web Design Options	Teacher candidates can set up an online learning space with a focus on readability and accessibility of materials.	Control over the online presentation of material requires teacher candidates to structure lessons that are accessible and engaging.
Selecting Content	Website Creation Tools	Teacher candidates can gather and manage the presentation of varied resources.	Curating online resources requires teacher candidates to review and select the most appropriate materials.

As teacher candidates develop their skills at designing instruction for online learning environments, perhaps by creating thematic online learning experiences, short lessons, or whole units, they will learn how to use the affordances of learning management systems to enable collaborative activities and develop increasingly refined methods of interacting with learners. Learning to use these tools complies with ISTE Standard 6:

> **Facilitator** Educators facilitate learning with technology to support student achievement of the ISTE Standards for Students. Educators:
> > **6b.** Manage the use of technology and student learning strategies in digital platforms, virtual environments, hands-on makerspaces, or in the field.

As colleges and schools of education infuse technology integration curriculum throughout their programs, specifically curriculum related to online instruction, it is important to note that teacher candidates are still in the process of developing basic competencies in curricular design for face-to-face classrooms. Adopting a pedagogical strategy in a classroom is clearly a novel activity for most teacher candidates at this stage of their development. Thinking about pedagogical strategies for online teaching can provide important opportunities to think deeply about teaching in general. Teacher functions such as providing resources, scaffolding learning activities, and becoming more deliberate about accommodations, differentiation, and personalization can be more thoughtfully planned, practiced, and developed in online platforms.

Conclusion

Colleges and schools of education have faculty with years of experience preparing teacher candidates for careers in face-to-face classrooms. As the potential for delivering learning experiences shifts into online environments, a solid understanding of the technologies and strategies for online teaching will become essential to the success of teacher candidates as they launch into their careers as certified teachers.

Online teaching should not be viewed as an add-on to teacher preparation programs; in fact, it is essential for a flourishing program that seeks to fully prepare the next generation of educators and should be infused throughout the entire preparation experience. By the time teacher candidates graduate, they should be versed in using tools and applications for teaching online. Learning to select and integrate technology tools and applications has the benefit of helping teacher candidates become better teachers in any learning environment. The instructional design skills needed to teach online are no different from the skills used to engage and assess students in traditional classrooms. CoI, the pedagogical framework discussed in this chapter, can assist teacher candidates as they curate content and resources, design for digital environments, and build their lessons around a supportive and interactive climate for learning with formative and summative assessments clearly aligned with instructional goals.

As I found in talking with graduates of my program, if teacher preparation programs prepare new teachers only for the face-to-face classroom, they are not preparing them to teach in today's world marked by digital connectivity. Colleges and schools of education must take the lead in providing a research-informed vision for online experiences in PK–12 teaching and for following through on that vision by addressing online teaching in their preparation programs. To do otherwise would be a critical lapse on our part.

Getting Started Resources

Boettcher, J. V., & Conrad, R. M. (2016). *The online teaching survival guide: Simple and practical pedagogical tips.* San Francisco, CA: Wiley.

Practical tips are very important for new teachers and teacher educators, and this well-reviewed book has plenty of them.

Darby, F. (2019). *How to be a better online teacher: Advice guide.* The Chronicle of Higher Education.
chronicle.com/interactives/advice-online-teaching

Teacher educators must begin to improve their own practice as online educators even if they have only a few online supplemental or enrichment activities as part of their teaching. This online webpage is a simple and straightforward list of suggestions for reflecting on practice.

iNACOL. (2011). *National standards for quality online teaching.* bit.ly/2y4gBNL

iNACOL (now known as the Aurora Institute) is grounded in identifying the best practices in online education. In addition to the iNACOL standards, the Blended Learning Teacher

Competencies (i.e., mindsets, qualities, adaptive skills, technical skills) may be valuable to teacher preparation coursework: bit.ly/3aksmOn

International Society for Technology in Education, Online and Blended Learning Network.
connect.iste.org/community/learningnetworks

Teacher educators who are also members of ISTE can participate in or follow conversations in the Online and Blended
Learning Network, which could prove beneficial in helping faculty teaching in technology-infused programs get creative about how to support teacher candidates learning how to teach online.

Quality Matters. qualitymatters.org

Quality Matters has synthesized research and best practices
into a set of standards for reviewing online courses for both
higher education and K–12. The rubrics in their Resources
section offer a glimpse of the goals we should aspire to in
online course design. Quality Matters has been adopted by more than 900
universities in North America and has implications for the design of PK–12
online courses.

References

Akyol, Z., & Garrison, D. R. (2013). *Educational communities of inquiry: Theoretical framework, research and practice.* doi.org/10.4018/978-1-4666-2110-7

Archambault, L., Kennedy, K., Shelton, C., Dalal, M., McAllister, L., & Huyett, S. (2016). Incremental progress: Re-examining field experiences in K–12 online learning contexts in the United States. *Journal of Online Learning Research, 2*(3), 303–326.

Bell, R. L., Maeng, J. L., & Binns, I. C. (2013). Learning in context: Technology integration in a teacher preparation program informed by situated learning theory. *Journal of Research in Science Teaching, 50*(3), 348–379.

Brinkerhoff, J. (2006). Effects of a long-duration, professional development academy on technology skills, computer self-efficacy, and technology integration beliefs and practices. *Journal of Research on Technology in Education, 39*(1), 22–43.

Carpenter, J. P., & Krutka, D. G. (2015). Engagement through microblogging: Educator professional development via Twitter. *Professional Development in Education, 41*(4), 707–728.

Consortium for School Networking. (2018). CoSN's 2018 Annual Infrastructure Survey Report. www.cosn.org/Infrastructure

Digital Learning Collaborative. (2018). *Online learning graduation requirements.* www.digitallearningcollab.com/online-learning-graduation-requirements

Foulger, T. S., Graziano, K. J., Schmidt-Crawford, D., & Slykhuis, D. A. (2017). Teacher educator technology competencies. *Journal of Technology and Teacher Education, 25*(4), 413–448. www.learntechlib.org/p/181966/

Garrison, D. R., Anderson, T., & Archer, W. (1999). Critical inquiry in a text-based environment: Computer conferencing in higher education. *The Internet and Higher Education, 2*(2–3), 87–105.

Graziano, K. J., & Bryans-Bongey, S. (2018). Surveying the national landscape of online teacher training in K–12 teacher preparation programs. *Journal of Digital Learning in Teacher Education, 34*(4), 259–277.

International Society for Technology in Education. (2017). ISTE Standards for Educators. www.iste.org/standards/for-educators

Kim, Y. C. (2016). *Shadow education and the curriculum and culture of schooling in South Korea.* New York, NY: Palgrave Macmillan.

Milman, N. B. (2014). Snow days: Is distance education a solution in PK–12 schools? *Distance Learning, 11*(2), 45.

Miron, G., Shank, C., & Davidson, C. (2018). Full-time virtual and blended schools: Enrollment, student characteristics, and performance. Boulder, CO: National Education Policy Center. nepc.colorado.edu/publication/virtual-schoolsannual-2018

Mishra, P., & Koehler, M. J. (2006). Technological pedagogical content knowledge: A framework for teacher knowledge. *Teachers College Record, 108*(6), 1017.

Moore, M. G. (1973). Toward a theory of independent learning and teaching. *The Journal of Higher Education, 44*(9), 661–679.

Norris, C., Hossain, A., & Soloway, E. (2011). Using smartphones as essential tools for learning. *Educational Technology, 51*(3), 18–25.

Pegrum, M., Oakley, G., & Faulkner, R. (2013). Schools going mobile: A study of the adoption of mobile handheld technologies in Western Australian independent schools. *Australasian Journal of Educational Technology, 29*(1).

Reiser, R. A., & Dempsey, J. V. (Eds.). (2018). *Trends and issues in instructional design and technology.* Boston, MA: Pearson.

Scalise, K., & Gifford, B. (2006). Computer-based assessment in e-learning: A framework for constructing "intermediate constraint" questions and tasks for technology platforms. *Journal of Technology, Learning, and Assessment, 4*(6), 45.

Shea, P., & Bidjerano, T. (2009). Community of inquiry as a theoretical framework to foster "epistemic engagement" and "cognitive presence" in online education. *Computers & Education, 52*(3), 543–553.

Sointu, E. T., Valtonen, T., Hirsto, L., Kankaanpää, J., Saarelainen, M., Mäkitalo, K., … Manninen, J. (2019). Teachers as users of ICT from the student perspective in higher education flipped classroom classes. *Seminar.net, 15*(1), 1–15.

Thomas, L. G., & Knezek, D. G. (2008). Information, communications, and educational technology standards for students, teachers, and school leaders. In *International Handbook of Information Technology in Primary and Secondary Education* (pp. 333–348). Boston, MA: Springer.

U.S. Department of Education. (2011). *Use of technology in teaching and learning.* www.ed.gov/oii-news/use-technology-teaching-and-learning

CHAPTER 7

Technology Infusion in Clinical Experiences

DEBRA R. SPRAGUE
SETH A. PARSONS
AUDRA K. PARKER
GEORGE MASON UNIVERSITY

Overview

Since the National Council for the Accreditation of Teacher Education (NCATE) published its Blue Ribbon Panel Report in 2010, teacher preparation has experienced a shift to re-situate clinical experiences at the core of teacher preparation. Inherent in this turn toward clinically centered teacher preparation are mutually beneficial school-university partnerships. One outcome of these efforts is an opportunity to support theory-to-practice connections. In this chapter, we, three teacher educators in the George Mason University (GMU) Elementary Education Program, explore how clinically centered teacher preparation affords opportunities for a program-wide and program-deep approach to address technology infusion. We suggest school-university partnerships afford teacher preparation programs opportunities to actualize technology infusion through both course-based field assignments as well as field experiences (e.g., student teaching) to help teacher candidates develop their ability to integrate technology.

Introduction

As researchers in the field of teacher preparation contemplate adopting a technology infusion model (Foulger, Buss, Wetzel, & Lindsey, 2015), one consideration is how this shift interacts with the burgeoning emphasis on clinically centered teacher preparation. The critical role of fieldwork in helping teacher candidates learn to teach with technology is highlighted in the literature. For example, Brenner and Brill (2016) reviewed literature on best practices in teacher education programs with regard to how teacher candidates learned to teach with technology and discovered three common themes: (a) technology training should be embedded in content-specific courses as well as technology courses, (b) certification programs should provide opportunities for teacher candidates to develop their own technology projects as well as reflect on and critique their projects, and (c) technology-rich experiences in coursework and field experience should be supported by teacher educators, instructional technology faculty, and the inservice teachers.

Similarly, Fleming, Motamedi, and May (2007) conducted survey research on seventy-nine teacher candidates' perceptions of their computer technology skills and factors that influenced those perceptions. They found that teacher candidates were most likely to report high levels of confidence with technology if they saw technology modeled and had the opportunity to use technology during clinical practice.

The recognition of the role of clinical experiences in supporting acquisition of skills and efficacy is not confined to technology. In fact, the broader field of teacher preparation has affirmed the powerful role clinical experiences play in preparing teachers. Following the release of the NCATE (2010) Blue Ribbon Panel Report, teacher education experienced a strategic shift (Burns, Jacobs, Baker, & Donahue, 2016; Hollins, 2015). Recognizing the traditional disconnect between theory and practice and between university coursework and real-world classrooms, teacher educators have made a variety of attempts to shift toward a clinically centered orientation. This philosophical shift resulted in a vision for teacher education that placed clinical practice at the heart of preparation, guided by both university-based and school-based teacher educators whose respective academic and practical understandings of theory are equally valued. Such a change to the tenets of teacher education does not happen without significant reorientations to how PK–12 schools and universities partner in the shared endeavor of teacher preparation.

This chapter will explore the intersection of clinically centered teacher preparation and technology. Specifically, we will discuss how the establishment of mutually beneficial school-university partnerships focused on clinical teacher preparation, shared inquiry, PK–6 student learning, and stakeholder (e.g., mentor teachers, administrators, instructional coaches) professional development support opportunities for technology infusion. We begin with a brief examination of clinical practice and a description of our Elementary Education Professional Development School (PDS) Network at GMU and how we have sought to actualize the tenets of clinical practice. We then describe opportunities for technology infusion through purposefully designed field experiences and in support of virtual clinical experiences. We close with recommendations for other colleges/schools of education who seek to adopt a technology infusion approach and want to leverage clinical experiences in efforts to help teacher candidates become proficient in teaching with technology.

Clinical Practice

In 2016, the American Association of Colleges for Teacher Education (AACTE) created the Clinical Practice Commission, which included scholars and teacher educators from across the United States. The Commission's charge was to synthesize the research base on clinical practice and make recommendations for the future of teacher education that is clinically embedded. In 2018, the Clinical Practice Commission released its report: *A Pivot Toward Clinical Practice, Its Lexicon, and the Renewal of Teacher Education* (2018). With the intention to actualize the NCATE Blue Ribbon Panel Report, this report further clarified clinical practice for school-university partnerships. In Table 7.1, we present the report's ten Proclamations, which outline a bold future for clinically centered teacher education, along with ideas for technology integration. This table, therefore, provides guidance for teacher preparation programs seeking to infuse technology into a clinically centered approach.

Table 7.1   AACTE Clinical Practice Commission's Proclamations as Applied to the Infusion of Technology

AACTE Clinical Practice Commission Proclamations (2018)	Possible Application of Proclamations in a Technology-Infused Program
Proclamation 1. Clinical practice is central to high-quality teacher education.	Use webinars and online courses to provide professional development for mentor teachers, site facilitators, and university faculty. Online professional development may be leveraged to limit attrition, support newcomers, and increase participation.
Proclamation 2. As pedagogy is the science of teaching, the intentional integration of pedagogical training into an educator preparation program is the cornerstone of effective clinical practice.	Infuse program-wide and program-deep technology integration curriculum. Use the ISTE Standards for Educators and the ISTE Standards for Students to help guide how teacher candidates develop efficacy and intentionality using technology with their PK–12 students.
Proclamation 3. Clinical practice includes, supports, and complements the innovative and requisite skills, strategies, and tools that improve teacher preparation by using high-leverage practices as part of a commitment to continuous renewal for all learning sites.	Create opportunities for practice with technology tools and skills. Use video coding programs to allow teacher educators the opportunity to view video of instruction and provide written feedback on the video.
Proclamation 4. Clinical partnerships are the foundation of highly effective clinical practice.	Explore technology integration models in university and school settings. Use email, chat, and videoconferencing tools to nurture such partnerships. They allow for ongoing communication between the university and school-based teacher educators.
Proclamation 5. Sustainable and shared infrastructure is required for successful clinical partnership.	Use email, chats, webinars, and videoconferencing tools to share ideas and sustain the governance of the program.
Proclamation 6. Clinical partnerships are facilitated and supported through an understanding of the continuum of development and growth that typifies successful, mutually beneficial collaborations.	Use webinars and online classes to keep school-based teacher educators and university faculty informed about new technologies and best practices. Allow co-teaching at the university and in the K–12 school so that knowledge can be shared among stakeholders.
Proclamation 7. As emerging professionals, teacher candidates are essential contributors and collaborators within clinical programs and partnerships.	Present new ideas and the latest research about technology integration into the classroom and school.

AACTE Clinical Practice Commission Proclamations (2018)	Possible Application of Proclamations in a Technology-Infused Program
Proclamation 8. Boundary-spanners, school-based teacher educators, and university-based teacher educators play necessary, vital, and synergistic roles in clinical educator preparation.	Use email, chats, and videoconferencing to communicate among stakeholders and maintain the partnership. Consistent and open communication among stakeholders is essential for mutually beneficial school-university partnerships, and technology can facilitate such communication.
Proclamation 9. Coalescing the language of teacher preparation and teaching around a common lexicon facilitates a shared understanding of and reference to the roles, responsibilities, and experiences essential to high-quality clinical preparation.	Use a website to define terms and roles and to house handbooks and forms as a common source of information.
Proclamation 10. Teaching is a profession requiring specialized knowledge and preparation. Educators are the pedagogical and content experts. It is through the assertion and application of this expertise that they can inform the process and vision for renewing educator preparation.	Give equal credence to technological knowledge as well as pedagogical and content knowledge. Support teacher candidates to develop all three knowledge bases as well as the practical knowledge of how all three are woven into teaching. The partnership, including candidates, can collaborate on research to investigate the impact of technology in teaching and learning and what works well.

How the proclamations are implemented in school-university partnerships will look different across contexts. The AACTE report recognizes teacher residencies and PDSs as exemplary models for enacting clinically centered teacher education. Residencies are partnerships where teacher candidates are residents, teaching in a classroom with close apprenticeship; it is typically a paid position that is accompanied by teacher education coursework. The PDS movement emphasizes mutually beneficial school-university partnerships that are guided by four purposes: teacher preparation, teacher professional development, student learning, and inquiry, as depicted in the following scenario.

Scenario at GMU

Amy looked around the classroom with excitement and some trepidation. Today she was going to teach a lesson that integrated technology and literacy instruction. She was nervous because she was not very comfortable with technology—somehow everything always went wrong when she tried to use a computer. In addition, adding to her nervousness, her university professor was coming today to do a formal observation.

Despite her nervousness, Amy knew she was well prepared and students would enjoy the activity. Students had been learning about the parts of a story: characters, plot, conflict, and resolution. They were working in pairs, and each pair used a graphic organizer as a scaffold for planning their own story. Today they were going to create an e-book of their story. Amy was happy that her mentor teacher, Miss Wellington, was willing to let students create an e-book instead of writing by hand. Miss Wellington had students read e-books online, but she had never had students create their own. Amy knew Miss Wellington was eager to see how students would do with this lesson.

Amy worked with the school-based technology specialists (SBTS) to reserve the computer lab for the lesson. SBTS were responsible for working with teachers on ways to integrate technology into instruction. Amy had all the computers booted up with StoryJumper (www.storyjumper.com), a free website that lets students write their own storybook, displayed on the screens.

Amy set up the tripod so she could record her lesson. She had borrowed a video camera from the university. As she set up the camera, she thought about Jimmy, whose parents had signed a form saying he was not to be video-recorded; she needed to plan carefully where to place the camera so he did not appear in the video. At first, she placed the camera so it would capture only her. She moved the camera later to show the students working. She knew her technology instructor would want to see students using the computers, so she needed to record that. As she was setting everything up, her university professor walked in. She would watch Amy teach the lesson and then watch the video and provide feedback afterward. Because the technology instructor would also provide feedback on the lesson, Amy would get guidance from both individuals.

When the students came in and settled down, Amy showed them how to navigate StoryJumper and how to begin writing their stories. She moved the camera to capture two of the groups as they wrote their stories. Everything went well for a while, but then Tommy and Mary seemed upset. Amy went to check on them and discovered they had accidentally shut the web browser and lost their story. Amy brought the browser back up and opened up StoryJumper again. She logged the students in and found their story for them. She sighed with relief that she was able to recover the story. Tommy could be difficult to handle when he got upset, so she was proud that she had avoided a meltdown.

Upon completion of the lesson, Amy met with her mentor teacher and her university professor. They discussed the lesson and the outcome. It was evident the students were excited to use the technology and were focused on the lesson. However, Miss Wellington expressed concern. She felt students spent too much time playing with StoryJumper and creating the pictures for the e-book and not enough time writing. She also was concerned about the situation with Tommy and Mary. She made a point of telling Amy that if the students had written by hand, as they usually do, Tommy would not have been upset and they would not have risked a meltdown. Amy pointed out that although students spent much time exploring the images the program offered, only two groups did not complete the story. One group was Tommy and Mary, who had experienced a technical glitch, and the other group consisted of David and Alejandro, two English language learners. They were creating a story with images and limited words.

Amy explained to Miss Wellington that technical glitches can happen when using technology but that she was prepared to handle those glitches. Amy explained that her technology instructor felt it would be appropriate for students to play with the website to become familiar with it, learn from mistakes, and figure out how to fix problems on their own. She said she had prepared to handle this particular glitch because she had deliberately closed the web browser while writing a story over the weekend in order to see if she could recover what she was writing. Once she figured out how to recover the story, she knew she was prepared to face that situation while teaching the lesson.

Our Context

GMU's Elementary Education PDS Program provides one example of how a teacher preparation program seeks to enact the tenets of the Blue Ribbon Panel Report (National Council for the Accreditation of Teacher Education, 2010) and the Report of the Clinical Practice Commission (2018). All aspects of the Elementary Education Program are contextualized within the PDS philosophy that embodies a genuine, mutually beneficial partnership between schools of education and PK–6 schools (Parsons et al., 2017). Because a clinical orientation is central to our program, teacher candidates are placed in PDS sites early in the program for observations and to work with students. This enables teacher candidates to engage in authentic learning experiences. Rigorous coursework is integrated with clinical experiences in diverse and effective schools and classrooms and in partnership with PK–6 school-based teacher educators. It is within this context that a vision for technology infusion can be actualized. Below we outline the governance structures, PDS network organizational framework, and program description for the purpose of contextualizing this work and providing elements that may be generalizable to teacher educators exploring clinical teacher preparation in their technology infusion efforts.

GMU's Elementary Education Program has a number of shared roles and governance structures that guide the work of the partnership (Parker, Parsons, Groth, Bean, & Slattery, in press), including a formal Memorandum of Understanding (MOU) with three local school districts. Schools within these districts complete an application process expressing their interest in collaborative work on a five-year cycle. Through this application process, school leaders ascertain staff commitment to the four purposes of PDS partnerships. Demographic information is also determined to ensure a diversity of school experiences for candidates. In addition, the level of technology and internet access available within the school is also addressed.

Part of the agreement between GMU's Elementary Education Program and its PK–6 partners requires schools to commit to shared roles and participation in governance structures (Parker, Parsons, Groth, & Brown, 2016). Partners in this effort include:

- a university facilitator,
- site facilitators (school teacher or administrator who acts as a liaison between the school and university),
- mentor teachers, and
- school-based teacher educators.

As a part of participation in the PDS network, these stakeholders contribute through a variety of governance structures. These include an advisory committee of representative stakeholders, a yearly principals' breakfast, regular role-specific meetings, and site-based meetings.

The GMU Elementary PDS Network provides the framework within which the elementary program functions. As a thirty-nine-credit post-baccalaureate, initial licensure program, elementary teacher candidates, organized in cohorts, complete coursework in both general and content-specific methods, which culminates in either a semester-long or yearlong student teaching internship. Because GMU faculty have a shared vision for the importance of partnership work, university faculty scaffold field assignments using theories and other ideas from readings with the intention to develop teacher candidates' commitments to practices such as inquiry, technology integration, culturally responsive pedagogies, and reflective teaching.

Infusion of Technology into Clinical Practice

Clinically centered teacher preparation programs provide multiple opportunities for the infusion of technology. Initial opportunities for collaboration begin as partnerships are established. For example, as part of our PDS application process, elementary schools are asked to reflect on the ways they integrate technology into the classroom. Because many of the schools GMU works with are Title I schools, the emphasis is not on the types of technology available or the ratio of the number of computers per student. Instead, GMU faculty are looking for a level of commitment to technology that will allow the teacher candidates to see ways to use technology for teaching and learning in a PK–6 classroom.

Once schools are selected, technology faculty meet with the SBTS in schools that expressed a commitment to technology use. The purpose of the meeting is to discuss what teacher candidates need to know about technology before completing their teacher preparation program. With this shared ideal, the SBTS work with technology faculty to design technology experiences for teacher candidates. This initial collaborative endeavor conveys to school-based partners their important role in teacher preparation and technology infusion.

The expertise represented within a partnership guides technology infusion across the Elementary Education PDS Program. Using an intentional and scaffolded approach, technology infusion is a key thread in each course and supports the development of teacher candidate knowledge for teaching with technology. For example, in our first course block, candidates are introduced to the ISTE Standards, the SAMR

Model, and developmentally appropriate technology integration practices for PK–6 learners. Faculty model the integration of technology tools into course activities.

Similarly, in both general and content-specific methods course blocks, teacher candidates are introduced to technology and web-based applications as instructional strategies, and instructors model the integration of these tools into their course instruction. This begins with candidates completing a technology audit and targeted observation of technology use in their field placements. In addition, throughout the methods blocks, teacher candidates in GMU's PDS Program are required to integrate technology as part of their lesson planning. They plan for the integration of technology and to teach the lesson they created, which is possible given the strong clinical partnership. Teacher candidates are encouraged to go beyond the use of interactive whiteboards for presentations and to instead place technology in the hands of the PK–6 students. These lessons have resulted in the PK–6 students writing their own e-books, using virtual manipulatives to understand math concepts, creating math-related videos, and exploring content using augmented reality.

GMU's teacher preparation program uses GoReact (get.goreact.com), a video coding platform, for teacher candidates to record a lesson and submit it to the technology faculty member who evaluates the effectiveness of the use of technology in the lessons. GoReact enables teacher candidates to upload videos to a secure server and then watch, reflect, and post comments on their videos. Faculty can also post comments on candidates' videos, as can anyone else the candidate chooses to invite (e.g., a classmate or a mentor teacher) (Zurawski, Sprague, Porter, & Williams, 2018). By using GoReact, faculty are able to provide teacher candidates extensive feedback, directed at specific points in their teaching experience. As the tool is used in several teacher preparation courses and during their internship, teacher candidates purchase a five-year subscription. Since the videos are housed on GoReact's servers, GMU provides limited technical assistance to students. This allows faculty to focus on the use of the video tool within the learning environment.

In the prior scenario, the teacher candidate, Amy, planned and taught a lesson on writing stories using an online e-book creator called StoryJumper. Amy did her homework and came to the lesson well prepared. She talked to Miss Wellington and showed her how easy it was to create an e-book. She also spoke with the SBTS to make sure the website she wanted to use was on the school district's approved list of sites. She made sure she was familiar with the website, trying it out ahead of time.

She had everything set up before the students arrived. Such preparation is needed prior to teaching a lesson with technology. Knowing what to do when something goes wrong is just as important as knowing how to use the technology. It is also important to note that the clinically embedded nature of our program helped Amy have a realistic understanding of the context and concerns when using technology with students and to be proactive where possible. For example, the teacher candidate was given the freedom to integrate technology into her lesson, even though the mentor teacher was unfamiliar with the technology being used.

Virtual Clinical Practice

The beginning of this chapter focused on technology infusion in field experiences where university faculty purposefully design classroom-based assignments in collaboration with clinical partners. This current section looks at ways in which technology can be used to help those who are supervising clinical experiences from a distance. These tools are key in supporting teacher candidates' integration skills as they facilitate more frequent and scaffolded theory-to-practice connections in a cost-effective manner.

Given the importance that teacher candidates place on their field experiences, particularly their final internship and the supporting mentor teacher (Valencia, Martin, Place, & Grossman, 2009), finding quality school field placements, face to face or virtual, is essential. Placement in classrooms not conducive to this vision can result in teacher candidates being overly frustrated by inhibiting factors related to using technology in teaching or in learning ineffective teaching strategies. To ensure teacher candidates are able to see connections between university courses that support them learning how to teach with technology and their field experiences, Beach, Martinussen, Poliszczuk, and Willows (2018) recommend using virtual classrooms. Virtual classrooms provide a prerecorded 360-degree view of a classroom where visitors can zoom in and out to examine various elements. Clicking on a "hot spot" in the video activates a callout video of the teacher explaining the purpose of an activity and how it supports student learning. A link for the virtual classroom tour website is available in the Getting Started Resources section at the end of this chapter.

There are multiple ways to use technology to supervise teacher candidates in clinical practice. Capturing teacher candidates in action allows teacher candidates and their instructors opportunities to revisit the experience multiple times and from varied perspectives. For example, video coding programs allow a supervisor to make observations available to teacher candidates throughout a lesson. This same tool supports teacher candidates in self-observation activities that, when scaffolded appropriately, support growth and development through in-depth reflection on their own lessons (Zurawski et al., 2018). Another way to observe, give feedback on, and/or evaluate a recorded lesson is through the use of VoiceThread (voicethread.com). Lilienthal, Potthoff, and Anderson (2017) used VoiceThread in an online, graduate practicum course. VoiceThread allows users to upload, share, and hold asynchronous discussions using documents, videos, presentations, images, and files. It is a cloud application that can be used across multiple platforms.

Video archives of practice teaching experiences have helped teacher candidates by triggering the cognitive dissonance needed to enable them to reflect more realistically on their practice (Colasante, 2011; Heafner, Petty, & Hartshorne, 2011; Shewell, 2014; Sonmez & Hakverdi-Can, 2012). However, video can also afford clinical supervisors and university faculty the opportunity to pause, view multiple times, jump ahead, and thus more deeply reflect about the event in the observation, which has been shown to improve their feedback to teacher candidates (Baecher, Browne Graves, & Ghailan, 2018). The clinical supervisors in Baecher et al.'s study used video conferencing to meet with peers to review recordings of post-observation conferences of other clinical supervisors. Results suggested that conducting video-based observations is a promising approach for helping clinical supervisors improve their post-observation conferencing skills (Baecher et al., 2018). This finding is important, especially for those conducting virtual supervision, as it may be difficult to interpret a person's intent when providing feedback at a distance, especially if the feedback is text-based (e.g., email, chat).

Although video is effective for capturing teacher candidates' teaching and helps to promote reflective practice, it is not without limitations. For example, video may not capture all aspects of a lesson, such as what might be happening off screen (Heafner et al., 2011). A solution to offset this limitation is Swivl (www.swivl.com). Swivl is an intelligent robot that rotates to follow the teacher candidate. It captures video and audio and uploads the file to the Swivl server. For optimal recording, the Swivl device and a lanyard transmitter (which is worn by the teacher candidate and provides a tracking device) must be unobstructed, meaning that the teacher candidate should make sure that they are not behind a desk or bookcase (Kesterson Franklin et al., 2017).

The technology explored thus far allows university faculty to view a video after the teacher candidate has completed the lesson. Therefore, feedback is delayed. E-coaching technology, such as Bug-in-Ear, allows a university faculty member to view the lesson in real time and provide immediate feedback. The teacher candidate wears an earpiece and can hear the feedback from the facilitator who, in real time, is viewing the lesson remotely (Rock, Zigmond, Gregg, & Gable, 2011). E-coaching technology allows university faculty to provide behavior-specific praise and address any concerns immediately, which allows teacher candidates to make midcourse corrections without interrupting the lesson (Schaefer & Ottley, 2018). Coogle, Ottley, Rahn, and Storie (2018) found that teachers' communication was enhanced with the use of e-coaching.

It is important to note that the use of video as a tool for supervision and coaching is enhanced in a situation where committed, clinical partnerships exist. Clarity of expectations, openness toward the use of video for observations, permissions for video recording of teachers and students, support for technical requirements, and scaffolding of expectations must all be facilitated for successful clinical context. Furthermore, university and school-based teacher educators should collaboratively design how video-recording tasks will be incorporated into field-based experiences. Ultimately, all these factors combine to provide the support teacher candidates' needs as they develop their teaching practice in a technology-infused program.

Consider These Action Steps

The following are recommendations for technology-infused teacher preparation programs that are clinically centered.

> **Partnerships.** Establish mutually beneficial partnerships that value the expertise of school-based teacher educators. A teacher preparation program does not need to be a PDS to build a relationship. Reach out to graduates of the program who are teaching in the schools. They may be willing to serve as clinical supervisors. Engage in conversations regarding shared interests and goals and establish areas in which school-based teacher educators' expertise can be tapped. Partnerships are premised on mutual respect and collaboration. Exploring how both university and school-based teacher educators can contribute to the shared vision of teacher preparation and teacher professional development is key.

Professional Development for Faculty and Mentors. Collaborate with colleagues to purposefully plan for and support technology infusion. For example, GMU provides an array of technology-focused professional development opportunities for faculty. These include tools to be used by faculty in course instruction that have direct application to PK–12 teaching and learning. By creating a road map for how technology infusion will be scaffolded across a program, faculty can work together to identify areas of need and capitalize on areas of expertise. Ongoing dialogue can support exploration of new technology tools. In fact, this is how our program's use of video coding to support supervision became a fixture in our work. These efforts should include school-based teacher educators. For example, GMU engages expert mentor teachers in designing and implementing advanced mentor training, including opportunities to explore video coding and other feedback tools for working with teacher candidates. Routinely, school-based teacher educators are invited to copresent at conferences and to coauthor articles based on their engagement in program innovations related to our technology infusion effort (e.g., Parsons et al., 2015).

Partnerships for Program Design. Engage school-based teacher educators in program design and revision. For example, we invited SBTS to provide feedback on technology experiences because the expert voices of school-based teacher educators were needed to inform GMU's technology education efforts. More broadly, school-based teacher educators serve on the program's advisory board, in leading the advanced mentor training, and in leadership roles such as site facilitation.

Leverage PK-12 Classroom-Based Technology. Integrate the tools that are commonly available in partner school sites into coursework experiences and clinical work. GMU's Elementary Education Program purchased iPad Minis to use in their methods courses. Teacher candidates are allowed to check these out to use for their technology lessons as needed. In addition, GMU has video cameras that teacher candidates can check out to record observations. Although many use their personal cell phones, some teacher candidates have had difficulty with the quality of the sound, while others have had the video stop in the middle of the lesson because the file was too big for the amount of space available on the phone. Although technological glitches should be expected, providing the teacher candidates with suitable cameras can alleviate these types of problems.

Conclusion

Mutually beneficial partnerships in technology-infused programs that situate teacher candidates in clinical contexts capitalize on the expertise of school-based teacher educators. Teacher candidates participating in field experiences where strong relationships exist among stakeholders are provided with opportunities for support in their growth and development as they practice teaching with technology. Engaged stakeholders who contribute to a shared mission of teacher preparation and who claim the importance of field experience in technology-infused programs realize that professional development, new ideas, experimentation, and risk-taking need to be accepted norms. Each of these elements creates opportunities for faculty, teacher candidates, and mentor teachers/school-based teacher educators to explore the role technology can play in student learning. Clinical partnerships that are a part of a technology-infused program are ripe for supporting the development of teacher candidates who can enter the teaching workforce confident in their ability to infuse technology. Through a strong clinical foundation, as outlined by AACTE's Clinical Practice Commission, teacher preparation programs can create avenues for teacher candidates to enter the field as tech-savvy educators.

Getting Started Resources

American Association of Colleges for Teacher Education, Clinical Practice Commission. (2018). *A pivot toward clinical practice, its lexicon, and the renewal of teacher education.* **bit.ly/2UsyQp2**

This commission report presents the outcomes of an effort to synthesize what is known about clinical practice in teacher education and to suggest a vision for clinically rich educator preparation. The report offers ten proclamations to support teacher preparation programs.

Hollins, E. R. (2015). *Rethinking field experiences in preservice teacher preparation: Meeting new challenges for accountability.* New York, NY: Routledge.

This book addresses key issues in clinical teacher preparation, including the recommendations for teacher preparation programs for maximizing field experiences and models for learning to teach in diverse contexts. Of particular note are chapters describing residency, rotations, and community-based experiences as models of clinical teacher preparation.

Parker, A. K., Parsons, S. A., Groth, L, & Levine-Brown, E. (2016). Pathways to partnership: A developmental framework for building PDS relationships. *School University Partnerships, 9*(3), 34–48.

This article shares an innovative structure for school-university partnerships that is differentiated and developmental. GMU's Elementary Education Program has three "pathways to partnership": partner schools, clinical practice schools, and collaborative inquiry schools. Each level of participation involves varying degrees of participation in the partnership structure, with the PDS model being the guiding framework for all partnerships.

Virtual Classroom Tours. bit.ly/2xCpKwK

This website provides virtual classroom tours as models of teaching. Clicking on hot spots activates videos of the teacher explaining the purpose of an activity and how it supports children's learning.

References

Baecher, L., Browne Graves, S., & Ghailan, F. (2018). Supervisor learning through collaborative video inquiry: It's not just for teacher candidates. *Contemporary Issues in Technology and Teacher Education, 18*(3), 556–577.

Beach, P., Martinussen, R., Poliszczuk, D., & Willows, D. (2018). A window into the classroom: Examining the use of virtual classrooms in teacher education. *Contemporary Issues in Technology and Teacher Education, 18*(3), 578–600.

Brenner, A. M., & Brill, J. M. (2016). Investigating practices in teacher education that promote and inhibit technology integration transfer in early career teachers. *Tech Trends, 60*(1), 136–144. doi.org/10.1007/s11528-016-0025-8

Burns, R. W., Jacobs, J., Baker, W., & Donahue, D. (2016). Making muffins: Identifying core ingredients of school-university partnerships. *School-University Partnerships, 9*(3), 81–95.

Clinical Practice Commission. (2018). *A pivot toward clinical practice, its lexicon, and the renewal of educator preparation.* Washington, DC: American Association for Colleges of Teacher Education. nysed.gov/common/nysed/files/cpc-aactecpcreport.pdf

Colasante, M. (2011). Using video annotation to reflect on and evaluate physical education pre-service teaching practice. *Australasian Journal of Educational Technology, 27*(1), 66–88. doi.org/10.14742/ajet.983

Coogle, C. G., Ottley, J. R., Rahn, N. L., & Storie, S. (2018). Bug-in-ear eCoaching: Impacts on novice early childhood special education teachers. *Journal of Early Intervention, 40*(1), 87–103. doi.org/10.1177/1053815117748692

Fleming, L., Motamedi, V., & May, L. (2007). Predicting preservice teacher competence in computer technology: Modeling and application in training environments. *Journal of Technology and Teacher Education, 15*(2), 207–231. www.learntechlib.org/primary/p/19848

Foulger, T. S., Buss, R. R., Wetzel, K., & Lindsey, L. (2015). Instructors' growth in TPACK: Teaching technology-infused methods courses to preservice teachers. *Journal of Digital Learning in Teacher Education, 31*(4), 134–147. doi.org/10.1080/21532974.2015.1055010

Heafner, T. L., Petty, T. M., & Hartshorne, R. (2011). Evaluating modes of teacher preparation: A comparison of face-to-face and remote observations of graduate interns. *Journal of Digital Learning in Teacher Education, 27*(4), 154–164. doi.org/10.1080/21532974.2011.10784672

Hollins, E. R. (2015). *Rethinking field experiences in preservice teacher preparation: Meeting new challenges for accountability.* New York, NY: Routledge.

Kesterson Franklin, R., O'Neill Mitchell, J., Siko Walters, K., Livingston, B., Blake Lineberger, M., Putman, C., & Karges-Bone, L. (2017). Using Swivl robotic technology in teacher education preparation: A pilot study. *TechTrends, 62*, 1–6. doi.org/10.1007/s11528-017-0246-5

Lilienthal, L. K., Potthoff, D., & Anderson, K. E. (2017). The development of an online, graduate practicum course. *Delta Kappa Gamma Bulletin, 84*(1), 42–52.

National Council for the Accreditation of Teacher Education (NCATE). (2010). *Transforming teacher education through clinical practice: A national strategy to prepare effective teachers.* A report of the Blue Ribbon Panel on clinical preparation and partnership for improved student learning. bit.ly/33XhgfS

Parker, A. K., Parsons, S. A., Groth, L., & Brown, E. (2016). Pathways to partnership: A developmental framework for building PDS relationships. *School-University Partnerships, 9*(3), 34–48.

Parker, A. K., Parsons, S., Groth, L., Bean, A., & Slattery, C. (in press). George Mason University's Elementary Education PDS program: Structures for shared governance, reflection and collaboration. In E. Garin & R. Burns (Eds.), *The NAPDS Nine Essentials in action: Cases of professional development schools.* Charlotte, NC: Information Age Publishing.

Parsons, S. A., Groth, L. A., Parker, A. K., Brown, E. L., Sell, C., & Sprague, D. (2017). Elementary teacher preparation at George Mason University: Evolution of our program. In R. Flessner & D. Lecklider (Eds.), *Case studies of clinical preparation in teacher education.* Lanham, MD: Rowman & Littlefield.

Parsons, S. A., Parker, A. K., Zenkov, K., DeGregory, C., Taylor, L., Kye, D., & Haury, S. (2015). Exploring the use of video and Edthena in literacy/English teacher preparation. In E. Ortlieb, L. Shanahan, & M. McVee (Eds.), *Video research in disciplinary literacies* (pp. 269–285). Bingley, United Kingdom: Emerald Press.

Rock, M. L., Zigmond, N. P., Gregg, M., & Gable, R. A. (2011). The power of virtual coaching. *Educational Leadership, 69*(2), 42–48.

Schaefer, J. M., & Ottley, J. R. (2018). Evaluating immediate feedback via Bug-in-Ear as an evidence-based practice for professional development. *Journal of Special Education Technology, 33*(4), 247–258.

Shewell, J. (2014). Collecting video-based evidence in teacher evaluation via the DataCapture mobile application. *Journal of Applied Learning Technology, 4*(2), 6–14.

Sonmez, D., & Hakverdi-Can, M. (2012). Videos as an instructional tool in pre-service science teacher education. *Egitim Arastirmalari-Eurasian Journal of Educational Research, 46,* 141–158.

Valencia, S. W., Martin, S. D., Place, N. A., & Grossman, P. (2009). Complex interaction in student teaching: Lost opportunities for learning. *Journal of Teacher Education, 60*(3), 304–322.

Zurawski, L., Sprague, D., Porter, A., & Williams, K. (2018). Evaluating university facilitators' perceptions of video as an observational tool. In E. Langran & J. Borup (Eds.), *Proceedings of Society for Information Technology & Teacher Education International Conference* (pp. 600–606). Washington, DC: Association for the Advancement of Computing in Education (AACE). www.learntechlib.org/primary/p/182589

Technology Integration in the Induction Years: The Importance of PK–12 Partnerships

JO WILLIAMSON
JULIE MOORE
KENNESAW STATE UNIVERSITY

Overview

It is easy to think that teacher induction is exclusively the purview of PK–12 schools and districts, but this landscape is changing. In this chapter, we assert that a program-deep and program-wide technology preparation experience will transition into a graduate's first few years of teaching. To help teacher educators envision new roles and responsibilities related to graduates' early career success, this chapter provides a review of what is known about teacher induction and new teachers' technology use. The chapter concludes with three practical strategies and meaningful resources to help teacher preparation programs support inductees' technology integration.

Scenario: The Tale of Two New Teachers

Jill and Marcus were classmates in their teacher preparation program. They took a required instructional technology class where they learned to create engaging, student-centered lessons using web-based collaborative projects, productivity tools, and content-based instructional software. In addition, technology was infused throughout their methods courses, and they were required to teach with technology in their clinical experiences. They felt they were ready for the profession!

After graduation, Jill took a position as a fifth grade teacher in a local school with a 1:1 initiative. As students came into her room each day, they sat in clusters, pulled out their Chromebooks, and logged on. Jill reflected on the first time she saw a Chromebook in her elementary language arts methods course in college and remembered her initial trepidation at incorporating technology into her teaching. However, her educational technology and methods courses raised her skill and comfort levels. At her new job, she needed only a few tips from her mentor to begin using technology thoughtfully and meaningfully in her lessons. She was lucky. Her school not only had technology and technology support but it also had an administration and a school culture that supported innovation surrounding the use of technology. This school was a good match for her, and she could see herself teaching there for quite a while.

Marcus also accepted a fifth grade teaching position but in another school district. He was given a teacher laptop and his classroom was equipped with a projector and two desktop computers. The school also had a twenty-station computer lab. Although there was a class set of iPads he checked out on occasion, he seemed to be the only teacher doing so. Since his preservice training used Chromebooks, he was somewhat unfamiliar with iPads. When he took his students to the computer lab for the first time, he had great plans. However, the computers were slow. Some wouldn't connect to the internet. His mentor and other veteran teachers at the school couldn't offer much support because they didn't use technology very much. Despite being interested in using technology, the access, support, and school culture did not promote it. As time went by, Marcus observed that his interest in using technology in his teaching decreased.

Traditionally, the responsibilities of teacher preparation programs have been perceived as ending when candidates graduate, but this concept is evolving. Universities have come under increased pressure to produce high-quality graduates with the relevant skills and staying power to become successful, established teachers. For example, US institutions seeking accreditation from the Council for the Accreditation of Educator Preparation (CAEP) must provide "valid and reliable data, and including employment milestones such as promotion and retention, that employers are satisfied with the completers' preparation for their assigned responsibilities in working with P–12 students" (Standard 4.3). Preservice institutions must also demonstrate that their teacher graduates perceive their preparation as "effective" and "relevant" to their jobs in PK–12 schools (Standard 4.4) (Council for Accreditation of Educator Preparation, 2016).

The US Department of Education seems to echo these standards. The *Advancing Educational Technology in Teacher Preparation Policy Brief* states that PK–12 students deserve to have teachers, including new teachers, who are fully prepared to implement technology "immediately upon entering the classroom" (Office of Educational Technology, 2016, p. 4). The National Education Technology Plan (NETP) challenges educator preparation programs to graduate teachers who are fully prepared, digital educators who do not need retraining by school systems who hire them (Office of Educational Technology, 2017).

CAEP and the US Department of Education appropriately place the onus on teacher preparation programs to produce high-quality graduates. However, Marcus's scenario presents a noteworthy dilemma. While Jill and Marcus both had solid teacher preparation experiences, their ability to integrate technology during their first year of teaching differed greatly. As a result, Jill's students had a greater opportunity to develop technology literacy and benefit from the additional resources afforded by a digital-age learning environment. Marcus's limited ability to use the technology integration skills he acquired in his undergraduate program is unfortunate, but what could his professors have done to better prepare him for this reality? Was his increasingly limited motivation toward technology use in the classroom the fault of his PK–12 school? To what extent is his preparation to blame?

We posit that the best approach to ensuring new teachers' successful technology integration is shared responsibility and problem solving instead of blame. A truly program-deep, program-wide preservice technology initiative will include meaningful partnerships with PK–12 schools, beyond a teacher candidate's graduation date, to ensure new teachers are successful at integrating technology as they enter the field and through their induction years.

What We Know about Induction

The early years in the profession are difficult ones for new teachers as shown by the high attrition rate (44%), nationally, for teachers within their first five years of teaching (Ingersoll, Merrill, Stuckey, & Collins, 2018). Concern about the attrition rates of new teachers has led to a proliferation of induction programs over the past twenty years. According to a New Teacher Center Policy Report (Goldrick, 2016), twenty-nine states in the US now require school districts to provide support for first-year teachers; of those, fifteen require support beyond the first year. Sixteen states provide dedicated funding for teacher induction. Even without state-level policy or funding, most new teachers participate in an induction program of some form (Ingersoll, 2012). Comprehensive induction programs include high-quality mentoring, common planning time, ongoing professional development, participation in professional learning communities, and standards-based teacher evaluation (Alliance for Excellent Education, 2004; Ingersoll, 2012).

We know that induction programs are effective at keeping teachers in the field (Carver-Thomas & Darling-Hammond, 2017; Ronfeldt & McQueen, 2017) as well as strengthening their practice in those first few years. In their review of research on induction programs, Ingersoll and Strong (2011) found that

> beginning teachers who participated in some kind of induction performed better at various aspects of teaching, such as keeping students on task, developing workable lesson plans, using effective student questioning practices, adjusting classroom activities to meet students' interest, maintaining a positive classroom atmosphere, and demonstrating successful classroom management. (p. 201)

Most importantly, teachers in induction programs had higher job satisfaction and retention, and their students had higher scores on achievement tests (Ingersoll & Strong, 2011).

While much can be learned from one's teacher preparation experience, it pales in comparison to the learning that takes place on the job. Indeed, the importance of learning about teaching and becoming a teacher while *in situ* cannot be underestimated. Many of the most common teacher induction practices (e.g., pairing a new teacher with a mentor, getting new teachers into professional learning communities, and providing co-planning time) are expressions of several tenets of sociocultural theories of learning. Vygotsky's (1978) precept of learning with a more knowledgeable other within the zone of proximal development is particularly applicable to teacher induction programs. The more knowledgeable veteran teacher uses her or his experience to help the new teacher acclimate to the profession. In this case, opportunities to strengthen a teacher's practice happen not only in the classroom but also in the hallways, teacher's lounge, administrative offices, and extracurricular events. The veteran teacher, often an assigned mentor, helps the new teacher navigate these spaces, shares lesson plans, gives advice, and models social norms. Similarly, other popular induction activities, such as placing the new teacher in a professional learning community and providing co-planning time, help the new teacher to successfully transition into the school and the profession. Each of these induction program features emphasize the importance of others in one's own learning and the enculturation process of becoming a teacher.

The extent to which teacher preparation programs can mimic these types of induction program structures and provide contextualized experiences using technology will help build a critical bridge from the preservice experience to the induction years. This bridge can be created by introducing preservice teachers to the concept and practice of professional learning communities, as well as expecting and supporting the use of technology during field experiences and student teaching placements. While several states have set standards for teacher induction programs, until recently there have been no national standards for teacher induction.

The New Teacher Center, a national, nonprofit organization dedicated to new teacher induction and mentor training, has been working to improve induction process and training induction mentors for over twenty years. The New Teacher Center released Teacher Induction Program Standards in 2018 (New Teacher Center, 2018). These forty-seven standards, aimed at school districts and school district personnel, are used broadly in the US and other countries. The standards are organized into three areas: Foundational elements (vision, leadership, engagement); Structural elements (mentor roles, professional learning, assessment of practice, and onboarding); and Instructional elements (assessment of practice and instructional mentoring). Standard 2.3 encourages schools to work with universities "to ensure that their graduates are prepared to succeed in the induction program"

(p. 9). Standard 9.4 focuses on helping mentors and beginning teachers to support instructional use of technology in the classroom to meet the diverse needs of every student. Guiding questions of Standard 9.4 include the following:

- How do we ensure that mentors and beginning teachers have equitable access to and are proficient with technology?

- In what ways do mentors encourage teachers to use technology to scaffold instruction and/or provide varied learning pathways to meet the needs of every student?

- In what ways do we appropriately use technology to support mentor and beginning teacher development and instructional practice? (p. 21)

While there is little mention in the literature induction practices related to technology use in teaching and learning, at least two research studies found that technology was not adequately addressed in induction programs and that beginning teachers desired more professional development in this area (Sherman, 2014; Slaouti & Barton, 2007). Two other research studies suggested that using technology as a delivery method for inducting new teachers may be one of the best ways to help them understand the power of technology to support learning. In one evaluation of a district-level induction program, Taranto (2011) found that Web 2.0 and other online tools were effective methods for delivering induction content. In a five-year study of ninety-five early career science teachers in five states, Bang and Luft (2013) found that beginning teachers who participated in an induction program with a strong e-mentoring component used the internet most for finding ideas to improve their teaching practices, whereas those who participated in a face-to-face program used internet resources the least.

What We Know about New Teachers' Technology Use

Our review of the research on novice teachers' technology use began with searches in academic databases for articles published in peer-reviewed academic journals since 2010. Terms such as novice teacher, beginning teacher, early career teacher, and technology were used in the subject fields. Next, search results were limited to empirical research studies with technology use as the focus of inquiry and early career teachers as participants. The bibliographies of these remaining articles were reviewed to identify other studies meeting criteria, including frequently cited studies prior to 2010. This process yielded thirteen research reports, eight conducted in the US and five in other countries (Belgium, England, Israel, New Zealand, and Singapore).

While the research on early career teachers' technology use is thin, there are some consistent patterns emerging. As discussed in the following section, these studies suggest that new teachers often struggle to integrate technology effectively, and to be successful, they need a unique combination of (1) adequate preservice technology preparation, (2) positive school culture and induction support, and (3) access to technology resources such as operable computers, robust internet access, and instructional software. The stronger each of these components, the more likely it is that the new teacher will integrate technology into their teaching. The weaker the components, the less likely they are to use technology. These components will be discussed in the following sections.

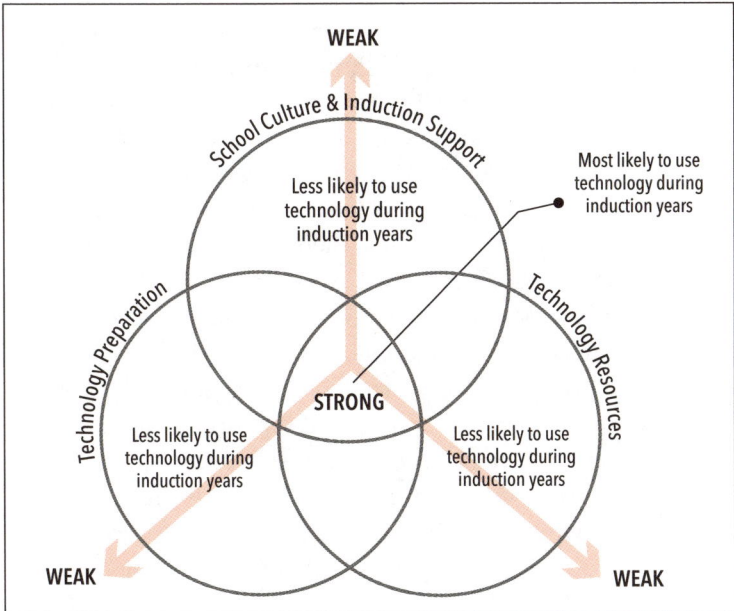

Figure 8.1 Three components necessary to support technology integration during induction years.

Adequate Preservice Technology Preparation

Several research studies explored the critical connection between strategies used in preservice technology programs and novice teachers' ability to integrate technology in their classrooms. Two studies asked new teachers to identify the most helpful technology-related components of their preparation programs. Six new teachers surveyed by Brenner and Brill (2016) selected the following as their most beneficial preservice experiences: (1) faculty modeling technology integration, (2) reflecting on learning activities that used technology, and (3) practicing and experimenting with integrating technology into lessons. These results echoed Sutton's (2011) interview study where novice teachers recommended relevant experiences with technology integration beyond a required technology course.

Other studies attempted to make an even stronger link between specific technology preparation strategies and graduates' effective technology use during their induction years. Modeling technology-supported instruction in methods courses is frequently cited as one effective strategy (Fraser & Garofalo, 2015; Gurevich, Stein, & Gorev, 2017; Hseih, 2018; Tondeur, Roblin, van Braak, Voogt, & Prestridge, 2017). In some cases, these methods courses were taught by content specialists (Fraser & Garofalo, 2015; Gurevich et al., 2017; Hseih, 2018). In Tondeur et al. (2017), the methods courses were co-taught by an instructional technology faculty member who also maintained an up-to-date website of technology resources for candidates. Other promising strategies included having teacher candidates complete technology-based internships, proving extra technology courses for a computer educator license, and using an e-portfolio system to showcase their technology integration projects (Alexander & Kjellstrom, 2014; Ottenbreit-Leftwich, Liao, Sadik, & Ertmer, 2018). In some of these successful cases, skill-based technology classes were eliminated in favor of infusing technology integration topics into other coursework (Tondeur et al., 2017). In other instances, a technology integration course was combined with other strategies to provide additional support (Alexander & Kjellstrom, 2014; Ottenbreit-Leftwich, et al., 2018). Less effective strategies included (1) having a skill-based, stand-alone technology course without infusing technology throughout the rest of the program and (2) eliminating the technology course when infusion efforts in other courses were poorly implemented (Tondeur et al., 2017).

While these studies do not point to one specific technology preparation strategy as superior, they do suggest that preservice teachers need authentic opportunities to observe, design, implement, and reflect upon technology-supported instruction throughout their preparation programs. Yet, researchers are careful to point out high-quality preservice teacher preparation does not ensure novice teacher technology use. School environments can hinder, or halt, new teachers' integration practices, even when teachers have been involved in extraordinary preparation attempts such as extra field experiences, assignments, and coursework (Alexander & Kjellstrom, 2014; Ottenbreit-Leftwich et al., 2018).

Positive School Culture and Induction Support

In alignment with the research on induction, most new teachers need social support to successfully implement technology. New teachers tend to perform better when technology is valued or expected at their school and there are support structures in place to help them implement technology-supported instruction. This support can come from formal mentors who codesign curriculum or responsive technology coordinators who assist new teachers with managing technology in the classroom (Clausen, 2007). New teachers can also benefit from tech-savvy colleagues who share ideas (Ottenbreit-Leftwich et al., 2018) and administrators who encourage and recognize new teachers' technology use (Slaouti and Barton, 2007). Starkey (2010) noted how novice teachers in New Zealand benefited from educational technology mentors beyond their own schools when subject matter expertise was not available locally. Social media and online professional learning networks are other promising conduits for new teacher technology support (Hseih, 2018; Tondeur et al., 2017; Ottenbreit-Leftwich et al., 2018).

When mentoring, co-planning, and reflection were not present, new teachers struggled with the logistics of managing technology in their classrooms and labs (Clausen, 2007; Starkey, 2010). In many cases, the narratives of new teachers' technology use were commingled with first-year induction challenges. Overwhelmed with student behavior and the never-ending cycle of planning, grading, and learning about their new schools, new teachers often reported they had little time or energy to plan for technology use in their classrooms (Gao, Wong, Choy, & Wu, 2011; Tondeur et al., 2017). If new teachers found themselves in cultures where there was little support for technology, some began to view what they had learned in their preparation program as simply not practical for real schools. They succumbed to rather than transformed their culture (Gao et al., 2011; Tondeur et al., 2017).

Access to Technology Resources

Access to reliable, modern technologies was found to be a third critical prerequisite for technology integration by new teachers. When access issues plagued a school, the barriers to technology use seemed to be nearly impossible for novice teachers to overcome. Some researchers documented cases of traditional access issues such as lack of hardware or infrastructure (Ottenbreit-Leftwich et al., 2018), but more subtle access issues were also described. Some new teachers had computers in their classrooms, but not enough. Others were not able to schedule labs as often as they needed or did not have time to set up classroom-based laptops (Slaouti & Barton, 2007). Some beginning teachers were not assigned their own classrooms and encountered different technologies and configurations as they moved from room to room (Alexander & Kjellstrom, 2014; Starkey, 2010). Researchers also documented cases where new teachers were unaware of how to gain access to websites blocked via internet filtering software (Ottenbreit-Leftwich et al., 2018; Starkey, 2010). Some teachers reported students' lack of internet access at home as a deterrent to using technology in the classroom (Alexander & Kjellstrom, 2014; Ottenbreit-Leftwich et al., 2018). Except for isolated cases where novice teachers sought technical help, purchased their own equipment, or asked for specific types of software, most new teachers did not try to address or change the access situation in their schools. They expressed disappointment, but either lived with it or moved to another school (Ottenbreit-Leftwich et al., 2018; Slaouti & Barton, 2007; Starkey, 2010).

Strategies for Supporting New Teachers' Technology Integration

The research clearly shows that new teachers' technology use is influenced by their preparation and environmental factors in PK–12 schools. While some of the PK–12 conditions may be beyond the control of teacher educators, there are several strategies teacher preparation programs can use to better support inductees' technology integration. These strategies include (1) offering a more authentic preservice technology curriculum, (2) influencing the content and delivery of PK–12 induction programs, and (3) partnering with schools to conduct additional research on new teachers' technology use. These strategies are discussed in the following sections.

Strategy One: Authentic Preservice Technology Curriculum

Research on new teacher technology integration suggests that preservice teachers need a deeper understanding of actual contexts in schools, whether ideal or not. To achieve this goal, preparation programs can match their technologies as much as possible to that of major employers (Starkey, 2010). Preservice teachers can also be educated on possible configurations in schools and how to manage technology in classrooms (Brenner & Brill, 2016). By adding this authentic content to teacher preparation programs, preservice teachers begin their induction into PK–12 schools even before they graduate.

Designing and implementing an authentic technology curriculum requires working closely with school partners to stay abreast of their current technologies and initiatives. To accomplish this task, the Instructional Technology Department at Kennesaw State University (KSU), north of Atlanta, Georgia, uses an advisory board to learn about technology initiatives in PK–12 schools and to keep the college's preservice technology curriculum aligned to practice. The advisory board, consisting of technology directors and coaches from twelve surrounding school districts, reviews and provides feedback on program ideas and changes. Faculty believe the board's input has been invaluable to their programs and work. The instructional technology department holds annual meetings with the board and speaks to individual members often.

Advisory board members are motivated to partner with their local teacher prepa-ration program because they are highly invested in creating a technology-proficient workforce for their districts. In addition to seeing their feedback integrated into teacher preparation programs, members also enjoy hearing about technology initia-tives in other school districts and calling on the instructional technology faculty for advice when they need support.

The advisory board keeps faculty updated concerning the types of initiatives, equip-ment, software, and web-based products their teachers are using in their schools. With this information, teacher preparation faculty makes as many relevant tools available to preservice teachers as possible. Special attention is given to web-based products that preservice teachers can access anywhere, anytime. This allows preser-vice teachers to make instructional materials at home and use them at their clinical placement schools, just as their collaborating inservice teachers do on a daily basis.

Collaboration with districts has resulted in other positive changes to the curriculum. For example, data literacy has become a stronger component since new teachers are expected to track and monitor student progress. To help preservice teachers understand the policies and procedures of partner districts, the department has interwoven into preservice teacher education programs information about the Children's Internet Protection Act (CIPA), the Children's Online Privacy and Protection Act (COPPA), the Family Educational Rights and Privacy Act (FERPA), the Individuals with Disabilities Education Act (IDEA), and the Copyright Act. Preservice teachers read sample acceptable use policies from partner districts and discuss ways to keep data secure and students safe while still using the internet in collaborative and creative ways. The advisory board helps faculty understand the policy decisions made in their districts. The faculty, as well, are often asked to share recent research, discuss issues, and offer potential solutions.

At KSU, the Instructional Technology Department primarily interacts with technology personnel from partner schools and shares this information with the rest of the teacher preparation program faculty. However, at other institutions, advisory boards are more broadly structured to include representatives from other departments in the colleges of education, sciences, and liberal arts. Deans or other leaders could chair the committee as well. Advisory committees might also benefit from parent, teacher, and community representation.

Strategy Two: Technology-Infused PK-12 Induction Programs

In addition to improving the authenticity of preservice technology programs, faculty can advocate for infusing technology content into existing school-based induction programs and using technology as a mode of delivery.

The Center for Teacher Innovation (CTI) at the Riverside County Office of Education provides a model of how to infuse technology in both the content and delivery of teacher induction programs. In California, new teachers are required to complete a state-approved induction program in their first year of employment to receive a renewable teaching certificate. The state does not provide dedicated resources for induction, so school districts usually cover the cost with discretionary local, state, or federal funds. In cases where districts do not provide new teachers with induction services, new teachers are able to absorb the cost themselves. While there are many providers of state-approved induction programs, CTI is the largest in the state, annually serving more than 3,000 teachers and contracting with 220 school districts for induction support for their teachers. The center also serves teachers throughout the US and internationally. New teachers participating in the program are provided with learning content and a coach to help them throughout the year. CTI develops and delivers the content for new teachers and comprehensive training for coaches.

CTI's induction content for new teachers is provided in the form of online modules and consists of optional pathways for participants. New teachers can personalize their experience by choosing various topics based on their learning needs. One of the in-depth learning topics is technology integration, but new teachers receive technology-related content whether they choose that module or not. Technology content and resources are infused into all other modules as well. The center provides training for induction coaches via a face-to-face or fully online format. Most of the actual coaching with new teachers is completed face-to-face, but CTI does provide online coaches in cases where a coach cannot be found locally.

Higher education faculty serve on the center's governance board and participate in the implementation of CTI's new teacher induction programs. Professors at California State University, San Bernardino helped write the content and often serve as facilitators for the face-to-face version of coaches' training. Professors at the University of California, Riverside collect data on the program, including participant surveys, and complete end-of-the-year reports for the center. They are also in the process of conducting research on CTI's induction efforts.

Involvement in large-scale induction programs may not be feasible for some teacher preparation programs, but faculty may be able to communicate with recent graduates through social media such as blogs, Twitter, and Facebook. Hopefully, candidates can use social media to establish connections with faculty, peers, and other professional learning resources during their preservice program and use them to stay abreast of current technology trends as they enter the profession.

Strategy Three: PK–12 Research Partnerships

Existing research on teachers' technology use during critical induction years is enlightening but limited in the number of participants, duration, and data collection methods. The studies on new teachers' technology use are mostly case studies of a few individual teachers. While these smaller scale, qualitative studies offer great insight into the context of schools, Gao et al. (2011) have called for more research with longer time frames and larger sample sizes.

As the research on new teachers' technology integration moves forward, it is important to include PK–12 schools as research partners (Ottenbreit-Leftwich et al., 2018). Both teacher preparation programs and schools play critical roles in new teachers' technology use. PK–12 schools as well as teacher preparation programs should design and update their new teacher support strategies based on research. Forging partnerships will help bridge the gap between preparation and practice, resulting in a more effective, seamless support system for new teachers.

Future research will likely follow the lead of those exploring how specific preservice technology preparation strategies transfer to new teachers' practice (Alexander & Kjellstrom, 2014; Brenner & Brill, 2016; Ottenbreit-Leftwich et al., 2018; Tondeur et al., 2017). As Brenner & Brill (2016) posit, teacher educators can learn a great deal by seeking to understand the experiences of their recent graduates, specifically aspects of preparation programs that influenced their technology implementation (p. 142). As evidenced by the limited availability of literature, research exploring the impact of technology preparation programs on graduates' early career practices is needed.

At the same time, school district partners can learn how to improve their support for beginning teachers' technology integration. Bang & Luft (2013) opened a fruitful line of inquiry into how various induction models affected the technology integration practices of new teachers. Ottenbreit-Leftwich et al. (2018) suggested focusing on technology-related mentoring practices for teacher inductees as well. Some researchers have noted that using technology to support students' higher-order thinking, problem solving, and creativity is rare. For this reason, it seems especially important for future research to (1) better describe how new teachers are using technology for teaching and learning in their classrooms and (2) explore instructional strategies during preservice preparation and early career professional development to help new teachers use technology to support instructional models such as inquiry-based, problem-based, or project-based learning.

Conclusion

In our opening scenario, Jill and Marcus had the advantage of going through a technology-rich and technology-infused teacher preparation program. Their preparation laid a strong foundation for them to become technology integrating teachers, but the unique characteristics of the schools Jill and Marcus were hired at resulted in very different outcomes in terms of their integration of technology in their fifth grade classrooms. Available research consistently shows that new teacher technology use also depends on the school culture and technology access. Supported through a preservice preparation partnership with his PK–12 school, Marcus could have been better prepared to face the realities of his employment situation. In the best-case scenario, such a partnership could have helped improve the technology situation at his school. This chapter provided concrete strategies to begin that work. Even though it is challenging, teacher preparation programs must start to view teacher induction as beginning with the preservice experience and extending into the inservice classroom so that our vision of technology use in schools can be more fully realized.

Getting Started Resources

California's Commission on Teacher Credentialing.
ctc.ca.gov/educator-prep/ca-teacher-induction

The California Commission on Teacher Credentialing publishes Teacher Induction Standards, Standards for the Teaching Profession, and a Continuum of Practice rubric for teachers. These documents provide an example of how one state supports teacher induction and professional growth.

ISTE Essential Conditions. **iste.org/standards/essential-conditions**

ISTE Essential Conditions are a set of fourteen Essential Conditions necessary to support the effective use of technology in school settings. This resource, published by ISTE, would be helpful for school leaders striving to establish the environmental conditions necessary for new teachers to successfully integrate technology.

The New Teacher Center. **newteachercenter.org/resources**

> The New Teacher Center strives to support early career teachers. The resource section contains induction standards, mentor standards, and coaching standards. There is also a white paper on how to establish teacher learning communities.

The William and Ida Friday Institute for Educational Innovation. **place.fi.ncsu.edu**

> The William and Ida Friday Institute for Educational Innovation hosts a MOOC on coaching digital learning. This could be a useful resource for induction coaches or preservice clinical supervisors responsible for coaching technology integration. Other free, self-directed MOOCs are offered.

Twitter Chats

Twitter Chats are real-time chats that occur over Twitter using a specific hashtag. Teacher preparation programs can help preservice teachers establish personal learning networks (PLNs) before entering the profession by either encouraging participation in existing chats or creating chats of their own for current candidates and alumni. The following Twitter Chats are especially relevant to preservice teachers, new teachers, and technology using teachers:

#pretchat Chat for Preservice Teachers: Thursdays, 7 p.m. EST

#ntchat Chat for New Teachers: First and third Wednesdays, 8 p.m. EST

#edtechchat Chat for Technology-Using Educators: Mondays, 8 p.m. EST

See the ISTE blog post "40 Education Twitter Chats Worth Your Time" for a list of fourty top education Twitter hashtags and chats. bit.ly/39rGsfT

Also see Kappanonline.org "Enhancing Teacher Education with Twitter" for a discussion of how to use Twitter and Twitter Chats in teacher education courses and programs. bit.ly/2WNd2pA

References

Alexander, C., & Kjellstrom, W. (2014). The influence of a technology-based internship on first-year teachers' instructional decision-making. *Journal of Technology and Teacher Education, 22*(3), 265–285.

Alliance for Excellent Education. (2004). *Tapping the potential: Retaining and developing high-quality new teachers.* Washington, DC: Alliance for Excellent Education. all4ed.org/wp-content/uploads/2007/07/TappingThePotential.pdf

Bang, E., & Luft, J. A. (2013). Secondary science teachers' use of technology in the classroom during their first 5 years. *Journal of Digital Learning in Teacher Education, 29*(4), 118–126. doi.org/10.1080/21532974.2013.10784715

Brenner, A., & Brill, J. (2016). Investigating practices in teacher education that promote and inhibit technology integration transfer in early career teachers. *TechTrends, 60,* 136–144. doi.org/10.1007/s11528-016-0025-8

Carver-Thomas, D., & Darling-Hammond, L. (2017). *Teacher turnover: Why it matters and what we can do about it.* Palo Alto, CA: Learning Policy Institute.

Clausen, J. M. (2007). Beginning teachers' technology use: First-year teacher development and the institutional context's effect on new teachers' instructional technology use with students. *Journal of Research on Technology in Education, 39*(3), 245–261.

Council for the Accreditation of Educator Preparation. (2016). *2013 CAEP standards: Adapted in 2016.* caepnet.org/~/media/Files/caep/standards/caep-standards-one-pager-0219.pdf?la=en

Fraser, V., & Garofalo, J. (2015). Novice mathematics teachers' use of technology to enhance student engagement, questioning, generalization, and conceptual understanding. *Journal of Technology and Teacher Education, 23*(1), 29–51.

Gao, P., Wong, A. F. L., Choy, D., & Wu, J. (2011). Beginning teachers' understanding performances of technology integration. *Asia Pacific Journal of Education, 31*(2), 211–223. doi.org/10.1080/02188791.2011.567003

Goldrick, L. (2016). *Support from the start: A 50-state review of policies on new educator induction and mentoring.* Santa Cruz, CA: New Teacher Policy Center. newteachercenter.org/wp-content/uploads/2016CompleteReportStatePolicies.pdf

Gurevich, I., Stein, H., & Gorev, D. (2017). Tracking professional development of novice teachers when integrating technology into teaching mathematics. *Computers in the Schools, 54*(4), 267–283.

Hsieh, B. (2018) This is how we do it: Authentic and strategic technology use by novice English teachers. *Contemporary Issues in Technology and Teacher Education, 18*(2), 271–288.

Ingersoll, R. M. (2012). Beginning teacher induction: What the data tell us. *Phi Delta Kappan, 92*(8), 47–51.

Ingersoll, R. M., Merrill, E., Stuckey, D., & Collins, G. (2018). Seven trends: The transformation of the teaching force – Updated October 2018. CPRE Research Reports. repository.upenn.edu/cpre_researchreports/108

Ingersoll, R. M., & Strong, M. (2011). The impact of induction and mentoring programs for beginning teachers: A critical review of the research. *Review of Educational Research, 81*(2), 201–233.

New Teacher Center. (2018). *Teacher induction program standards.* Santa Cruz, CA: New Teacher Center.

Office of Educational Technology. (2016). *Advancing educational technology in teacher preparation: Policy brief.* tech.ed.gov/teacherprep/

Office of Educational Technology. (2017). *Reimagining the role of technology in education: 2017 National Education Technology Plan update.* tech.ed.gov/files/2017/01/NETP17.pdf

Ottenbreit-Leftwich, A., Liao, J. Y., Sadik, O., & Ertmer, P. (2018). Evolution of teachers' technology integration knowledge, beliefs, and practices: How can we support beginning teachers, use of technology? *Journal of Research on Technology in Education, 50*(4), 282–304. doi.org/10.1080/15391523.2018.1487350

Ronfeldt, M., & McQueen K. (2017). Does new teacher induction really improve retention? *Journal of Teacher Education, 68*(4), 394–410. doi.org/10.1177/0022487117702583

Sherman, D. B. (2014). *New teacher induction programs: A case study of an exemplary school district, and how it prepares its new teachers for the use of instructional technology in the classroom* (Unpublished doctoral dissertation). Loyola University Chicago, Chicago, IL. ecommons.luc.edu/luc_diss/915/

Slaouti, D., & Barton, A. (2007). Opportunities for practice and development: Newly qualified teachers and the use of information and communications technologies in teaching foreign languages in English secondary school contexts. *Journal of In-Service Education, 33*(4), 405–424. doi.org/10.1080/13674580701687807

Starkey, L. (2010). Supporting the digitally able beginning teacher. *Teaching and Teacher Education, 26*(7), 1429–1438. doi.org/10.1016/j.tate.2010.05.002

Sutton, S. (2011). The preservice technology training experiences of novice teachers. *Journal of Digital Learning in Teacher Education, 28*(1), 39–47.

Taranto, G. (2011) New-teacher induction 2.0. *Journal of Digital Learning in Teacher Education, 28*(1), 4–15. doi.org/10.1080/21532974.2011.10784675

Tondeur, J., Roblin, N., van Braak, J., Voogt, J., & Prestridge, S. (2017). Preparing beginning teachers for technology integration in education: Ready for take-off? *Technology, Pedagogy and Education, 26*(2), 157–177. doi.org/10.1080/1475939X.2016.1193556

Vygotsky, L. S. (1978). *Mind in society: The development of higher psychological processes.* Cambridge, MA: Harvard University Press.

SECTION III

Evaluating Technology Infusion

The chapters in this section share methods and guidance for assessing candidate outcomes and program- and college-level processes and progress.

CHAPTER 9

Leadership for Technology Infusion: Guiding Change and Sustaining Progress in Teacher Preparation

JON M. CLAUSEN
BALL STATE UNIVERSITY

Overview

In order for technology infusion to be successful, leaders at the upper administrative levels within teacher preparation programs must facilitate change, prioritize competing initiatives, and shape the change process for faculty and teacher candidates. Education leaders can draw on several theories, frameworks, and tools to support change. In this chapter, I discuss the essential role of leadership for those who seek to promote and support the advancement of technology infusion within their teacher preparation programs, and I offer suggestions for how education leaders can initiate the process of transformational change for technology infusion.

Scenario

Dean Smith leads a teacher preparation program (TPP) that seeks to prepare teacher candidates to enter their future classrooms with the knowledge and skills that will make them successful educators. The TPP requires candidates take a variety of courses that emphasize content knowledge, meeting the needs of diverse learners, and understanding the communities where children live. The TPP has never had a required educational technology course.

In the past, there have been several attempts to introduce different technologies within the TPP, including a required laptop initiative, digital portfolio require-ment, and grant-funded projects that made new technologies and support available to faculty and teacher candidates. The assumption by leaders was that access to technology and development of a digital portfolio would translate into candidates' understanding how to integrate technology within their own classrooms. During this period, faculty took teacher candidates to a portfolio lab at the beginning and end of the semester where support personnel assisted them in uploading content and publishing their portfolios. These efforts resulted in an archive of digital materials for accreditation but lacked a comprehensive emphasis on modeling tech-nology use and integration by faculty. In fact, faculty relied on support personnel to teach candidates about technology and assist them with portfolio develop-ment, forfeiting their own responsibility to learn and model technology use with candidates.

Faculty professional development was targeted to specific technologies and skills but was not ongoing and lacked connection to coursework activities, curricular needs, and faculty interests. Teacher candidates frequently interpreted portfolio requirements as something they "had to do" as a function of course assessment protocol but saw little connection between uploading files to their portfolio and improving their instructional practices. Artifacts for their required portfolio were low-level uses of technology and included word-processed papers, lesson plans, and presentations given to the class. Consequently, technology use by faculty and candidates was inconsistent throughout the TPP. Teacher candidate experiences integrating technology within their teaching practice, or being modeled for them by faculty, were dependent on the course section they were enrolled in and whether faculty were comfortable in the technical knowledge and pedagogical practices that allowed candidates to explore technology integration.

Recent surveys of faculty and teacher candidates found addressing technology within the preparation program was viewed as important, but not a priority in learning how to teach. Survey results also indicated a lack of an overriding vision for how faculty and candidates are expected to integrate technology within their instructional practices, or further, how technology should be infused throughout the program. In fact, communication with school partners and alumni indicated teacher candidates did not possess positive attitudes about technology, were unable to think critically about technology use with PK–12 students, and were slow to adapt to district expectations for technology use with students.

The survey results provided Dean Smith and TPP leadership an opportunity to rethink how technology was leveraged within the TPP. This included an understanding of the role of technology in teaching and learning and the kinds of things TPP leadership could do to build capacity for technology to be addressed throughout the TPP in a program-deep and program-wide, infused approach. However, competing demands on the dean such as budget shortfalls, declining enrollment, state legislative decisions about alternative licensure, and reducing credit hours for licensure created challenges for moving forward.

Dean Smith was inundated with a variety of demands that pushed and pulled on her attention and TPP resources. In order to address the challenge of preparing all candidates within the teacher preparation program to teach with technology, Dean Smith needed to make the case as to why technology infusion was a priority. The dean decided to regroup in order to provide leadership with a compelling argument for a technology infusion initiative, including ways to empower and support faculty as they engage in their own change process, and how to prioritize resources so that the change process would be successful.

Building Capacity

Building capacity for technology infusion is much more than receiving grant funds, acquiring technology, and providing short-term professional development focused on technical skills—all efforts from past eras that have helped the field get to where technology can be posed as a priority in teacher preparation. But technology infusion involves moving beyond those important baseline efforts to transforming teacher preparation programs encompassing a stronger emphasis for teacher candidates on learning to effectively teach with technology, as well as the curriculum elements and instructional practices of faculty that will be required for this to happen. As discussed in other chapters, building capacity for technology infusion requires thoughtful consideration of many organizational factors that involve curricular design of coursework and instructional practices of faculty. Education leaders face an array of decisions related to both the short- and long-term objectives for the programs they lead. In many cases, TPP leaders are responding to shifting dynamics within their college, university, or state that they have little control over. However, education leaders within TPPs retain significant control in developing a context that articulates a shared vision for the program, structuring initiatives to support that vision, and providing resources that can lead to change. In this chapter, I deconstruct the scenario about Dean Smith and offer ways education leaders can support the rationale for technology infusion throughout teacher preparation programs.

Making the Case

In the scenario, Dean Smith is presented with an opportunity to address alumni and K–12 employer concerns regarding candidates' readiness to use technology within their instructional practices. The dean is supported by external factors that can help make the case to faculty for technology infusion. In 2016, the Office of Educational Technology released a policy brief that documented teacher candidates lack preparation to enter classrooms and use technology to support student learning. The brief identified four guiding principles for teacher education programs to consider and challenged programs to improve candidate preparation. The guiding principles were as follows:

- Focus on the active use of technology to enable learning and teaching.

- Build sustainable, program-wide systems of professional learning for higher education instructors.

- Ensure preservice teachers' experiences with educational technology are program-deep and program-wide.

- Align efforts with research-based standards, frameworks, and credentials. (p. 9)

For Dean Smith, these four principles provide direction to move away from what the college had traditionally done to introduce technology within the TPP. Instead of focusing on technology-specific solutions, these principles emphasize development of the instructional context throughout the TPP and a challenge for faculty to transform instructional practices that provide opportunities for teacher candidates and their students to use technology to support learning and teaching. Dean Smith interprets her role in achieving these principles as the individual who can best help to establish the context for programmatic and instructional change. Specifically, she interprets the principles for "building program-wide systems" and experiences that are "program-deep and program-wide" as ones she has the most direct control over. She believes that if the opportunities and systems are in place, there will be a greater chance that faculty and candidates will embrace the change process. She also understands a "technology" initiative may be met with resistance by various factions vying for scarce resources.

Along with the US Department of Education's Office of Educational Technology policy brief, Dean Smith is bolstered by accreditation, professional standards, and licensure language that supports technology infusion throughout the TPP. The Council for the Accreditation of Educator Preparation (CAEP) (2016) identified technology as a "cross-cutting theme" and specifically mentions candidate technology use in Standard 1.5:

> Providers ensure that candidates model and apply technology standards as they design, implement, and assess learning experiences to engage students and improve learning; and enrich professional practice.

The Council of Chief State School Officers Interstate New Teacher Assessment and Support Consortium (InTASC) standards also identify technology integration as a set of cross-disciplinary skills in a developing teacher's knowledge, dispositions, and performance (Council of Chief State School Officers, 2013). Content area standards have embraced technology use to explore content, test hypotheses, and research (e.g., National Council for the Social Studies, 2010; National Council of Teachers of Mathematics, 2015; National Research Council, 2013). Further, standards put forth by the International Society for Technology in Education (ISTE) focus on how educators can best use technology to support their professional practice and development (2017a).

Dean Smith is beginning to understand that technology infusion involves a transformational change process for the entire TPP. This not only includes restructuring dedicated resources but also engaging faculty in a change process themselves. She realizes a change process requires faculty to:

- critically reflect about their own technology use and instructional practices with candidates,

- support teacher candidates as they learn how to teach with technology,

- provide teacher candidates with models of good technology use in PK–12, and

- provide teacher candidates with opportunities to practice teaching with technology within teacher education courses.

The dean's leadership in this change process will require her to provide others with a rationale for change and provide opportunities for the various factions within TPP to see themselves in the changes that need to occur.

As Dean Smith contemplates how she will establish priorities and lead this long-term change process, she understands that top-down decision making has been met with resistance in the past. Previous initiatives left many important stakeholders feeling left out instead of being a part of the process. There are several theoretical frameworks and resources that can further her thinking as she moves forward. In the next section, I provide an overview of frameworks and resources that can help education leaders understand the change process and develop a context supportive of technology infusion.

Understanding the Change Process

Change Theory and Models to Guide Leaders

There are several frameworks and resources available to guide leaders like Dean Smith in a change process, including Rogers's (2003) Diffusion of Innovations Theory, Fullan's (2007) three-phase process for change, and Hall and Hord's Concerns-Based Adoption Model (2015). Additional information about the role of context within the technological, pedagogical, and content knowledge (TPACK) framework can also provide guidance to education leaders (Mishra, 2019; Mishra & Koehler, 2006).

Rogers's (2003) Diffusion of Innovation Theory explains how, why, and at what rate a new innovation (ideas or technology) might spread through cultures. Key elements to the theory are the innovations, the adopters, communication channels, time, and the social system that may influence the potential adopter.

Fullan (2007) suggests that the change process involves three phases. The process is complex, and what happens at one stage strongly affects the following stages. Initiation is the first phase. This phase is about deciding to begin the change process and requires developing a commitment toward the process. The initiation phase involves the leader taking several factors into consideration including access to information, faculty, and community. Each can act as a change agent in the process. Implementation is the second phase and is the part of the process where action plans are carried out and progress is monitored or adjusted. Continuation is the third phase and is the part of the process where the leader plays a pivotal role in whether or not to continue implementing the initiative.

The Concerns-Based Adoption Model (C-BAM) by Hall and Hord (2015) also provides leaders with a process for implementing change. Leaders should consider a variety of factors that can aid or hinder their efforts. The C-BAM model for change emphasizes that any meaningful change requires a developmental process and takes three to five years to fully implement. By understanding the Stages of Concern (SoC) and Levels of Use (LoU), Innovation Configurations (IC) are developed to facilitate change. Hall & Hord (2015) describe this change process through the development of an Implementation Bridge. The bridge highlights existing practices and the implementation process needed in order for new practices to take hold. All stakeholders in the change process play a role in C-BAM, and the creation of professional development activities that support change is driven by information gathered from those stakeholders. How leaders advocate for, recognize, and incentivize faculty to participate in initiatives are key factors to help faculty prioritize these demands (Hall & Hord, 2015; Hord, 2017; Kolb, Kashef, Roberts, Terry, & Borthwick, 2018). Change agents' understanding of the organizational culture and context can also affect the success or failure of the change process.

The Importance of Context as Part of the Change Process

Educational leaders' ability to shape the context supporting technology use by teacher educators and teacher candidates requires examination of the role of context in building capacity for technology infusion. The TPACK framework recognizes that various contextual factors affect use of technology during teaching and learning. For example, Porras-Hernandez and Salinas-Amescua (2013) posited that contextual factors that affect TPACK can occur at micro (i.e., classroom), meso (i.e., school/institution), and macro (i.e., society) levels and can relate to the teacher and/or the students. Knowledge of contexts is therefore understood to be essential for effective technology integration (Rosenberg & Koehler, 2015; Swallow & Olofson, 2017).

Mishra (2019) acknowledged the importance of understanding contextual knowledge as its own knowledge domain within the TPACK diagram, which illustrates contextual knowledge (XK) as something that teachers, teacher educators, and education leaders "can act on, change, and help teachers develop" (p. 1). Understanding of contextual knowledge also "highlights the organizational and situational constraints that teachers work within. … This allows us to go beyond seeing teachers as designers within the classrooms but rather as *intrapreneurs*— knowing how their organization functions, and how the levers of power and influence can effect sustainable change" (p. 2). As education leaders work to build capacity for technology infusion and empower various stakeholders to engage in a change process, the XK that is unique to a particular course, department, college, university, PK–12 school and classroom, and community will affect the structure of that change. Use of the TPACK framework, and specifically the emphasis on XK, helps Dean Smith understand that building capacity will not be a one-size-fits-all solution. She must use and develop the strengths of the TPP and focus energies on elements of the change process that need greater attention.

Understanding the change process is important to Dean Smith. Prior to becoming dean, she was a successful social foundations faculty member. Her own experiences and conceptions about learning with technology are limited, and she assumes her level of technology knowledge is far behind some of the faculty and candidates. The previous ways the TPP had introduced technology had not led to sustainable change in how faculty and candidates use technology, and the technology integration that does exist is dependent on the course and instructor who teaches the course. Limitations due to credit requirements prevent her from adding a required educational technology course for all candidates in the TPP. In the absence of a required course, she seeks direction in how to move forward, set priorities, and work within the existing context to build capacity for technology infusion. As a leader, she needs to overcome these challenges and support the TPP in making this change. While the frameworks and resources for change are helpful, Dean Smith seeks additional tools that can help her to take action and initiate change.

Initiating the Change Process: Tools to Guide Change

ISTE Essential Conditions and Standards for Education Leaders

ISTE has developed materials identifying essential conditions and standards to aid education leaders in technology planning and systematic change. The ISTE Essential Conditions identify fourteen critical elements to leverage technology use for learning (ISTE, 2017b). From a leadership perspective, consideration of the Essential Conditions offers education leaders a variety of components to account for with regard to XK, including creating a shared vision for educational technology, empowering all stakeholders, consistent and adequate funding, and ongoing professional development. The ISTE Standards for Education Leaders specifically articulate ways to develop programs, empower faculty and staff, and establish goals (ISTE, 2018). For example, the Standards for Education Leaders allow leaders to inspire a culture of innovation and engage stakeholders in developing and adopting a shared vision for technology use. Specifically, the ISTE standards—including elements of being a Visionary Planner, Empowering Leader, and System Designer— provide leaders guidance in working collaboratively with others to establish a vision for infusion, creating a culture of innovation, and ensuring resources to support effective technology use for learning.

The TPACK Leadership Diagnostic Tool

The TPACK leadership diagnostic tool (Graziano, Herring, Carpenter, Smaldino, & Finsness, 2017) was developed by the American Association of Colleges of Teacher Education (AACTE) Committee on Innovation and Technology to support education leaders in their efforts to infuse technology throughout their teacher preparation program. Details on the development and research of the diagnostic tool can be found in existing literature (Clausen, Finsness, Borthwick, Graziano, Carpenter, & Herring, 2019; Graziano et al., 2017; Thomas, Herring, Redmond, & Smaldino, 2013). Examination of the TPACK leadership diagnostic tool can be helpful for education leaders, such as Dean Smith, who seek a process for taking action toward building capacity for technology infusion. The diagnostic tool is grounded in the theory of action (Argyris, Putnam, & McLain Smith, 1985; Argyris & Schon, 1974) and the transformational leadership framework (Day, Sammons, Leithwood, & Kington, 2008; Leithwood, Harris, & Hopkins, 2008; Leithwood & Jantzi, 2008).

The TPACK leadership diagnostic tool "was developed as a self-assessment tool to serve the individual institution in its decision-making process" (Graziano et al., 2017, p. 37). The diagnostic tool uses the theory of action to facilitate examination of

- various factors affecting an initiative (favorable policy environment, additional resources, faculty time and attention, school partners, scalability),

- elements within their context the leader can control (human resources, fiscal resources, personal resources, engagement with internal/external partners), and

- resources the leader has available to initiate, support, and sustain the change (vision statement, faculty capacity, organizational redesign).

Each section of the diagnostic tool is defined by a range of statements that provide leaders with a way to assess where the TPP may be while initiating change (beginning, developing, acceptable, leading). The range of statements provides a sliding scale the education leader can use to gauge the status of various factors that effect change and the progress of the college/school of education or program within the process.

In a case study of institutions that used the diagnostic tool during TPACK initiatives, Clausen et al. (2019) discovered that education leaders found all components of the diagnostic tool relevant as they planned and implemented their initiatives. "Leaders used various components of the diagnostic tool to engage with others, to consider how physical spaces and personnel could be repurposed in support of the initiative, and to think critically about prioritizing competing political, financial, and contextual demands" (p. 64). Results of the study illustrated that leadership decision making was instrumental in the planning and implementation of TPACK initiatives. Clausen et al. (2019) concluded that

[w]ithout guidance for leaders to understand and participate in the change process, leaders may be left chasing grant funding for technology or undertaking a vision based on the determination of a single individual. Neither is optimal if the goal is transformational and sustainable change for effective technology use by teacher education faculty and candidates to enhance PK–12 learning. Leaders need to thoughtfully reflect on how competing priorities and resources, faculty time and attention, involvement of school partners, and the ever-critical policy environment can impact the development and implementation of their TPACK based initiatives. Making time to consult elements, such as those outlined in the TPACK leadership diagnostic tool, while leading the change process of TPACK-focused initiatives can help ensure that the initiatives are successful. (p. 66)

The TPACK leadership diagnostic tool is a great resource for Dean Smith because it provides her the means to keep a broad perspective on the change process and allows her to reflect on areas of the context that need attention. The dean will need to successfully communicate that the process of building capacity for technology infusion is unlike previous technology initiatives and something that involves all operations of the TPP. The role of faculty in the change process is one of the major challenges Dean Smith foresees as she moves forward. Organizing professional development and learning opportunities for faculty will be an important element in the process. As discussed elsewhere in this book, the Teacher Education Technology Competencies (TETCs) (Foulger, Graziano, Schmidt-Crawford, & Slykhuis, 2017) and the ISTE Standards for Educators are additional resources Dean Smith can use to support faculty development. In addition to the competencies and standards, the ADKAR model (Hiatt, 2006), introduced and discussed in the following section, can help direct professional learning opportunities because it focuses on outcomes that reinforce growth.

ADKAR Organizational Change Management Model

ADKAR is an acronym that represents five outcomes individuals need to achieve lasting change: Awareness, Desire, Knowledge, Ability, and Reinforcement (Hiatt, 2006). The ADKAR model is a goal-oriented change management framework for organizations. ADKAR focuses on individuals as the key to the change process (Hiatt, 2006). As discussed earlier, individual stakeholders (e.g., program chairs, full-time faculty, adjunct faculty, school principals, cooperating teachers) can determine the success or failure of a change initiative. Having a model that empha-sizes the personal role in a change process can support both individual growth and sustainability of the change the organization is hoping to achieve. It can also help guide professional development activities to strengthen faculty in their use and modeling of technology.

Leadership Moving Technology Infusion Forward

In this section, I recommend two specific areas education leaders should focus on to help them succeed in the process of change for technology infusion. They include developing a vision for technology infusion and constructing a context that supports infusion.

Developing a Vision for Technology Infusion

Education leaders like Dean Smith face a complex process of transformational change. There are multiple standards, frameworks, and tools that can support her as she begins to move forward in the process. Now that she is ready to take action, she asks herself, "What is technology infusion going to look like at this institution?" Several of the frameworks and resources underscore that a leader should have a vision that guides the initiative implementation, supports professional development, and addresses the management of resources (Graziano et al., 2017; ISTE, 2017b; ISTE, 2018). A challenge for Dean Smith is that she is unclear what that vision should look like.

Developing a vision for technology infusion should not be something foisted onto a single individual or small committee. Whether the leader of the change process is the dean, or an individual or group appointed by the dean, developing a vision for technology infusion should involve a leadership team of change agents with clearly articulated roles focused on supporting technology infusion throughout the TPP. As in the scenario at the beginning of this chapter, education leaders do not always understand what is meant by technology integration or what it means to infuse technology in a program-deep and program-wide manner. As research has shown, leaders in the past have spent significant resources only to have them underused (Epstein, 2019). Leaders need to educate themselves, seek input, and listen to recommendations from educational technology faculty, who can help to expand their understanding of what technology infusion might look like and what kinds of resources, personnel, restructuring of physical spaces, and professional development might be required to make the process successful. The leaders must put themselves in the place of those being asked to make changes. They must also participate in the change process, engage with stakeholders, listen to concerns, and celebrate the achievements of those working to infuse technology throughout the teacher education program (Clausen et al., 2019).

The leadership team should include educational technology faculty familiar with technology integration and infusion and the standards, frameworks, and models mentioned throughout this chapter. Additional personnel and stakeholders may include technology support personnel who are familiar with purchasing, servicing, and managing hardware and software; content and grade-level faculty to share information about their instructional goals and existing pedagogical practices; and community partners to share their expertise and needs as they look to hire future educators. This leadership team should focus on technology infusion broadly to develop and implement a vision for how technology can be embedded within the professional education sequence of courses. The leadership team should then develop structures to scaffold faculty as they model technology within instructional practices and provide opportunities for candidates to use and practice technology integration within courses and field experiences, including student teaching. Once the team is established, the question remains, "How will we get there?" The answer is, "It depends."

Constructing the Instructional Context for Technology Infusion

Local contexts are the reason why technology infusion will look different each time an education leader attempts to address the challenge of technology infusion. Creating a team to establish an initial vision is an important first step; the next is engaging with faculty and other stakeholders to establish buy-in of a shared vision. Using change models like the Concerns-Based Adoption Model (Hall and Hord, 2015) provides leaders and their teams a process for facilitating change. As part of this process, leaders must engage faculty in critical and highly reflective conversations about content, pedagogical practices, and technology's role in learning, teaching, and assessment. In order for these kinds of conversations to take place, a leader must cultivate a context that is supportive, collaborative, and encourages creative risk-taking.

Education leaders' decision making about personnel, restructuring of physical spaces, and prioritizing budgetary concerns is extremely important in creating a situation where both faculty and teacher candidates feel empowered to be creative and take pedagogical risks with technology. Creating physical and/or online spaces that support faculty and candidate exploration with technology also creates opportunities for engagement with others about pedagogical practices and content. These spaces promote faculty empowerment by supporting growth of their technology knowledge and can also be opportunities for faculty to engage with others (students, faculty, technology integration specialists, etc.). These informal spaces are often the places where collaborations are started, ideas are hatched, and deeper thinking about infusion can take place. It is in these kinds of spaces that faculty, or various factions within the teacher preparation program who are resistant to or do not fully understand the need for technology infusion, can interact with others to think critically about issues like social justice, diversity, and community engagement. From there, they can think creatively about how various technologies can support student exploration of these issues, allow for candidates to demonstrate their knowledge and understanding, and provide opportunities for candidates to represent and share their knowledge with others. The ideal would be to create a learning community focused on improvement of the teacher education program through technology infusion. One outcome of this process might be a curriculum map of the teacher education program, existing assessments, and an explanation of how various technologies can support existing instructional practices. Faculty can work with others to modify, restructure, or create new opportunities for candidates that emphasize knowledge construction enhanced through affordances of technology.

To make this happen, education leaders will need to provide sustained supports like an annual budget, targeted professional development, and continuous support for faculty instructional change. This may require consideration of hiring technology integration specialists, shifting faculty loads to enable their participation in professional development activities, and/or development of a faculty technology mentoring program to enhance faculty members' technology knowledge in relation to their content and pedagogical approaches. This will help all faculty understand that technology infusion touches on all content areas and all pedagogical practices—vital aspects of their professional endeavors.

Conclusion

Technology infusion will vary from one teacher education program to the next. The size of the teacher education program, the number of teacher education faculty, the available financial resources, and the flexibility of the education leader to initiate change, along with other factors, will determine how a technology infusion change effort can move forward. Some institutions may decide an initial first step is to restructure the curriculum so that content methods courses are blocked with a required educational technology course that also has a practicum component; this will ensure that candidates have opportunities to put into practice what they are learning about content and technology integration. Another institution may do away with a required educational technology course, but then repurpose educational technology faculty to design learning opportunities with content area and methods faculty to integrate technology within coursework and specific assignments throughout the program. A third institution may restructure physical spaces and personnel to create a context for innovation, empowering and building faculty capacity to model technology use with candidates. Educational technology faculty could then work closely with faculty to create a series of micro-credentials mapped to redesigned course assignments throughout the program, where candidates demonstrate they have met both content and pedagogical standards, along with the ISTE Standards for Educators. Success of these and other configurations will depend on leadership and insightful decision making.

In order to take hold, a technology infusion effort will require sustained support from leadership that creates instructional contexts that empower faculty to spearhead and actively participate in the change process. Leaders who understand the value in producing shared meaning for change will collaborate with others to create a vision of how technology infusion supports faculty and candidate development and TPP goals. Beyond creating a vision, it is essential that leaders prioritize infusion by holding true to long-term plans that include budgetary, structural, and personnel decisions that enable that vision to come to fruition. This can be done only by creating spaces and supports for all stakeholders to engage in critical conversation about instructional practices and how technology can be used to support learning and teaching. Through these efforts, education leaders such as Dean Smith may initiate a transformational change process that leads to technology infusion within their teacher education programs.

Getting Started Resources

Hall, G. E., & Hord, S. M. (2015). *Implementing change: Patterns, principles, and potholes* (4th ed.). Upper Saddle River, NJ: Pearson.

> The concerns-based adoption model is discussed in depth in this book. The authors provide details about the change process, research, and case studies to aid readers as they undergo their own change initiatives.

Graziano, K. J., Herring, M. C., Carpenter, J. P., Smaldino, S., & Finsness, E. S. (2017). A TPACK diagnostic tool for teacher education leaders. *TechTrends, 61*(4), 372–379. doi.org/10.1007/s11528-017-0171-7

> The AACTE TPACK leadership diagnostic tool provides leaders with a means to gauge and reflect on how an educator preparation program is using technology, prioritizing resources, and developing the instructional context for technology infusion. This article includes a copy of the tool.

ISTE Essential Conditions. iste.org/standards/essential-conditions

> The ISTE Essential Conditions identify fourteen critical elements for leveraging technology for learning. Leaders can use the conditions to reflect on the various components needed for technology infusion.

ISTE Standards for Education Leaders.
iste.org/standards/for-education-leaders

> Refreshed in 2018, the ISTE Standards for Education Leaders focus on the knowledge and behaviors of leaders so they are able to support and empower teacher and student technology use. These standards emphasize the role of leaders for planning strategically, advocating for equity and inclusion, empowering teachers and learners, designing sustainable systems, and connecting with others.

Kolb, L., Kashef, F., Roberts, C., Terry, C., & Borthwick, A. (2018). *Challenges to creating and sustaining effective technology integration in teacher education programs.* tech.ed.gov/edtechtprep

> This white paper was written by the Building Sustainable Systems Working Group. This group of researchers, organized during the 2016 US Department of Education's Office of Educational Technology Teacher

Education Summit in 2016, examined how teacher education programs might build sustainable, program-wide systems of professional learning for higher education instructors.

References

Argyris, C., Putnam, R., & McLain Smith, D. (1985). *Action science: concepts, methods, and skills for research and intervention.* San Francisco: Jossey-Bass.

Argyris, C., & Schon, D. (1974). *Theory in practice: Increasing professional effectiveness.* San Francisco, CA: Jossey-Bass.

Clausen, J. M., Finsness, E. S., Borthwick, A. C., Graziano, K. J., Carpenter, J., & Herring, M. (2019). TPACK leadership diagnostic tool: Adoption and implementation by teacher education leaders. *Journal of Digital Learning in Teacher Education, 35*(1), 54–72. doi.org/10.1080/21532974.2018.1537818

Council for the Accreditation of Educator Preparation. (2016). *CAEP standards for initial-licensure programs.* caepnet.org

Council of Chief State School Officers. (2013, April). *Interstate Teacher Assessment and Support Consortium InTASC Model Core Teaching Standards 1.0: A resource for state dialogue.* Washington, DC: Author.

Day, C., Sammons, P., Leithwood, K., & Kington, A. (2008). Research into the impact of school leadership on pupil outcomes: Policy and research contexts. *School Leadership & Management: Formerly School Organization, 28,* 5–25.

Epstein, B. (2019). Calling all "somebodies" to solve the edtech collective action problem. In C. Crawford, D. Willis, R. Carlsen, I. Gibson, K. McFerrin, J. Price & R. Weber (Eds.), *Proceedings of Society for Information Technology & Teacher Education International Conference 2019.* Association for the Advancement of Computing in Education (AACE). learntechlib.org/primary/p/208640

Foulger, T. S., Graziano, K. J., Schmidt-Crawford, D. A., & Slykhuis, D. A. (2017). Teacher educator technology competencies. *Journal of Technology and Teacher Education, 25*(4), 413–448.

Fullan, M. (2007). *The new meaning of educational change* (4th ed.). New York, NY: Teachers College Press.

Graziano, K. J., Herring, M. C., Carpenter, J. P., Smaldino, S., & Finsness, E. S. (2017). A TPACK diagnostic tool for teacher education leaders. *TechTrends, 61*(4), 372–379. doi.org/10.1007/s11528-017-0171-7

Hall, G. E., & Hord, S. M. (2015). *Implementing change: Patterns, principles, and potholes.* Upper Saddle River, NJ: Pearson.

Hiatt, J. (2006). *ADKAR: A model for change in business, government, and our community.* Loveland, CO: Prosci Learning Center Publications.

Hord, S. (2017). Learning together for leading together. In K. S. Louis, S. M. Hord, & V. Von Frank (Eds.), *Reach the highest standard in professional learning.* Thousand Oaks, CA: Corwin/Leaning Forward.

International Society for Technology in Education. (2017a). ISTE Standards for Educators. iste.org/standards/for-educators

International Society for Technology in Education. (2017b). ISTE Essential Conditions. iste.org/standards/essential-conditions

International Society for Technology in Education. (2018). ISTE Standards for Education Leaders. iste.org/standards/for-education-leaders

Kolb, L., Kashef, F., Roberts, C., Terry, C., & Borthwick, A. (2018). *Challenges to creating and sustaining effective technology integration in teacher education programs.* bit.ly/2LJ6kdL

Leithwood, K., Harris, A., & Hopkins, D. (2008). Seven strong claims about successful school leadership. *School Leadership and Management, 28*(1), 27–42.

Leithwood, K., & Jantzi, D. (2008). Linking leadership to student learning: The contributions of leader efficacy. *Educational Administration Quarterly, 44*(4), 496–528.

Mishra, P. (2019). Considering contextual knowledge: The TPACK diagram gets an upgrade. *Journal of Digital Learning in Teacher Education, 35*(2). doi.org/10.1080/21532974.2019.1588611

Mishra, P., & Koehler, M. J. (2006). Technological pedagogical content knowledge: A framework for integrating technology in teacher knowledge. *Teachers College Record, 108*(6), 1017–1054.

National Council for the Social Studies. (2010). *National curriculum standards for social studies: A framework for teaching, learning, and assessment.* Silver Spring, MD. socialstudies.org/standards

National Council of Teachers of Mathematics. (2015, July). *Strategic use of technology in teaching and learning mathematics.* bit.ly/2UrTTrJ

National Research Council. (2013). *Next Generation Science Standards: For states, by states.* doi.org/10.17226/18290

Office of Educational Technology. (2016). *Advancing educational technology in teacher preparation: Policy brief.* tech.ed.gov/teacherprep

Porras-Hernandez, L. H., & Salinas-Amescua, B. (2013). Strengthening TPACK: A broader notion of context and the use of teacher's narratives to reveal knowledge construction. *Journal of Educational Computing Research, 48,* 223–244. doi.org/10.2190/ec.48.2.f

Rogers, E. M. (2003). *Diffusion of innovations.* New York, NY: Free Press.

Rosenberg, J. M., & Koehler, M. J. (2015). Context and technological pedagogical content knowledge (TPACK): A systematic review. *Journal of Research on Technology in Education, 47*(3), 186–210.

Swallow, J. C., & Olofson, M. W. (2017). Contextual understandings in the TPACK framework. *Journal of Research on Technology in Education, 49*(3–4), 228–244. doi.org/10.1080/15391523.2017.1347537

Thomas, T., Herring, M., Redmond, P., & Smaldino, S. (2013). Innovation, change, and technology: The evolution of a leadership module to develop TPACK ready teacher candidates. *TechTrends, 57*(5), 55–63.

CHAPTER 10

Evaluating Technology Infusion: Teacher Candidate and Program Outcomes

RAY R. BUSS
ARIZONA STATE UNIVERSITY

Overview

This chapter provides information for teacher educators and college/school of education leaders on two ways to assess the effectiveness of technology infusion. First, assessing teacher candidates' technology integration abilities is the primary focus of the chapter. The chapter describes four theoretical perspectives that have influenced assessment efforts related to technology integration: the Technological Pedagogical Content Knowledge (TPACK) framework, the self-efficacy perspective, the Theory of Planned Behavior, and the Decomposed Theory of Planned Behavior. Secondarily, and when applicable, complementary assessment work in which teacher candidates evaluate effectiveness of their technology-infused program is discussed. Authors of previous chapters have appropriately focused on *technology infusion* as a means to develop teacher candidates' abilities to teach with technology. By comparison, this chapter focuses on evaluating the ultimate outcome of technology infusion, the development of teacher candidates' *technology integration* abilities, defined as their capabilities to teach K–12 students using technology.

Scenario

For the moment, assume you are able to "sit in" on an elementary education department meeting where faculty members are discussing the benefits and costs of infusing technology throughout the elementary education teacher preparation program. The discussion has been going on for some time, and now it has turned to the matter of assessing outcomes with respect to infusing technology throughout the program to foster teacher candidates' technology integration.

Abigail comments: "So let's say we move forward with technology infusion to prepare teacher candidates to integrate technology into their instruction. How will we know whether it had any benefits? In other words, how will we assess its effectiveness?"

Benjamin responds: "That's a really good point. I've heard a lot about technology infusion, and the idea makes sense to me, but I have to admit I haven't seen much evidence about its benefits. Also, how could we use related assessment data to improve courses, the program, and provide targeted professional development to our instructors?"

Christa notes: "I spent a little time examining assessment of technology integration, and there are several approaches that have been employed. The first is TPACK, the model we thought about using to guide our technology infusion and instructional approaches as we prepare teacher candidates to use technology in their teaching. Others have assessed self-efficacy for technology integration, attitudes toward technology integration, and so on."

Turning to Christa, Daniel asks: "Have you seen any assessments of technology integration that included portfolios, course-embedded assessments, or micro-credentials like 'badging' as part of their assessments?"

Before Christa can respond, Abigail interjects: "In my own reading of the literature, I recall something called the Decomposed Theory of Planned Behavior. Does anyone else recall seeing that? And what about interviews? Is there any work on using interviews to assess technology integration by teacher candidates?"

The conversation moves on to other issues, but you are immersed in your own thoughts about the whole issue of assessment of the effectiveness of technology infusion and its influences on technology integration and efficacy of program delivery in your college/school of education. You have heard about some of these assessment processes, but others that were mentioned are very new to you, and you are interested in learning a bit more. Read on. In this chapter, I focus on various technology integration appraisal procedures appropriate for instructors and program leaders as you determine the effectiveness with which teacher candidates in your teacher preparation programs can integrate technology.

Consistent with the definition provided earlier in this book, *technology infusion* means incorporating technology throughout courses in teacher preparation programs so that it is "program-deep and program-wide" to support teacher candidates' learning to use technology in seamless ways as appropriate in their instruction to foster student learning. Thus, technology infusion is the means to an end. The end is *technology integration*, actions taken by teacher candidates to include appropriate technology in their instructional activities with students to foster deep understanding of the content. Moreover, in this chapter, assessment of technology integration is defined broadly to include such things as teacher candidates' (a) perceptions of their abilities to integrate technology, including technology skills and self-efficacy, and (b) intention to integrate technology in their future classrooms. Additionally, it includes teacher candidates' (c) descriptions of how they would use technology in their lesson plans and instruction, and (d) discussion of how they have asked K–12 students to use technology during instruction and learning. Finally, many of the efforts to assess technology integration have been based on employing "proxy" measures, which have served as "stand-in" measures because more direct measures of technology integration were not accessible. For example, using teacher candidates' intentions to integrate technology at the end of a teacher preparation program serves as a proxy measure rather than collecting actual instances of technology integration, which could be done only after they began their work in K–12 classrooms. Thus, teacher education programs have used a more cost-effective and easier way to obtain proxy measures of intention rather than obtaining actual technology integration data (e.g., through observations and review of lesson plans).

Theoretical Frameworks Related to Assessment of Technology Integration

Before discussing assessment procedures, it will be instructive to consider several theoretical frameworks that are useful with respect to instruction *and* assessment of technology infusion efforts within preparation programs. In this section, I have offered information about three theoretical perspectives. First, I consider the Technological Pedagogical Content Knowledge (TPACK) framework (Koehler & Mishra, 2008; Mishra & Koehler, 2006), which has had an extraordinary influence on technology infusion efforts as evidenced in the literature. Second, I offer a brief discussion about self-efficacy and attitudes and their influences on teacher candidates' technology integration. Third, I briefly describe Ajzen's Theory of Planned Behavior (TPB) and its role in assessing teacher candidates' intention to integrate technology, followed by a discussion of the Decomposed Theory of Planned Behavior (DTPB), an adaptation of Ajzen's TPB that is more closely focused on technology matters.

TPACK

As noted in the scenario, Christa expressed the important dual role TPACK has played in the technology integration literature. The TPACK framework is critical for two reasons. First, TPACK serves as an organizing structure for teaching teacher candidates to integrate technology. Second, TPACK serves as one means to assess teacher candidates' abilities to integrate technology, which is discussed later in this chapter.

Before contemplating TPACK as an organizing structure for technology infusion, let us quickly consider the TPACK framework. Briefly, Mishra and Koehler (2006; Koehler & Mishra, 2008) suggest TPACK is a framework that aids understanding of technology integration. Specifically, they argue that to teach effectively with technology, teachers must have strong content knowledge (CK), pedagogical knowledge (PK), and technological knowledge (TK). Moreover, teachers must learn to blend knowledge of these domains, leading to pedagogical content knowledge (PCK), technological content knowledge (TCK), and technological pedagogical knowledge (TPK). Finally, teachers who learn to weave these together seamlessly develop technological pedagogical content knowledge (TPACK). See Figure 10.1 for an illustration of the TPACK framework. Chapter 1 of this book provides a more comprehensive discussion of the TPACK framework.

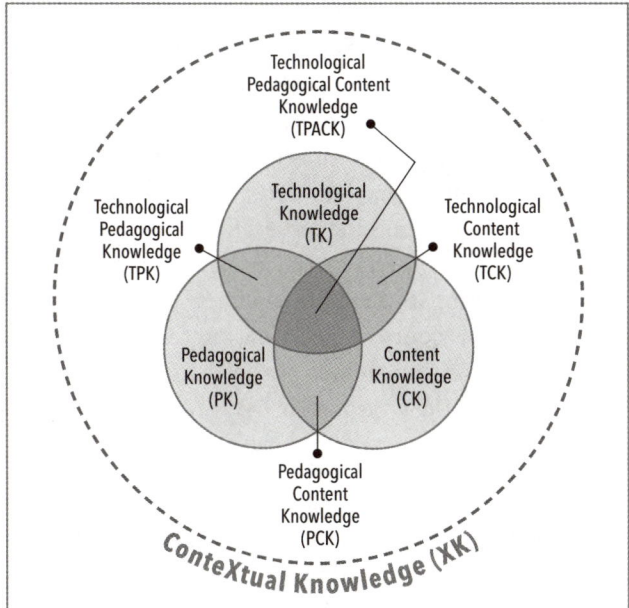

Figure 10.1   The TPACK model demonstrates the weaving together of content knowledge, pedagogical knowledge and technical knowledge, in teaching with technology. Revised version of the TPACK image. © Punya Mishra, 2018. Reproduced with permission.

Technology infusion is intended to be a program-deep and program-wide effort. At Arizona State University, my colleagues and I initiated a technology infusion approach in methods courses for two reasons. First, methods courses can deal with implications about TPACK content knowledge and pedagogical expertise, two prominent areas of the TPACK framework, while teacher candidates focus on developing their technology skills and technology integration abilities. We knew we needed to support the development of technology skills among instructors, so we offered a variety of carefully crafted professional development opportunities and supports (Buss, Foulger, Wetzel, & Lindsey, 2018; Buss, Wetzel, Foulger, & Lindsey, 2015; Foulger, Buss, Wetzel, & Lindsey, 2015; Wetzel, Buss, Foulger, & Lindsey, 2014). By incorporating technology into their methods courses, instructors modeled for our teacher candidates how they might use technology during instruction of science, language arts, mathematics, reading, social studies, and other content areas. As well, they helped teacher candidates learn how to teach with technology within their specific content.

Second, addressing technology integration in methods courses using TPACK as the framework served as an organizing tool by which teacher candidates could understand the merging of subject-matter content, pedagogy related to the content, and technology as an instructional tool *of that content*. Indeed, results from several studies confirmed teacher candidates used the framework to connect content knowledge (CK), pedagogical knowledge (PK), and technological knowledge (TK) and formed more complex understandings that helped them become more effective in integrating technology (Buss et al., 2015, 2018). Thus, TPACK served as a framework that guided instructors' and teacher candidates' developing understanding of how to integrate technology into instruction. During methods course instruction, our faculty members modeled the blending of technology with teaching methods to deliver content upon which teacher candidates built as they began their work with K–12 students.

Self-Efficacy and Attitudes

In other work on technology integration, researchers have found self-efficacy and attitudes were related to intentions to use technology (Abbitt, 2011; Teo & van Schaik, 2012; Tondeur, Scherer, Siddiq, & Baran, 2017). Bandura (1997, p. 3) defined self-efficacy as "beliefs in one's capabilities to organize and execute the courses of action required to produce given attainments." Self-efficacy, as typically used in this research, was the level of competency teacher candidates *expected* to attain when teaching with technology. Several researchers have found self-efficacy affected teacher candidates' intention to integrate technology (Abbitt, 2011; Teo & van Schaik, 2012; Wang, Ertmer, & Newby, 2004). In a study of preservice teachers, Wang et al. (2004) found teacher candidates who observed instructors' use of technology and teacher candidates who participated in goal setting with respect to technology integration were more likely to make positive judgments about self-efficacy related to technology integration.

With respect to attitudes, Teo (Teo, 2009; Teo & van Schaik, 2012) explored how attitude served as a mediating variable that influenced technology integration. Using the Technology Acceptance Model (TAM; Davis, Bagozzi, & Warshaw, 1989), one of the first models of technology acceptance that included psychological variables, Teo and Davis et al. found perceived usefulness of technology and perceived ease of use of technology influenced attitude toward technology use; these perceptions in turn affected intention to use technology. Proponents of the Theory of Planned Behavior (TPB) have employed a more comprehensive approach to examining how attitudes and other variables influence intention to integrate technology, which is described in the next section.

Theory of Planned Behavior and Decomposed Theory of Planned Behavior

The Theory of Planned Behavior (TPB; Ajzen, n.d.) provides a useful theoretical framework because it is a comprehensive approach to examining important factors that influence intentions to engage in a behavior. The rationale for using the TPB for technology infusion efforts is that teacher preparation programs can readily assess teacher candidates' intentions to integrate technology, but rarely can they measure subsequent performance of inservice teachers' (former teacher candidates') actual teaching using technology. Thus, the TPB has served as a proxy measure of technology integration by assessing intended technology integration—that is, *prospective use* of technology during future instruction. Moreover, the TPB is a more comprehensive model than other models because it includes examination of various kinds of beliefs, attitudes, others' influence through norms, perceived control or self-efficacy, and their influences on technology integration.

In the TPB, behavioral beliefs about the benefits of K–12 students' learning by using technology influence attitudes about technology integration. In turn, attitudes, the extent to which technology integration is valued, influence the intention to engage in technology integration. To understand the TPB, consider the following oversimplified example of a teacher candidate, Elizabeth, a hypothetical student in a teacher preparation program. Elizabeth thought, "Students will learn more if I teach with technology" (behavioral belief), which influenced her thought about herself, "I am positively disposed toward technology integration" (attitude), which increased her resolve to use technology, "I will use technology in my teaching" (intention).

Similarly, normative beliefs about perceived expectations of important reference groups such as other teachers or parents influence the subjective norms held by individuals about technology integration, which, in turn, influence intentions to integrate technology. Finally, control beliefs—opinions about factors that enable or hinder technology integration such as teacher candidates' own ability to use technology, access to technology, support and time, and so on—influence perceived behavioral control, "people's perceptions of their ability to perform a given behavior" (Ajzen, n.d., paragraph on Perceived Behavioral Control) and, subsequently, intention to integrate technology. Taken together, the TPB framework has been shown to be very useful in understanding how behavioral beliefs, attitudes, normative beliefs, subjective norms, behavioral control beliefs, and perceived behavioral control all have influenced intentions to engage in a behavior (in our case, technology integration).

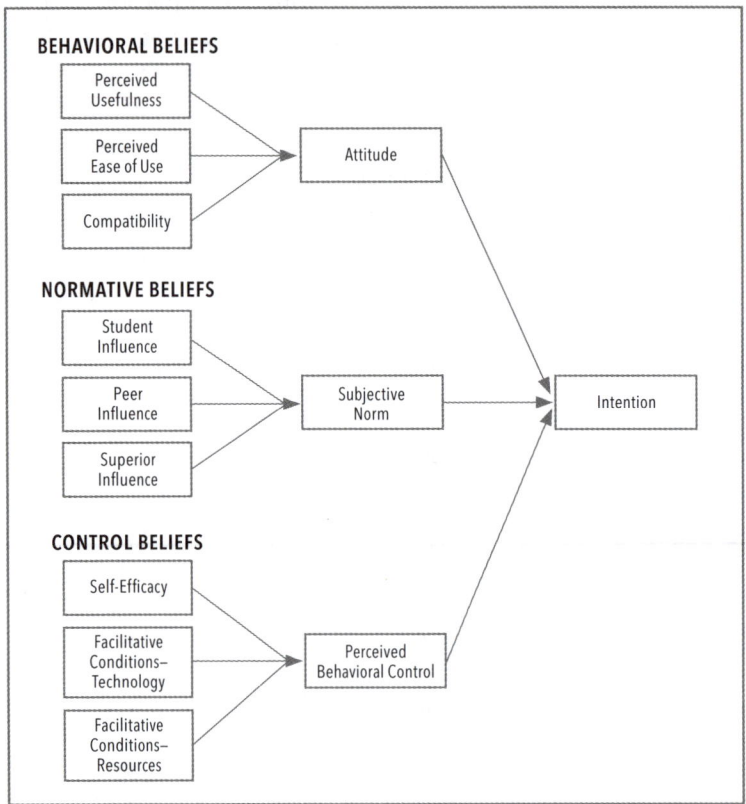

Figure 10.2 Decomposed Theory of Planned Behavior. Adapted from Sadaf, Newby, & Ertmer (2012, 2016).

Others conducting research on technology integration or more generally on the use of technology have revised the TPB, developing what they have called the Decomposed Theory of Planned Behavior (DTPB; Atsoglou & Jimoyiannis, 2012; Sadaf, Newby, & Ertmer, 2012, 2016; Taylor & Todd, 1995). In Figure 10.2, I have provided an illustration of the DTPB. In these decomposed or deconstructed frameworks of the TPB, researchers have parsed the behavioral beliefs, normative beliefs, and control beliefs into smaller, more particular constructs that are closely aligned with specific beliefs related to technology integration or using technology. For example, Sadaf et al. (2012, 2016) decomposed behavioral beliefs into perceived usefulness, perceived ease of use, and compatibility, which relate to the users' values and needs. Thus, behavioral beliefs are divided into finer grained factors influencing those beliefs.

Similarly, Sadaf et al. partitioned normative beliefs into student, superior, and peer influences. Finally, Sadaf et al. divided control beliefs into self-efficacy, facilitative conditions—technology (e.g., computers, software), and facilitative conditions—resources (e.g., time, support, etc.) as compared to the more general control beliefs that are assessed in the TPB. The decomposition approach used by Sadaf et al. (2012, 2016) was consistent with the work of other researchers who also examined intention to use technology with the DTPB (Atsoglou & Jimoyiannis, 2012; Taylor & Todd, 1995).

Assessing Technology Integration in Teacher Preparation Programs

For a moment, recall the scenario where faculty members discussed their concerns about assessing the effectiveness of technology infusion. They suggested several different methods. In this section, I describe various approaches to assess technology integration in teacher preparation programs, including assessment of TPACK, self-efficacy, and intention using the Theory of Planned Behavior or Decomposed Theory of Planned Behavior, plus use of portfolios, micro-credentials, and interviews. These methods have been used to evaluate teacher candidates' technology integration abilities and to gauge course and program effectiveness with respect to preparing teacher candidates to integrate technology.

Assessing Technology Integration Using TPACK

Assessing TPACK or some other set of variables that measures technology skills is foundational to the assessment of teacher candidates' technology integration abilities. In fact, careful consideration of the matter suggests such indices of skill development will be critical to determine the effectiveness of the instruction being provided to teacher candidates. Thus, a first step in measuring teacher candidates' abilities and skills related to technology integration is assessing the TPACK knowledge domains. Although there are many instruments in the literature that are used to measure a teacher's TPACK, Schmidt, Baran, Thompson, Mishra, Koehler, and

 Shin (2009) developed an instrument that accesses all seven of the TPACK domains: CK, PK, TK, PCK, TCK, TPK, and TPACK. The TPACK instrument is available at bit.ly/2Ju2qUB or by scanning the QR code.

The Schmidt et al. TPACK instrument includes fifty-seven Likert-type items that assess each of the TPACK domains separately. In addition, some demographic variables are gathered, and open-ended items are included, which are optional. This particular TPACK instrument is noteworthy because it has demonstrated sound reliabilities for the various TPACK domains, ranging from .78 to .93 (Schmidt et al., 2009). As currently constructed, the TPACK instrument is appropriate for use with teacher candidates who will be teaching in PK–8 settings, including those in early childhood, elementary, and special education programs. Recent studies suggest thoughtful consideration should be given to assessment of TPACK domains when evaluating teacher candidates' technology integration because some domains appear to be more relevant.

A brief caveat about using TPACK to assess technology integration is warranted. We should not confuse assessing TPACK, which includes foundational aspects for technology integration, with assessing actual technology integration. Thus, TPACK serves as a proxy, a stand-in measure, which assesses teacher candidates' perceptions about their technology integration skills. Therefore, TPACK domain knowledge should be regarded as a necessary but not sufficient indicator of technology integration. TPACK assessments should be used in combination with other assessments, triangulating data to more comprehensively assess teacher candidates' abilities to integrate technology. When colleges/schools of education are first implementing a technology infusion approach, it will be critical to measure TPACK domain knowledge as part of the assessment process to ensure technology infusion efforts are providing the necessary foundation to develop teacher candidates' technology integration abilities and skills (see, for example, Buss et al., 2018). In fact, when conducting assessments during the first several years of program implementation, the TPACK instrument may be appropriate as the primary instrument to be used along with interviews, for example, which may be crafted in a way to delve more deeply into teacher candidates' responses on the TPACK instrument, as well as assessing other aspects of technology infusion. In our work on technology infusion at ASU, we have used the TPACK instrument in combination with interviews to assess teacher candidates' technology integration (Buss et al., 2015, 2018). Quantitative results showed teacher candidates increased their TPACK domain scores and qualitative data were useful in further understanding the TPACK scores and adjusting/modifying the technology infusion program to be more effective.

Assessing Self-Efficacy for Technology Integration

As mentioned earlier in the chapter, Wang et al. (2004) examined self-efficacy for technology integration among teacher candidates. Results from that study showed the final, sixteen-item scale assessed students' self-efficacy related to their "abilities to use technology in strategic ways" (Wang et al., 2004, p. 235). Examples of the items include "I feel confident I have the skills necessary to use the computer for instruction," "I feel confident that I can successfully teach relevant content with appropriate use of technology," and "I feel confident I can mentor students in appropriate use of technology." When assessing technology integration, consideration should be given to measuring self-efficacy.

Assessing Intention to Integrate Technology Using TPB and DTPB

In the scenario at the beginning of the chapter, Abigail spoke about the Decomposed Theory of Planned Behavior (DTPB) and its use in assessing technology integration. Numerous studies have been conducted using the Theory of Planned Behavior (TPB) and DTPB to assess teacher candidates' intentions to integrate technology (Sadaf et al., 2012, 2016; Teo & van Schaik, 2012). The benefits of using the TPB include assessing various factors that influence intentions to integrate technology. As noted in the discussion above, those factors include beliefs, attitudes, normative influences, and perceived behavioral control, which are more comprehensive in scope and go beyond the knowledge-based assessment of TPACK.

Ajzen (n.d.) cautions that those using the TPB approach would be well advised to determine teacher candidates' responses within the local contextual setting. For example, a preliminary study is warranted to determine the types of responses that might come from your own teacher candidates prior to developing a TPB instrument tailored to assess your candidates' intentions to integrate technology. Thus, in creating the instrument, Ajzen suggests eliciting important beliefs, normative referents, and control factors from the group for whom you are designing the TPB instrument. In our efforts at ASU, my colleagues and I have undertaken this approach with our teacher candidates to develop a TPB survey to assess factors related to technology integration (Foulger, Buss, Su, Donner, & Wetzel, 2019). For example, with respect to normative beliefs and their influence, results showed our teacher candidates' believed principals, teacher colleagues, parents, *and* students would all expect them to integrate technology into their instruction. Thus, we created items that included students. For example, one item was, "When I become a teacher, my students will expect me to integrate technology into my instruction."

Sadaf et al. (2012, 2016) used the DTPB to assess teacher candidates' likelihood they would integrate technology using Web 2.0 tools. As noted in Figure 10.2, researchers using the DTPB approach divide behavioral, normative, and control beliefs of the TPB into finer grained components, many of which are focused on technology use, per se, rather than being more general as in the TPB. Sadaf et al. provided the items they used, which serve as a good beginning point for those interested in using the DTPB to assess technology integration. Nevertheless, some adaptation will be required for assessing technology infusion because their focus was solely on use of Web 2.0 technologies, not the broad defining factors of technology integration. Moreover, some of the constructs were assessed using only one item, which is inadequate based on test theory. Thus, some additional item construction would be required to apply the Sadaf assessment to a technology infusion program.

One final comment is warranted with respect to the use of TPB and DTPB for assessing teacher candidates' intentions to integrate technology. Assessing intention serves as a strong, readily obtainable proxy measure, a stand-in assessment of technology integration for teacher preparation programs. Moreover, given the goal of teacher preparation programs with respect to providing support to their teacher candidates' use of technology during instruction, use of the TPB or DTPB will provide a strong approach for developing an assessment of the effectiveness of that preparation.

Assessing Technology Integration Using Portfolios and Course-Embedded Assessments

Portfolio-based measures of teacher candidates' technology integration abilities capitalize on the use of artifacts or assignments, which are a natural part of course-work. Portfolios provide a means to assess the growth of technology integration over time and afford educators the opportunity to examine actual implementation of technology integration more closely. For example, teacher candidates can develop electronic portfolios that might include (a) lesson plans of technology integration and how those lesson plans are aligned with the International Society for Technology in Education (ISTE) Standards for Students and Educators or other content standards that promote technology. They could also include (b) videos of actual technology integration experiences they facilitate or help to facilitate in classrooms, (c) audio or written reflections on technology integration, and even (d) products of PK–12 students resulting from technology integration experiences the teacher candidate facilitated. Further, selected artifacts from portfolios could be used to assess the effectiveness of technology infusion instruction within courses. Additionally, teacher candidates might use portfolios to demonstrate their technology integration knowledge, skills, and dispositions to future employers. Teacher candidates can also use portfolios as a means to set goals and monitor and assess their growth with respect to technology integration.

Wetzel and Strudler (2006; Strudler & Wetzel, 2008, 2012) have thoughtfully discussed the costs and benefits of using electronic portfolios from the perspectives of students and faculty members, as well as employing portfolios for assessment and accreditation purposes. Various sites are available to teacher candidates, which they can use to create their portfolios, as well as garner suggestions about what to include in the portfolio such as ISTE Standards and other standards (Kappa Delta Pi, n.d.; Levin, 1996; Shaltry, Henriksen, Wu, & Dickson, 2013). The strength of course-embedded assessments such as portfolios is that these artifacts are already being completed by teacher candidates, so no additional resources are required to conduct this kind of assessment process. Nevertheless, use of this technique can make the technology integration assessment process a piecemeal evaluation procedure unless coordination occurs across the entire program. Thus, making assessment "program-deep and program-wide" to be consistent with technology infusion efforts would be essential. In particular, assessment of teacher candidates' technology integration abilities and program appraisal must be conducted frequently, not merely at the beginning and end of the program for a teacher candidate.

Assessing Technology Integration Using Micro-Credentialing with Badges

Recently, as noted in the scenario, micro-credentialing has become a means by which individuals demonstrate knowledge, skills, or competencies and then receive recognition for their attainments by earning a "badge." Micro-credentialing has its roots in the business and technology industry, but recently it has been employed in teacher preparation settings. For example, Randall, Harrison, and West (2013) implemented a micro-credentialing procedure in a secondary education program. Students received lower-level (tech activities) badges and project-level badges, which culminated in a course-level badge. Moving beyond the course level, students earned strategy, applied-level, and a top-level badge for technology integration. The authors suggested that badges are highly motivating to students because they earn badges as they go, rather than being rewarded at the end of the semester or program. Badges also provide teacher candidates and program faculty members with a way to monitor candidates' development of technology integration abilities.

Further, electronic badges are inexpensive. Nevertheless, a college/school that chooses to use micro-credentialing must carefully consider creating or revising and delivery of instruction, development of assessments. As well, they must account for the time involved for teacher candidates to earn a badge and for teacher educators to evaluate their work (Randall et al., 2013). Moreover, teacher educators and educational leaders considering the use of micro-credentialing should consider how competency-based aspects of such a process might shape or affect the curriculum. Finally, using badges that are connected to metadata—information about the actions required to earn a badge—warrants consideration because it provides detailed information about the micro-credentialing process including what teacher candidates learned. Another excellent source on badges is a book by Ifenthaler, Bellin-Mularski, and Mah (2016).

Assessing Technology Integration Using Interviews

As mentioned by Abigail in the scenario, interviews can be used to assess teacher candidates' technology integration. In our work on the effectiveness of technology infusion at Arizona State University, we use focus group interviews to gather qualitative data, which allows us to make better interpretations of the quantitative data we obtain using the TPACK instrument (Schmidt et al., 2009) and to inform our work in other ways (Buss et al., 2015, 2018). For example, during the interviews, teacher candidates (a) describe aspects of their lesson plans related to technology integration, (b) discuss how they integrated technology in their practicum or student teaching classrooms, and (c) review strengths and needs for revision of technology-infused coursework. The information gathered from students' interviews has informed course-level revisions to instructional strategies and assignments, established better connections to field experiences, and provided grounds for professional development for teacher educators to teach technology-infused courses. Examples of the questions we have used include the following:

1. What technology integration procedures have you seen modeled in your education courses and student teaching? What technologies? What activities?

2. Provide an example of how you would teach an elementary/middle school lesson with student use of technology. What would the students learn? Why would this approach be better than an approach without technology?

3. What factors account for your level of preparation in being able to integrate technology into your instruction? (Buss et al., 2018, pp. 149–150)

Conclusion: A Multistage Strategy for Assessing Technology Infusion Effectiveness

As you consider assessment of your technology infusion efforts, you may want to consider when to initiate your assessment processes. Should you assess your efforts immediately? Alternatively, should you wait for a few iterations before assessing? You will also want to consider using an action research approach, which because of its cyclical nature, adaptability to your context, and affordances with respect to reflection and implementation of modifications will allow you to improve your technology infusion efforts, provide feedback to various stakeholders, and increase teacher candidates' technology integration abilities.

When you implement assessment of technology infusion in your teacher preparation programs, you may want to begin with assessing teacher candidates' technology integration skills by using the TPACK assessment instrument or an adaptation of it (Schmidt et al., 2009; Tondeur et al., 2017). Using individual or focus group interviews along with the TPACK measures (Buss et al., 2015, 2018; Wetzel et al., 2014) will allow you to review your technology infusion efforts from teacher candidates' perspectives. Such an assessment approach is prudent because you will want to determine how effectively teacher candidates are acquiring knowledge of the various TPACK domains based on current program design. For example, are your technology infusion efforts affording effective teaching and learning of the TK, TPK, and TPACK components of your technology-infused approach? Moreover, early in the process, focus group interviews or individual interviews may provide for assessment of instructional effectiveness and offer information about additional professional development that may be warranted for instructional staff members delivering the technology-infused courses. Additionally, by using several assessment processes, you will be triangulating data to make increasingly sound assessments and decisions based on the data.

Later, after technology infusion has become more advanced and the instructional aspects of the technology infusion approach are on a solid footing, you may want to shift your efforts to using other approaches. For example, you might consider techniques such as micro-credentialing using badges that also serves as a motivating influence to teacher candidates or assessing teacher candidates' technology integration skills through portfolios, which move beyond self-report of technology integration abilities. Moreover, at the later stage, you may wish to assess teacher candidates' intentions to engage in technology integration by using Ajzen's (n.d.) Theory of Planned Behavior or the Decomposed Theory of Planned Behavior used by Sadaf et al. (2012, 2016) in combination with micro-credentialing or portfolio assessment.

Getting Started Resources

Ajzen, I. (n.d.). *Theory of Planned Behavior.*
people.umass.edu/aizen/tpb.diag.html

> At this website, Ajzen explains the Theory of Planned Behavior (TPB). Ajzen thoroughly describes the constructs and provides discussions of how various constructs are related and how they influence intention to perform a behavior. The diagram is interactive, and clicking on the various constructs provides details about the theory. Other components of this website offer, for example, additional information about the TPB, construction of a TPB measure, and research studies using the TPB.

Buss, R. R., Foulger, T. S., Wetzel, K. A., & Lindsey, L. (2018). Preparing teachers to integrate technology into K–12 instruction II: Examining the effects of technology-infused methods courses and student teaching. *Journal of Digital Learning in Teacher Education, 34*(3), 134–150.
doi.org/10.1080/21532974.2018.1437852

> The authors employed a mixed-methods approach to study the development of teacher candidates' technology integration skills. They used Schmidt et al.'s (2009) TPACK measure and focus group interviews to explore the growth of technology integration among teacher candidates over a two-year period. The focus group interviews were critical in explaining TPACK survey responses (quantitative data) and provided rich data related to the effectiveness of the technology infusion approach and professional development needed by instructors. An appendix includes the focus group questions.

Randall, D. L., Harrison, J. B., & West, R. E. (2013). Giving credit where credit is due: Designing open badges for a technology integration course. *TechTrends, 57*(6), 88–95.

The authors describe how they implemented a micro-credentialing process in their secondary education program. As the authors suggest, badges are highly motivating to students and low in cost (i.e., providing the electronic badges is inexpensive). Nevertheless, they note the costs to the college/school are in creating and delivering related instruction, devising the assessments, and accounting for the costs in "the time spent evaluating the work qualifying for a badge" (Randall et al., 2013, p. 90). Using badges that are connected to meta-data, information about the actions/skills/behaviors required of students to earn a badge, warrants consideration because it provides detailed information about the micro-credentialing process and what students learned.

Sadaf, A., Newby, T. J., & Ertmer, P. A. (2016). An investigation of the factors that influence preservice teachers' intentions and integration of Web 2.0 tools. *Educational Technology Research and Development, 64*, 37–64.

This article provides an example of the Decomposed Theory of Planned Behavior (DTPB). In it, the authors examine teacher candidates' intentions to use Web 2.0 technologies during their instruction. The authors provide items they used in assessing teacher candidates' beliefs, attitudes, norms, perceived behavioral control, and intention to use Web 2.0 technologies in the classroom; these items may be adapted for use in assessing factors influencing teacher candidates' intentions to integrate technology.

Tondeur, J., van Braak, J., Siddiq, F., & Scherer, R. (2016). Time for a new approach to prepare future teachers for educational technology use: Its meaning and measurement. *Computers & Education, 94*, 134–150.

The authors discuss the development and validation of a twenty-two-item survey instrument that "measure[s] pre-service teachers' perceptions of the extent to which they experience the support and training needed to integrate technology in their educational practice" (Tondeur et al., p. 148). The instrument assesses six strategies that may be used in teacher preparation programs, including (a) using role models, (b) affording reflection, (c) providing instructional design, (d) using authentic experiences, (e) collaborating with peers, and (f) providing feedback to teacher candidates.

References

Abbitt, J. T. (2011). An investigation of the relationship between self-efficacy beliefs and technology integration and technological pedagogical content knowledge (TPACK) among preservice teachers. *Journal of Digital Learning in Teacher Education, 27*(4), 134–143.

Ajzen, I. (n.d.). *Theory of Planned Behavior.* people.umass.edu/aizen/tpb.diag.html

Atsoglou, K., & Jimoyiannis, A. (2012). Teachers' decisions to use ICT in classroom practice: An investigation based on Decomposed Theory of Planned Behavior. *International Journal of Digital Literacy and Digital Competence, 3*(2), 20–37.

Bandura, A. (1997). *Self-efficacy: The exercise of control.* New York, NY: W. H. Freeman.

Buss, R. R., Foulger, T. S., Wetzel, K. A., & Lindsey, L. (2018). Preparing teachers to integrate technology into K–12 instruction II: Examining the effects of technology-infused methods courses and student teaching. *Journal of Digital Learning in Teacher Education, 34*(3), 134–150. doi.org/10.1080/21532974.2018.1437852

Buss, R. R., Wetzel, K., Foulger, T. S., & Lindsey, L. (2015). Preparing teachers to integrate technology into K–12 instruction: Comparing a stand-alone technology course with a technology-infused approach. *Journal of Digital Learning in Teacher Education, 31*(4), 160–172. doi.org/10.1080/21532974.2015.1055012

Davis, F. D., Bagozzi, R. P., & Warshaw, P. R. (1989). User acceptance of computer technology: A comparison of two theoretical models. *Management Science, 35,* 982–1003.

Drummond, A., & Sweeney, T. (2017). Can an objective measure of technological pedagogical content knowledge (TPACK) supplement existing TPACK measures? *British Journal of Educational Technology, 48*(4), 928–939. doi.org/10.1111/bjet.12473

Foulger, T. S., Buss, R. R., Su, M., Donner, J. L., & Wetzel, K. (2019). Predicting teacher candidates' future use of technology: Developing a survey using the theory of planned behavior. In K. Graziano (Ed.), *Proceedings of the Society for Information Technology and Teacher Education International Conference* (pp. 2177–2183). Chesapeake, VA: Association for the Advancement of Computing in Education (AACE). learntechlib.org/primary/p/207991

Foulger, T. S., Buss, R. R., Wetzel, K., & Lindsey, L. (2015). Instructors' growth in TPACK: Teaching technology-infused methods courses to preservice teachers. *Journal of Digital Learning in Teacher Education, 31*(4), 134–147. doi.org/10.1080/21532974.2015.1055010

Foulger, T. S., Wetzel, K., & Buss, R. R. (2019). Moving toward a technology infusion approach: Considerations for teacher preparation programs. *Journal of Digital Learning in Teacher Education.* doi.org/10.1080/21532974.2019.1568325

Ifenthaler, D., Bellin-Mularski, N., & Mah, D. (2016). *Foundations of digital badges and micro-credentials: Demonstrating and recognizing knowledge and competencies.* New York, NY: Springer.

Kappa Delta Pi. (n.d.) *Creating a portfolio.* kdp.org/resources/pdf/careercenter/Creating_a_Portfolio.pdf

Koehler, M., & Mishra, P. (2008). Introducing TPCK. In AACTE Committee on Innovation and Technology (Ed.), *The handbook of technological pedagogical content knowledge (TPCK) for educators* (pp. 3–29). New York, NY: American Association of Colleges of Teacher Education and Routledge.

Levin, B. B. (1996). Using portfolios to fulfill ISTE/NCATE technology requirements for preservice teacher candidates. *Journal of Computing in Teacher Education, 12*(3), 13–20.

Mishra, P., & Koehler, M. (2006). Technological pedagogical content knowledge: A framework for teacher knowledge. *Teacher College Record, 108*, 1017–1054.

Randall, D. L., Harrison, J. B., & West, R. E. (2013). Giving credit where credit is due: Designing open badges for a technology integration course. *TechTrends, 57*(6), 88–95.

Sadaf, A., Newby, T. J., & Ertmer, P. A. (2012). Exploring factors that predict preservice teachers' intentions to use Web 2.0 technologies using Decomposed Theory of Planned Behavior. *Journal of Research on Technology in Education, 45*(2), 171–195.

Sadaf, A., Newby, T. J., & Ertmer, P. A. (2016). An investigation of the factors that influence preservice teachers' intentions and integration of Web 2.0 tools. *Educational Technology Research and Development, 64,* 37–64.

Schmidt, D., Baran, E., Thompson, A., Mishra, P., Koehler, M. J., & Shin, T. (2009). Technological pedagogical content knowledge (TPACK): The development and validation of an assessment instrument for preservice teachers. *Journal of Research on Technology in Education, 42,* 123–149. doi.org/10.1080/15391523.2009.10782544

Shaltry, C., Henriksen, D., Wu, M. L., & Dickson, W. P. (2013). Situated learning with online portfolios, classroom websites, and Facebook. *TechTrends, 57*(3), 20–25.

Strudler, N., & Wetzel, K. (2008). Costs and benefits of electronic portfolios in teacher education: Faculty perspectives. *Journal of Computing in Teacher Education, 24*(4), 135–142.

Strudler, N., & Wetzel, K. (2012). Electronic portfolios in teacher education: Forging a middle ground. *Journal of Research on Technology in Education, 44*(2), 161–173.

Taylor, S., & Todd, P. A. (1995). Understanding technology usage: A test of competing models. *Information Systems Research, 6*(2), 144–176.

Teo, T. (2009). Modeling technology acceptance in education: A study of pre-service teachers. *Computers & Education, 52,* 302–312.

Teo, T., & van Schaik, P. (2012). Understanding the intention to use technology by preservice teachers: An empirical test of competing theoretical models. *International Journal of Human-Computer Interaction, 28,* 178–188.

Tondeur, J., Scherer, R., Siddiq, F., & Baran, E. (2017). A comprehensive investigation of TPACK within pre-service teachers' ICT profiles: Mind the gap! *Australasian Journal of Educational Technology, 33*(3), 46–58.

Tondeur, J., van Braak, J., Siddiq, F., & Scherer, R. (2016). Time for a new approach to prepare future teachers for educational technology use: Its meaning and measurement. *Computers & Education, 94,* 134–150.

Wang, L., Ertmer, P. A., & Newby, T. (2004). Increasing preservice teachers' self-efficacy beliefs for technology integration. *Journal of Research on Technology in Education, 36*(3), 231–250.

Wetzel, K., Buss, R. R., Foulger, T. S., & Lindsey, L. (2014). Infusing educational technology in teaching methods courses: Successes and dilemmas. *Journal of Digital Learning in Teacher Education, 30*(3), 89–103. doi.org/10.1080/21532974.2014.891877

Wetzel, K., & Strudler, N. (2006). Costs and benefits of electronic portfolios in teacher education: Student voices. *Journal of Computing in Teacher Education, 22*(3), 99–108.

SECTION IV

Advancing Technology Infusion

The chapter in this section shares a vision and action steps for nationwide collaboration for technology infusion in teacher preparation.

CHAPTER 11

What Can We Achieve Together? A Call to Action for the Future of Technology Infusion in Teacher Preparation Programs

JOSEPH B. SOUTH
CHIEF LEARNING OFFICER, ISTE

JI SOO SONG
SENIOR POLICY AND ADVOCACY ASSOCIATE, ISTE

Overview

In the past decade, an explosion of access to technology in American schools has contributed to a fundamental change in the teaching environment. More classrooms than ever are equipped with the connectivity and devices necessary to leverage digital teaching opportunities. Yet, teachers continue to report that they do not feel well prepared to integrate new technologies across student learning experiences. As highlighted throughout *Championing Technology Infusion in Teacher Preparation*, teacher preparation represents a critical juncture in tackling this issue. This concluding chapter highlights five key areas that stakeholders from the public, private, and nonprofit sectors can collaboratively engage to systemically and sustainably improve teacher preparation pipelines and ensure that all teachers are prepared to use technology effectively from day one: setting a vision, incentivizing mastery, building capacity, prioritizing funds, and leveraging accountability.

Educators Are Our Nation's Most Vital Strategic Resource

We may have no greater strategic resource than our educators to ensure the long-term prosperity of our nation. Outside of individual and family factors, they are the most influential factor in a child's academic achievement (RAND, 2012). In one landmark longitudinal study, researchers at Harvard University and Columbia University found that high-quality educators have a lasting impact on students even after they leave the PK–12 system. Students assigned to highly effective educators were more likely to attend college, earn higher incomes, and experience an overall better quality of life (Chetty, Friedman, & Rockoff, 2014).

However, our educators' teaching environments are rapidly changing to more align with larger changes in the workforce landscape that increasingly require advanced technological skills (Bughin et al., 2018). Various policies and programs in the US have fundamentally reconfigured and updated schools' and libraries' technology infrastructure, making significant steps in closing the "digital divide," defined in the US Department of Education's National Educational Technology Plan as the "gap between students who [have] access to the Internet and devices at school . . . and those who [do] not" (Office of Educational Technology, 2017, p. 7). For example, access to broadband jumped from under 30% of US classrooms to upward of 99% in the last six years. Forty-two million more students can now access the internet routinely at school (Marwell, 2019). Furthermore, according to the Consortium for School Networking (CoSN), the proportion of districts achieving a 1:1 student-to-device ratio increased from 23% in 2014 to 49% in 2018 (Maylahn, 2018). Thus, as noted in Chapter 3, increasing numbers of students have at their fingertips the power to access a wide variety of information in different formats.

Although these figures paint a hopeful picture for digital equity, mere access to technology does not necessarily guarantee increased learning for all students. Massive investments into devices and infrastructure set a reasonable expectation among community stakeholders and government agencies that the technology will be used for effective teaching, and failure to do so represents a colossal waste of public resources. Unfortunately, research continues to show that many educators do not feel well prepared to integrate technology across student learning experiences. As mentioned in the preface, according to an international survey on teachers' perceptions of their preparation programs, only 45% of American educators felt "well prepared" or "very well prepared" to use information and communications technology (ICT) for teaching (Organisation for Economic Co-operation and Development, 2019). Figures are even more dire when considering specific technology skills such as "data analytics, computer programming languages, website design/creation, and robotics," which only about 10% of educators are confident using in classrooms (Schuyler & Buckley, 2018, p. 2).

A major factor contributing to this phenomenon is that many teacher preparation programs do not have the capacity to adequately train teacher candidates. Researchers note that "[t]eacher educators … need to … effectively connect technology, pedagogy, and content in relation to specific teaching goals for specific goals of students," yet "studies indicate that many teacher educators are uncertain about their ability to use educational technology" (Uerz, Volman, & Kral, 2018, p. 19). For example, surveys of postsecondary faculty conducted by the Bill and Melinda Gates Foundation found that while most faculty are familiar with pedagogical approaches involving technology, they do not apply them in their own teaching (McGoldrick, Watts, & Economou, 2015).

In their literature review of teacher educators' technology competencies, Uerz et al. (2018) also emphasize the importance of training for teacher educators on technology integration, noting that "teacher educators need to be able to be innovative, collaborative, and researching professionals in order to enhance their own teaching with technology" (p. 20). However, in a national study of about 1,500 four-year institutions, 83% of respondents reported that their faculty's lack of training was a barrier to integrating technology within teacher preparation programs (Kleiner, Thomas, & Lewis, 2007). Another national survey of higher education faculty found that approximately half do not believe that their institution provides "good" or "excellent" professional development opportunities to integrate technology (Dahlstrom, 2015).

Furthermore, researchers note that a "majority of teacher education programs use a one-course model to prepare teachers to use technology," and such models, which require teacher candidates to simply pass a one-off class, "lack strong pedagogical knowledge on how to best integrate technology to support learning" (Kolb, Kashef, Roberts, Terry, & Borthwick, 2018, p. 2). This current structure of teacher preparation programs, coupled with the fact that educators who lack strong, comprehensive preparation in pedagogical methods are more likely at risk for attrition (Carver-Thomas & Darling-Hammond, 2017; Ingersoll, Merrill, & May, 2014), adds another layer or urgency.

The lack of adequate preparation is not effectively alleviated through professional development opportunities for inservice educators. Surveys have found that about half of inservice educators identified "lack of training" as one of the biggest barriers to incorporating technology into their teaching (Pressey, 2013). Another analysis conducted by the Education Week Research Center found that less than half of educators believe that their school or district provides training that supports classroom innovation with technology (Harold, 2019). Disadvantaged students are especially likely to have educators who lack access to necessary professional development opportunities. A Pew Research Center study found that 70% of educators in higher-income areas "say their school does a 'good job' providing … the resources and support they need to incorporate digital tools in the classroom," compared to just 50% of educators in lower-income areas (Purcell, Heaps, Buchanan, & Friedrich, 2013, p. 4).

Because of these shortcomings, the burden of responsibility currently falls on cash-strapped districts and schools to draw from their limited budgets to train incoming educators and to retrain inservice educators. This model is simply unsustainable. A new approach to solving this issue must involve multiple stakeholders from across sectors who collaborate to ensure that teachers arrive in the classroom fully prepared.

Systemically and Sustainably Infusing Technology into Teacher Preparation Programs

By improving how current teacher preparation programs support teacher candidates to teach with technology, we can accomplish three primary goals:

1. Reap the benefits of the devices and infrastructure investments that have been made to enhance student learning experiences.

2. Staff every classroom with an educator who has the knowledge, skills, and mindset to keep pace with the rapidly changing technology landscape.

3. Enable schools to reinvest funds otherwise spent on retraining teachers into other priority areas that directly support student learning.

As emphasized in Chapter 2, such a fundamental shift requires a deliberate, coordinated effort that involves forward-thinking leadership and develops organizational capacities across sectors. Teacher preparation programs represent the most obvious and essential agents of change. But to implement sustainable change at scale, those programs must have the support of various stakeholders, including the federal government, state and district leaders, and nongovernmental organizations (NGOs).

Each entity must be involved in accomplishing the following five key steps. Noteworthy examples of these steps already in action are also provided below. The efforts of the International Society for Technology in Education (ISTE) are highlighted as a model for the types of activities that NGOs can pursue to support technology infusion in teacher preparation. And because ISTE is presently making a concerted effort in this area, examples involving ISTE appear under several steps.

1. Establish Competencies Aligned to a Shared Vision

Stakeholders must agree on a set of independent standards that clearly establish the knowledge, skills, and mindsets all educators should master in order to use technology effectively in the classroom.

The federal government can articulate a national vision around what an effective teacher preparation program looks like. For example, the US Department of Education's "Advancing Educational Technology in Teacher Preparation" policy brief highlights examples of innovative teacher preparation programs from around the country. The brief additionally outlines four guiding principles that colleges/schools of education can use to improve current teacher preparation programs: focusing on the active use of technology, building professional development pathways for faculty, ensuring that teacher candidates' experiences with technology are program-deep and program-wide, and aligning efforts with research-based standards (Office of Educational Technology, 2016).

State leaders can adopt specific, evidence-based competencies around technology that educators must master prior to entering the classroom. The recent ISTE (2019a) analysis of state teaching standards show that many states are not currently calling for educators to be proficient in evidence-based uses of technology for learning. However, state policymakers can meet school districts' demand for teachers who know how to use technology effectively by incorporating this expectation in their educator licensure, advancement, and renewal requirements. As noted in Chapter 8, more rigorous licensure requirements can help educators find meaningful ways to infuse technology into student learning experiences, especially during teachers' first years in the classroom. For example, the Texas State Legislature requires all teacher candidates undergo "instruction in digital learning ... aligned with the International Society for Technology in Education's standards for teachers" (Tex. Education Code § 21.044, 2017).

NGOs, in consultation with educators, education leaders, educational technology experts, and researchers, can develop and continuously update an independent set of standards around educational technology. These standards should set the bar for the knowledge, skills, and mindsets PK–12 educators must master in order to use technology effectively in the classroom. For example, the ISTE Standards for Students, Educators, Education Leaders, and Coaches all provide a research-based pedagogical framework for how technology can be used as a tool to advance students' learning in a variety of content areas. As of this writing, seventeen US states have formally adopted, adapted, or endorsed the latest iteration of the ISTE Standards. All fifty states have used past iterations of the standards in an official capacity (ISTE, 2019e). The Getting Started resources in Chapter 6 identified several sets of standards and competencies that NGOs have developed to increase the quality of current teacher preparation programs. For instance, iNACOL (now the Aurora Institute) and the Learning Accelerator (learningaccelerator.org), both of which provide resources to support personalized, blended learning strategies in schools, collaborated in the development of the *Blended Learning Teacher Competency Framework* (Powell, Rabbitt, & Kennedy, 2014). The framework serves as a "starting point around which to observe emerging practice and organize teacher development and training resources" (p. 5).

NGOs and colleges/schools of education can also collaboratively lead the development and continuous updating of competencies required specifically of teacher preparation program faculty. As mentioned in Chapter 5, education researchers, with the advisement of various organizations—including the ISTE Teacher Education Network (TEN), Council for the Accreditation of Educator Programs (CAEP), the National Technology Leadership Coalition (NTLC), the Society for Information Technology and Teacher Education (SITE), and the American Association of Colleges for Teacher Education (AACTE)—developed the Teacher Educator Technology Competencies (TETCs). While these organizations did not provide specific input on the TETCs themselves, they met frequently with the researchers, informing the research methodology (Foulger, Graziano, Schmidt-Crawford, & Slykhuis, 2017). The TETCs outline the knowledge, skills, and mindsets that all teacher educators must possess to ensure that teacher candidates graduate from their programs well prepared to use technology effectively.

Finally, **NGOs** can guide policymakers in adopting those competencies. Many NGOs work at both the state and national levels to assist policymakers, as government entities—such as the state education agency, state board of education, or state legislature—seek to advance their educational technology goals.

2. Incentivize the Achievement of Mastery by Teacher Candidates

Stakeholders must design licensure, compensation, and professional advancement pathways to recognize and reward teacher candidates' mastery of essential educational technology competencies.

Colleges/schools of education can build incentive pathways for teacher candidates directly into their teacher preparation programs. As noted in Chapter 10, these incentives can take the form of badges or micro-credentials, which reward teacher candidates upon successful demonstration of certain competencies on assessments and thus provide a continuous, low-cost source of motivation throughout their completion of the program. Research has demonstrated that educators enjoy opportunities to earn micro-credentials and transfer their learning into teaching practices (ISTE, 2018b).

NGOs can develop programs that provide pathways for teacher candidates to achieve and showcase mastery of essential competencies. For example, the ISTE Certification for Educators is a competency-based, device-neutral program that unpacks the ISTE Standards for Educators. This blended learning, competency-based program offers educators an opportunity to reimagine the use of educational technology in meaningful and transformative ways. As of this writing, more than 1,900 educators are on their way to earning an ISTE Certification.

State and district leaders can leverage various policies to incentivize mastery of essential competencies. They can tie initial licensure requirements, license renewal requirements, hiring preferences, educator compensation, and career advancement pathways to the demonstration of those competencies. The Utah State Board of Education (2017) incentivizes educators to build their proficiency in the effective use of technology by providing a state endorsement tied to salary increases. The state permits educators to meet the requirements for this endorsement in a variety of ways. For example, educators may participate in the Leadership in Blended and Digital Learning program and the ISTE Certification for Educators program, both provided through the Utah Education Network (Norville, 2019). In Newport News Public Schools (2018) in Virginia, the district gives hiring preference to instructional technology coaches who hold an ISTE Certification.

3. Build Capacity for Technology Infusion in Colleges/Schools of Education

Program leaders and faculty at colleges/schools of education must develop their capacity to infuse educational technology into teacher preparation programs.

As highlighted in Chapter 1, a technology-infused program supports teacher candidates in a manner that is program-deep, with faculty who understand how technology can be comprehensively incorporated into a given course. A technology-infused approach is also program-wide, transitioning away from a single-course model to one that involves all parts of the system in the process of helping teacher candidates become proficient in teaching with technology.

Colleges/schools of education and NGOs can partner to benchmark current teacher preparation programs. As outlined in Chapter 1, the goal of such an assessment would be to identify successful components of the existing program that should be maintained, as well as critical areas for improvement. It is important to note that colleges/schools of education are not monoliths. Each faces a wide variety of contextual challenges that affect the extent to which it may infuse technology into teacher preparation programs. Thus, program leaders must collaborate with faculty to determine which challenges are most critical and how strategic partnerships may relieve those bottlenecks. Examples of such contextual challenges, identified by Kolb et al. (2018), include the following:

1. Is the teacher preparation program currently using research-based structures and practices to best facilitate growth among teacher candidates?

2. Are faculty provided with adequate formal training, time, and incentives to improve their practices? Are they impeded by competing demands (e.g., research priorities)?

3. Are program leaders taking equal ownership of technology infusion by instilling a culture of innovation among faculty, improving their own understanding of effective pedagogy, and allocating financial investments into necessary training?

4. Do the districts who hire teacher candidates upon graduation continuously inform the teacher preparation program? For instance, are teacher candidates provided adequate opportunities to interact with a range of tools in a manner that is applicable to the realities of the teaching profession? Does a program's use of technology relate to teacher candidates' grade level and discipline?

The ISTE Higher Education Recognition Program is one example of a benchmarking method, that evaluates whether a particular teacher preparation program demonstrates alignment to the ISTE Standards for Educators. Various master of educational technology programs, such as those at California State University, Fullerton; Johns Hopkins University; and the American College of Education have undergone this evaluation, earning their marks as ISTE-recognized higher education programs (ISTE, 2019c; Cook, 2019).

Colleges/schools of education and NGOs can also partner to directly develop the capacity of program leaders and faculty. Such efforts can be grounded in the ISTE Standards for Education Leaders, which provide a framework of "knowledge and behaviors required … to empower teachers" and focus on critical topics in digital teaching and learning—including "equity, digital citizenship, visioneering, team and systems building, continuous improvement and professional growth." The Connected Learner standard specifically calls on program leaders and faculty to "[d]evelop the skills needed to lead and navigate change, advance systems and promote a mindset of continuous improvement for how technology can improve learning" (ISTE, 2018a, p. 2).

For example, as shown in Chapter 1, the first step of this process may be for the colleges/schools of educations' educational technologists and faculty to codevelop assignments, which require teacher candidates to think deeply about how technology can enhance learning. However, the broader vision for colleges/schools of education should be for all faculty, regardless of their subject area, to master the knowledge and skills to model and deliver instruction that prepares teacher candidates to use technology effectively. Organizations such as ISTE and AACTE have the capacity to convene teacher candidates, inservice educators, and teacher preparation program faculty to spark this type of conversation—for example, through the organizations' annual conferences.

ISTE is also currently working with Fairfield University to ensure that faculty members are ISTE-certified. At the same time, Fairfield's school of education is working to become a Certification Authorized Provider (CAP), which would allow graduates of their teacher preparation program to earn an ISTE Certification for Educators.

Fairfield University's Ongoing Efforts to Redesign Its Teacher Preparation Program

In 2016, Fairfield University's Graduate School of Education in Connecticut brought on board Joshua Elliott as its director of educational technology. With Elliott at the helm, the school began reflecting on how to improve its teacher preparation program. Faculty sought to design a program where coursework completed by teacher candidates would be as relevant as possible to the work they would be doing as classroom educators. They also wanted to build a program where technology would not be framed as an "add-on," but rather infused across different courses.

This work was further propelled through conversations at the state level led by the Connecticut Commission for Educational Technology (CCET), assembled by the Connecticut General Assembly to "envision, coordinate, and oversee the management and successful integration of technology in schools, libraries, colleges and universities" (Connecticut State Department of Administrative Services, 2019). Doug Casey, executive director of CCET, had already begun championing the ISTE Standards with unanimous endorsement among his commission members. He also observed that stakeholders in Connecticut actively sought educators who use technology effectively. He conducted a survey of parents, teachers, local school board members, and other education stakeholders, finding that "90 percent of respondents indicat[ed] that the [ISTE] Standards address well the skills and competencies that students need for college and careers" (Casey, 2019, p. 13). Casey's review of local school board policies corroborated this demand. For example, Newington Public Schools endorsed "student use of [technology] for learning and research … distance learning activities, asking questions of and consulting experts, [and] communicating with other students and individuals" (Newington Public Schools Board of Education Policy § 6141.321, 2009).

As noted in Chapter 9, a favorable political environment can provide the momentum necessary to spur action among teacher preparation programs. As such, CCET developed a set of policy recommendations for local school boards, including those that address teacher preparation and professional development, that would encourage adoption of the ISTE Standards. These recommendations, as well as other ISTE resources, helped Casey persuade the Connecticut State Board of Education to formally adopt the ISTE Standards for Students in 2018.

Casey met with Elliott and other Fairfield University faculty, who agreed that the ISTE Standards provided a vision through which they could begin improving their teacher preparation program. Fairfield is now undergoing several changes, including the introduction and continuous improvement of two courses that will be foundational to the infusion process. For example, every teacher candidate takes the Introduction to Educational Technology course grounded in the ISTE Standards for Students and Educators (Elliott, 2019). Through this course, teacher candidates have an opportunity to build tools and resources based on evidence-based frameworks such as Triple E (Kolb, 2017) and SAMR (Puentedura, 2014), both discussed in Chapter 4. Teacher candidates can also take an Emerging Technologies course, which examines how innovative technologies, such as augmented and virtual reality, can be used to advance student learning (Fairfield University, 2019). Fairfield faculty are further exploring how the Graduate School of Education can incorporate technology into other coursework.

Fairfield University is working to become an ISTE-recognized higher education program and a CAP. This work is beginning with Fairfield building its own capacity first, as Elliott and adjunct faculty are going through the ISTE Certification process. Elliott believes that the rigorous certification process allows faculty to think deeply about the courses currently offered in Fairfield's teacher preparation program. He also believes that the certification process allows faculty members to reflect on their own practices as educators and evaluate whether those practices encourage innovation among teacher candidates or inhibit them.

District leaders and colleges/schools of education can form mutually beneficial partnerships to provide meaningful practicum opportunities for teacher candidates. As noted in Chapter 7, such experiences can allow for teacher candidates to apply theory to practice and experiment with innovative ideas. Inservice teachers at the district should be actively involved in designing the structure of the partnership, outlining what their roles would be, as well as providing feedback to continuously improve clinical experiences. These partnerships can be grounded in the Systems Designer standard of the ISTE Standards for Education Leaders, which call for program leaders and faculty to "build teams and systems to implement, sustain and continually improve the use of technology to support learning" (ISTE, 2018a, p. 2).

For example, Towson University is working with Baltimore County Public Schools (BCPS) to provide authentic learning experiences for teacher candidates, where they can examine what it means to use technology effectively. As part of their Universal Design for Learning course, teacher candidates are partnered with an inservice educator at BCPS. The teacher candidates observe the inservice educator's class and identify learning barriers that may be alleviated through technology. Teacher candidates then have the opportunity to present their findings to BCPS inservice teachers and Towson University faculty (Office of Educational Technology, 2016).

The University of Michigan uses a similar model in partnership with Ann Arbor Public Schools (AAPS). Prior to their student-teaching practicum, teacher candidates, under the guidance of University of Michigan faculty, have an opportunity to design digital citizenship mini-lessons. These lessons, which address topics ranging from productive communication in online spaces to digital identity and safety, are presented to small groups of AAPS middle schoolers. Through this partnership, teacher candidates can reflect on elements of the lesson that worked and did not work, all while getting on-the-ground teaching experience (Office of Educational Technology, 2016).

4. Prioritize Funding

Stakeholders must sustain the necessary changes by adequately allocating funds or advocating for funds that support improvements to teacher preparation programs.

The federal government can assist with providing funding that stakeholders require in order to improve current teacher preparation programs. For example, the Higher

Education Act (HEA), which governs postsecondary programs in the United States, provides federal funds specifically to support teacher preparation programs (Hegji, 2017). The US Congress is currently debating its reauthorization (ISTE, 2019d).

State leaders can also provide funding that stakeholders require to improve current teacher preparation programs. As emphasized in Chapter 9, these grant opportunities should not simply focus on funding the acquisition of technology tools. For example, states can provide categorical grants for colleges/schools of education to redesign programs or for districts to partner with colleges/schools of education to collaboratively design and provide authentic clinical experiences for teacher candidates. Furthermore, Title II-A of the Every Student Succeeds Act (ESSA), which governs PK–12 education in the US, provides federal funds to "support reform efforts with the entities that oversee preparation standards" (US Department of Education, 2016, p. 9). State leaders can prioritize the use of Title II-A funds to meet this end, so that teacher candidates exit teacher preparation programs with the necessary competencies.

NGOs and colleges/schools of education can organize stakeholders and advocate for sustained funding. Coordinated advocacy is required to ensure that federal and state policymakers continue to appropriate funds that support teacher preparation programs. Advocacy efforts must highlight stories of impact, identifying innovative teacher preparation programs that have benefited educators and students due to access to public funds. For example, ISTE collaborates with the Consortium for School Networking and the State Education Technology Directors Association to speak with members of the US Congress about the importance of fully funding ESSA Title II-A funds (ISTE, 2019b).

5. Leverage Accountability Appropriately

Stakeholders must hold each entity in the system accountable for ensuring that every educator is fully prepared to use technology effectively in the classroom.

The federal government and state leaders can work with accreditation agencies to ensure that teacher preparation programs are expected to adequately prepare teacher candidates in essential educational technology competencies. Furthermore, ESSA requires that the use of Title II-A grants be evidence-based (US Department of Education, 2016). States can closely monitor grant implementation so that recipients are indeed using federal funds to promote teacher preparation programs' use of evidence-based strategies.

We Owe It to Our Students

Students across the world are living in a time where the workforce landscape has shifted significantly and is continuing to change at an accelerating rate, particularly due to the advent of advanced technologies such as artificial intelligence, robotics, and automation (ISTE, 2019f). Researchers predict that by 2030, American workers will increase time spent using advanced technologies by 50% (Bughin et al., 2018). Furthermore, hiring managers increasingly seek new employees who can use technology to collaborate with colleagues, design creative solutions, and thoughtfully communicate (Hart Research Association, 2018). Unless we strengthen the teacher preparation pipeline so that all educators have the knowledge, skills, and mindsets to help PK–12 students use technology for effective learning, many students, particularly those from disadvantaged communities, will not have access to society's growing opportunities.

This book serves to spark a critical discussion between educators, education leaders, colleges/schools of education, NGOs, and policymakers about reimagining the processes by which we train our educators. From highlighting the need for systemic change that addresses the current disconnect between teacher preparation programs and classroom realities to providing actionable recommendations grounded in evidence-based frameworks and suggestions around cross-sector partnership opportunities, *Championing Technology Infusion in Teacher Preparation* is a guide for ensuring that teacher candidates are ready to use technology effectively from day one. The time is now for individuals and organizations involved in teacher preparation to join this effort, so that all PK–12 students, regardless of background, have equitable access to high-quality instruction, where technology is used as an essential tool to accelerate learning.

Getting Started Resources

International Society for Technology in Education. (2019).
Transforming the teacher educator experience.
iste.org/learn/teacher-education

This ISTE webpage provides various resources that faculty
may use to build their own capacities, including access to The
ISTE Teacher Education Network, as well as an instructor's guide to using
technology effectively.

ISTE Higher Education Recognition Program.
iste.org/learn/highered-recognition

The ISTE Higher Education Recognition Program provides a
method for teacher preparation programs to benchmark their
current program against the ISTE Standards for Educators and identify areas of
improvement.

ISTE Standards. **iste.org/standards**

The ISTE Standards for Students, Educators, Education
Leaders, and Coaches provide a research-based pedagogical
framework for how technology can be used as a tool to advance
students' learning in a variety of content areas. Stakeholders
can use the ISTE Standards to redefine the types of competencies sought from
teacher candidates as they relate to the effective use of technology.

Kolb, L. (2017). *Learning first, technology second: The educator's
guide to designing authentic lessons.* Arlington, VA:
International Society for Technology in Education.
iste.org/learningfirst

Designed for educators, this book emphasizes that learning
with technology does not happen just because of a particular tool. The author
provides effective classroom strategies that leverage technology to create
authentic learning experiences for students, as well as supplemental case
studies and lesson planning templates.

Norville, V. (2019). *Utah banks on statewide approach to adopting educational technology.* Washington, DC: National Association of State Boards of Education. bit.ly/2WZfUjv

This case study details how Utah's leaders developed the Digital Teaching and Learning grant program and worked with the Utah Education Network to make the ISTE Certification for Educators program available to their educators. Policymakers can use this case study as a model for how educators' mastery of key educational technology competencies may be incentivized.

References

Bughin, J., Hazan, E., Lund, S., Dahlström, P., Wiesinger, A., & Subramaniam, A. (2018). *Skill shift: Automation and the future of the workforce.* New York, NY: McKinsey Global Institute. mck.co/2VWmJQo

Carver-Thomas, D., & Darling-Hammond, L. (2017). *Teacher turnover: Why it matters and what we can do about it.* Washington, DC: Learning Policy Institute. bit.ly/2SccZQW

Casey, D. (2019). *Annual report of the Connecticut Commission for Educational Technology.* Hartford, CT: Connecticut Commission for Educational Technology. bit.ly/3aIUJVK

Chetty, R., Friedman, J. N., & Rockoff, J. E. (2014). Measuring the impacts of teachers II: Teacher value-added and student outcomes in adulthood. *American Economic Review, 104*(9), 2633–2679. doi.org/10.1257/aer.104.9.2633

Connecticut State Department of Administrative Services. (2019). Connecticut Commission for Educational Technology. portal.ct.gov/DAS/CTEdTech/Commission-for-Educational-Technology

Cook, M. (2019). *ACE program is the first to receive ISTE recognition.* ace.edu/resources/news/newsitem/ace-program-receives-iste-recognition

Dahlstrom, E. (2015). *Educational technology and faculty development in higher education.* Louisville, CO: EDUCAUSE Center for Analysis and Research. library.educause.edu/-/media/files/library/2015/6/ers1507-pdf.pdf

Elliott, J. (2019). *MD 400: Introduction to educational technology.* Fairfield, CT: Fairfield University.

Fairfield University. (2019). Educational technology & school library media. bit.ly/2UsGXC4

Foulger, T. S., Graziano, K. J., Schmidt-Crawford, D., & Slykhuis, D. A. (2017). Teacher Educator Technology Competencies. *Journal of Technology and Teacher Education, 25*(4), 413–448. Waynesville, NC: Society for Information Technology & Teacher Education. learntechlib.org/p/181966/

Harold, B. (2019). *Ed-tech supporters promise innovations that can transform school. Teachers not seeing impact.* Bethesda, MD: Education Week. bit.ly/2wD6BLn

Hart Research Association. (2018). *Fulfilling the American dream: Liberal education and the future of work.* Washington, DC: Association of American Colleges and Universities. www.aacu.org/sites/default/files/files/LEAP/2018EmployerResearchReport.pdf

Hegji, A. (2017). *The Higher Education Act (HEA): A primer.* Washington, DC: Congressional Research Service. fas.org/sgp/crs/misc/R43351.pdf

Ingersoll, R., Merrill, L., & May, H. (2014). *What are the effects of teacher education and preparation on beginning teacher attrition?* Philadelphia, PA: Consortium for Policy Research in Education. cpre.org/sites/default/files/researchreport/2018_prepeffects2014.pdf

International Society for Technology in Education. (2018a). *ISTE Standards for Education Leaders.* iste.org/standards/for-education-leaders

International Society for Technology in Education. (2018b). *Using ESSA to fund edtech: Getting the most out of Title IV-A.* Arlington, VA: Author. iste.org/docs/advocacy-resources/title-iv-a-guide-2019.pdf

International Society for Technology in Education. (2019a). *Course of mind: Policy recommendations to activate learning sciences in your district.* Arlington, VA: Author. bit.ly/2JoFLt0

International Society for Technology in Education. (2019b). *2019 EdTech Advocacy and Policy Summit.* iste.org/advocacy?vvsrc=%2fcampaigns%2f61453%2frespond

International Society for Technology in Education. (2019c). *Higher ed recognition program.* iste.org/learn/highered-recognition

International Society for Technology in Education. (2019d). *ISTE policy principles: Higher ed modernization.* iste.org/advocacy/advocacy-platform

International Society for Technology in Education. (2019e). *ISTE Standards.* iste.org/standards

International Society for Technology in Education. (2019f). *SkillRise literature review: Advancing edtech and adult learning for the future of work.* Arlington, VA: Author. skillrise.org/themes/skillrise/assets/docs/skillrise-literature-review-2019.pdf

Kleiner, B., Thomas, N., & Lewis, L. (2007). *Educational technology in teacher education programs for initial licensure* (NCES 2008-040). Washington, DC: National Center for Education Statistics, Institute of Education Sciences, U.S. Department of Education. nces.ed.gov/pubs2008/2008040.pdf

Kolb, L. (2017). *Learning first, technology second.* Arlington, VA: International Society for Technology in Education.

Kolb, L., Kashef, F., Roberts, C., Terry, C., & Borthwick, A. (2018). *Challenges to creating and sustaining effective technology integration in teacher education programs.* Washington, DC: American Association of Colleges for Teacher Education. bit.ly/2LJ6kdL

Marwell, E. (2019). *2019 state of states: The classroom connectivity gap is closed.* San Francisco, CA: Education Superhighway. go.aws/3awaAYO

Maylahn, P. (2018). *2018-2019 annual infrastructure report.* Washington, DC: Consortium for School Networking. bit.ly/3bB8KWx

McGoldrick, B., Watts, J. S., & Economou, K. (2015). *U.S. postsecondary faculty in 2015: Diversity in people, goals and methods, but focused on students.* Seattle, WA: Bill and Melinda Gates Foundation. gates.ly/2UYAoXW

Newington Public Schools Board of Education Policy § 6141.321. (2009). z2policy.cabe.org/cabe/Z2Browser2.html?showset=newington

Newport News Public Schools. (2018). *Instructional technology coach.* Newport News, VA: Author. sbo.nn.k12.va.us/hr/jobs/descriptions/ITC.pdf

Norville, V. (2019). *Utah banks on statewide approach to adopting educational technology.* Washington, DC: National Association of State Boards of Education. nasbe.org/wp-content/uploads/2019/06/Norville_Utah-digital-learning_Final.pdf

Office of Educational Technology. (2016). *Advancing educational technology in teacher preparation: Policy brief.* tech.ed.gov/files/2016/12/Ed-Tech-in-Teacher-Preparation-Brief.pdf

Office of Educational Technology. (2017). *Reimagining the role of technology in education: 2017 National Education Technology Plan update.* tech.ed.gov/files/2017/01/NETP17.pdf

Organisation for Economic Co-operation and Development. (2019). *TALIS 2018 results (Volume I): Teachers and school leaders as lifelong learners.* Paris, France: OECD Publishing. doi.org/10.1787/1d0bc92a-en

Powell, A., Rabbitt, B., & Kennedy, K. (2014). *iNACOL blended learning teacher competency framework.* Vienna, VA: iNACOL. bit.ly/3c7kfoX

Pressey, B. (2013). *Comparative analysis of national teacher surveys.* New York, NY: Joan Ganz Cooney Center. files.eric.ed.gov/fulltext/ED555587.pdf

Puentedura, R. R. (2014). *Learning, technology and the SAMR model: Goals, processes and practice.* hippasus.com/rrpweblog/archives/2014/06/29/LearningTechnologySAMRModel.pdf

Purcell, K., Heaps, A., Buchanan, J., & Friedrich, L. (2013). *How teachers are using technology at home and in their classrooms.* Washington, DC: Pew Research Center. pewrsr.ch/2ydH3EJ

RAND Corporation. (2012). *Teachers matter: Understanding teachers' impact on student achievement.* Santa Monica, CA: RAND Corporation. rand.org/pubs/corporate_pubs/CP693z1-2012-09.html

Schuyler, S., & Buckley, E. (2018). *Technology in US schools: Are we preparing our kids for the jobs of tomorrow?* New York, NY: PricewaterhouseCoopers. pwc.to/3dAo1sF

Texas Education Code § 21.044. (2017). statutes.capitol.texas.gov/Docs/SDocs/EDUCATIONCODE.pdf

Uerz, D., Volman, M., & Kral, M. (2018). Teacher educators' competences in fostering teachers' proficiency in teaching and learning with technology: An overview of relevant research literature. *Teaching and Teacher Education, 70,* 12–23. doi.org/10.1016/j.tate.2017.11.005

U.S. Department of Education. (2016). *Non-regulatory guidance for Title II, Part A: Building systems of support for excellent teaching and leading.* www2.ed.gov/policy/elsec/leg/essa/essatitleiipartaguidance.pdf

Utah State Board of Education. (2017). *Checklist of minimum requirements for the educational technology endorsement.* Salt Lake City, UT: Author. bit.ly/2URnLwS

Index